Other Books by Robert Blumenfeld

Nonfiction

Accents: A Manual for Actors (1998; revised and expanded edition, 2002)

Acting with the Voice: The Art of Recording Books

All the Tricks of the Trade: Everything You Need to Know about Comedy: A Practical Handbook and Complete Performance Guide for Actors. Writers, and Directors

Blumenfeld's Dictionary of Acting and Show Business

Blumenfeld's Dictionary of Musical Theater: Opera, Operetta, Musical Comedy

Memories of a Vanished Time: A Tribute to My Mother and Father: A Page from American History

Using the Stanislavsky System: A Practical Guide to Character Creation and Period Styles

Stagecraft: Stanislavsky and External Acting Techniques: A Companion to Using the Stanislavsky System

Teach Yourself Accents: The British Isles: A Handbook for Young Actors and Speakers

Teach Yourself Accents: Europe: A Handbook for Young Actors and Writers

Teach Yourself Accents: North America: A Handbook for Young Actors and Writers

Tools and Techniques for Character Interpretation: A Handbook of Psychology for Actors, Writers, and Directors.

How to Rehearse When There Is No Rehearsal: Acting and the Media (by Alice Spivak, written in collaboration with Robert Blumenfeld)

Fiction

The Count of Sainte-Hélène, or The Lure of Infamy: A Novel of the Bourbon Restoration

The Vampires of Morève: A Family Chronicle

Two Plays: The Count of Sainte-Hélène: A Balzacian Melodrama; Interludes of the Heart: A Play about Marcel Proust

THE FIRST TIME I SAW PARIS

Memories of Dreams Come True

For my brilliant multitalented friend Henry Burby, Enjoy! compliments Rico Blumfld 02/19/2025

Robert Blumenfeld

The last time I saw Paris, her heart was warm and gay,
No matter how they change her, I'll remember her that way.
— Song, 1940, music by Jerome Kern,
lyrics by Oscar Hammerstein II

Library of Congress Control Number:		2025901997
ISBN:	Hardcover	979-8-3694-3968-5
	Softcover	979-8-3694-3967-8
	eBook	979-8-3694-3966-1

Front cover photo by the author: the view from room 44 of the Hôtel Michelet Odéon over the roofs of the place de l'Odéon on a May afternoon
Back cover author photo used by permission of Jean-Frédéric Guidoni-Tarissi

Print information available on the last page.

Rev. date: 01/30/2025

To order additional copies of this book, contact:
Xlibris
844-714-8691
www.Xlibris.com
Orders@Xlibris.com
863971

CONTENTS

Part Two
My Return to Paris and Other Trips

I dedicate this book to my brilliant, supportive, loving parents, who fostered and encouraged all my interests, and whom I miss every day: my mother, Ruth Blumenfeld (1915—2015) and my father Max David Blumenfeld (1911—1994); and to the wonderful Professor of French of Rutgers University, Serge Sobolevitch (1924—2001), my undergraduate adviser, who suggested the project that won me a Carnegie Foundation Fellowship, and my first trip to Paris.

Putting My Trip in Context: 1963, a Traumatic Year in a Turbulent Decade

THE FIRST TIME I went to Paris was in the summer of 1963 between my Junior and Senior years as a French major at Rutgers University in New Brunswick, NJ. I had been awarded a Carnegie Foundation Fellowship to spend three months abroad from May through July doing research for them on a topic that had won me the fellowship. After the trip, as one of the requirements of the award, I had to write a paper for the foundation detailing my findings. I was thrilled to be going to Europe for the first time, and especially excited at the prospect of visiting the city that I had long dreamed of and that is the center of French culture, history, literature, and art.

In 1963 the Cold War was raging and the Vietnam War was heating up. As the year went on, it proved to be traumatic, with a great deal of societal unrest and several deeply shocking and horrible events, although there were also some hopeful developments in the area of civil rights.

The 1960s in general was a decade of political disturbances, turbulence, and social upheavals, including those of that other particularly traumatic year 1968, of which you will read more farther on. That was the year when the May uprising in Paris appeared to be the beginning of another French Revolution. In retrospect, the political unrest I sensed around me in 1963 in Paris seemed a precursor of 1968. In that same year, students inspired by the French example occupied American university campus buildings, such as those at Columbia University in New York City, as a form of protest against governmental corruption, inequality, and the Vietnam War. I had earned my MA in French Language and Literature at Columbia in February, 1967, so of course I was no longer a member of the student body when the campus was taken over by the protestors, or I would no doubt have been one of them.

In 1963 the Cold War sometimes threatened to turn into a hot world war beyond the war in Southeast Asia, as the USA and the USSR vied for world hegemony and the triumph of each vast country's economic system. I could not help but be aware of everything that was going on, since we were bombarded with the television news that we watched every evening. Even before that, in the 1950s, we had suffered through the McCarthy era in American politics, and the persecution of people who had been or still were Communists, including the actors, screenwriters, and other victimized personnel on the infamous Hollywood blacklist.

In 1962 U.S. involvement in the Vietnam War had increased enormously, when President John F. Kennedy had sent approximately 23,000 American soldiers into the country, whereas before that, since 1955, there had been about a thousand military "advisers" to the South Vietnamese government. And on January 2, 1963 the Viet Cong, the North Vietnamese army, won its first major victory at An Bac.

As the war dragged on, the draft for men was instituted on December 1, 1969 (it ended officially in 1973) over protest, and some people who wanted to avoid service in what they considered a war that we should not be fighting fled to Canada, but from 1962 on, in the midst of antiwar protests over the next years, a minority had joined the growing hippie commune and "drop out" protest movement, with its famous "flower power," and the flower children's motto "Make peace, not war!" Drugs, especially marijuana, were also associated with this development, generally viewed by the majority with disapproval. The people involved tried to refuse to participate in a society that was economically unjust, that was involved in making war not peace, and that was racist to the core; or at least tried to refuse participation as much as it is ever really possible to do so. At the same time, there were many small and massive protests against the war, calling for an end to U.S. involvement, until the conflict finally ended in 1975, without a clear American victory. And I remember how terrible it was and how disheartening to watch the daily television news when the government announced the statistics of the latest number of dead and wounded. Of course, the Viet Cong number of deaths was always much higher than the total of Americans, if one could believe that. It certainly seemed like propaganda, presumably meant to indicate how well we were actually doing. The broadcasts were generally sickening, and all in the service of a war that so many of us thought should never have been undertaken.

I signed petitions calling for an end to the war, and participated in some of those protests, including a march on Washington, D.C., and campus protests when I was back at Rutgers in 1968 studying for a PhD in Comparative Literature that I never completed, although I took all my course work. People said that those of us who were against the war were against the people who served in the armed forces, but that wasn't true. On the contrary, I wanted every single one of them back home safe and sound.

On one of those protest marches on the bright sunny autumn day of October 21, 1967, with its high temperature a pleasant 66 degrees Fahrenheit in New York, I had an object lesson in government lies and propaganda. I drove to Washington with some friends, and the trip, which should have taken perhaps four and a half hours, took over six, with traffic particularly heavy as we approached the city. Later on, we were in the rear of the crowd that broke through the fence surrounding the Pentagon, and I observed the armed soldiers lining the steps. Shortly after we had broken through, I saw canisters launched at the crowd, and white smoke emanating from wherever they had landed: it was tear gas. Everyone started running away, and I ran with a handkerchief over my nose, even though I was far enough away not to have been affected by the gas. When we were on the way home, we turned on the car radio to listen to the news. The broadcaster said—and these are the only words I actually remember— "The Pentagon denies using tear gas," no doubt continuing with something like "this afternoon, on the unruly crowd that broke through the fence and stormed the Pentagon." Our jaws dropped open! We had been there! We had seen them use tear gas! This was the object lesson in government lies and propaganda.

In August, 1968 the Democratic National Convention was held in Chicago. Lyndon B. Johnson's vice president, Hubert H. Humphrey, was the party's presidential nominee in this election year, and the convention was the scene of massive protests and riots because of the Vietnam War, which the Johnson administration had continued to expand. The riots outside the convention hall were sometimes brutally put down by the police, and the "Chicago Seven" anti-war protestors in particular became famous when they were convicted for crossing state lines to incite a riot, a verdict later overturned. Chicago was run by the autocratic Mayor Richard J. Daley, a career politician who served as mayor beginning in 1955, and who was frequently criticized for corruption, racism, and police brutality.

I should make it clear that although I adamantly opposed the war, I have every sympathy for those who were obliged to fight in it, many of whom never returned. I honor them, and the government owes veterans and their families all possible benefits. The vast majority of them had very little choice: they were drafted and they had to go. Fleeing to Canada cannot ever have been an easy thing to do: It must have been wrenching to leave one's home and family behind, and only total opposition to the war could explain why people fled. But most people were simply required to serve in the armed forces even if they disagreed with the war or else they risked a long jail sentence. I myself did not pass the army physical and received a 4-F notice partly because of the physical disability of flat feet and fallen arches. All told, there were approximately 3.8 million killed, including civilians in North and South Vietnam. Among the dead were 58,200 American military personnel, and there were so many who returned from Vietnam maimed physically and/or psychologically for life. I had a couple of college friends who served and came back home deeply traumatized. Those veterans deserve all our compassion and sympathy.

In the Middle East, the increasingly fraught situation there would lead to the 1967 war, when Israel took over East Jerusalem and occupied the West Bank of the Jordan River, which was part of Jordan.

As for France, the Indochinese War the French were fighting to maintain their colonialist hold on what came to be called South

Vietnam ended with the French defeat at Dien Bien Phu in 1954. Indochina being divided in two, the north part of the country became North Vietnam, and was under Communist rule, while South Vietnam remained a capitalist democracy, and in 1955 the United States began sending those aforementioned "advisers," mainly to ensure that rubber, tin, and oil supplies could continue to be exploited by and exported to American companies, and in pursuance of preventing South Vietnam from falling into Communist hands, as per the "domino theory"—long discredited—espoused by President Eisenhower's Secretary of State John Foster Dulles: that Communism in one country—in this case North Vietnam—would lead inevitably to its spread into neighboring countries. It didn't help matters when on April 7, 1963 Josip Broz Tito, who had fought the Nazis in World War Two, was named President for Life of Yugoslavia, a previously rather loose federation of Balkan states established in 1946 as a Socialist, i.e., Communist Federal Republic, thus cementing the idea in many people's minds that dictatorship was the order of the day, and was spreading rapidly under the aegis of the USSR.

The Algerian War of Independence had begun in 1954, with its consequent unrest in French society, and many calling for a negotiated peace and many others agitating for Algerian independence. The war that was sapping the French economy and that was responsible for so many deaths had helped to bring about the fall of the Fourth Republic in 1958, and then in October of that year, the establishment of the Fifth Republic, with its new Constitution, and with Charles de Gaulle as president, serving the first of two five-year terms. In March six people were condemned to death for an assassination attempt against De Gaulle, and five were pardoned, while one was executed by firing squad. De Gaulle resigned in 1969, rather than serving a third unconstitutional term because he maintained that he did not wish to be a dictator, and that he wanted to ensure the continuation of democracy and of a proper French Republic.

De Gaulle had been much revered when he led the Free French resistance to the Nazis in World War Two, from his base in London. But during his presidency, he managed to alienate Great Britain by vetoing its entry into the European Common Market, precursor to the European Union. And he created further unrest when he encouraged the Québec separatist movement that wanted the largely francophone province of Québec to secede from Canada.

The Algerian War ended in 1962 with decolonialization and Algerian independence, but that was not the end of conflicted feelings about what had happened ever since France had occupied Algeria in 1830, not completely securing its colonialist rule there until 1903. Nor was it the end of French prejudice against Algerians who wanted to live in France, after having been told that French culture was superior and more desirable than their own. French had become a second language to many whose first languages were Arabic and/or Kabyle, but they were not always welcomed in France. Nor were those people of French origin who had moved to Algeria or descended from those who had moved there.

In the United States, the Civil Rights movement was gathering steam, and on August 28, 1963 Dr. Martin Luther King, Jr. delivered his celebrated, pivotal "I Have a Dream" speech on the steps of the Lincoln Memorial to an audience of probably 250,000 who had participated in the March on Washington for Jobs and Freedom. It was the single largest protest gathering in American history up to that point.

On September 15 the monstrous terrorist bombing of the African American 16th Street Baptist Church in Birmingham, AL was committed by white supremacists who were members of the KKK, and four teenage girls were killed. Dr. King called it "one of the most vicious and tragic crimes ever perpetrated against humanity." Sixty years later, as I write these lines, it's not news that we still have a long way to go in establishing true equality and equal justice for all.

On August 5, the Soviet Union, Great Britain, and the United States had already signed the Nuclear Nonproliferation Treaty. Nevertheless, 1963 also saw the Cuban missile crisis from October 16 to October 28, several months after Fidel Castro's visit to the USSR in May. To forestall an American invasion, which may have been secretly discussed by the inner circles of the American government, the USSR installed long-range missiles in Communist Cuba, threatening the United

States, which already had missiles installed in Italy and Turkey, so that the Soviet Union itself felt threatened. On February 8, all travel and commercial transactions with Communist Cuba had been made illegal for American citizens. And now, in 1963, President Kennedy made it plain to the Soviets that they had to withdraw the missiles, or else. War seemed imminent, or at least possible, particularly when the U.S. Navy invaded the Bay of Pigs in Cuba. The Soviets backed down and withdrew the missiles.

On Friday, November 22 President John F. Kennedy was assassinated in Dallas and died in hospital later that day. His Vice President Lyndon B. Johnson was sworn in as president immediately following Kennedy's death. Americans, especially perhaps those of us who were alive at the time, have never quite recovered from this trauma, nor from the assassination of his brother Robert F. Kennedy on June 5, 1968, and his death on June 6; or from the assassination of Dr. Martin Luther King, Jr. on April 4, 1968 at the Lorraine Motel in Memphis, TN. I stayed at that motel when I was on tour as an actor in the mid-1970s with the National Theater of the Deaf, and even staying there was unnerving.

Many of the events of 1963 mentioned here happened after my return from Europe, obviously, but I was very aware of all those that had occurred before and during my trip, about some of which you will read more below. I enjoyed that trip immensely in spite of everything, isolated as I was from the horrors happening far away from me. Personally, I was fine, after all, and privileged, not in harm's way, and with no worries about where my next meal was coming from or whether I would have shelter and a good night's sleep.

AUTHOR'S NOTE

U NFORTUNATELY, I DIDN'T start keeping travel journals until 1984. Fortunately, I have kept them ever since, so I could easily find information about my trips to the USSR and Greece, recounted in this volume. My memory is excellent, but a journal with details about people and places certainly would have helped me write the first part of this book, and the section about my trip to Scotland in the second part. I don't remember the names of people I met during those trips in most cases. However, I have told people quite a number of the anecdotes in these sections over the years so that they have naturally stayed with me. And since I have been to Paris so many times over the last forty years, and stayed in the same St.-Germain neighborhood almost every time, I am completely familiar with and knowledgeable about the streets and avenues in that area, and elsewhere in Paris as well.

I have also done research regarding the history detailed in the preface, as I obviously couldn't have relied on my memory when presenting all the facts. And for the same reason, I have researched the history in other parts of the book; for instance, that of the chateaux of the Loire, told to us on the guided tours; and of the 1745 rebellion in Scotland, about which I have read a great deal. I thought it would be fun for the reader to learn something about the early history of Paris, where the name came from, a little about the history of the language, and so forth, so I have included some salient information at the opening of chapter two. I have also included information about my background and some of my beliefs to provide the reader with further perspective on my perceptions.

All translations from foreign languages are my own.

I am delighted to acknowledge my incalculable debt to my French teachers at Princeton High School, and to the professors at Rutgers, who taught me French language and literature, and to those at Columbia University as well. All three departments were wonderful, offering very interesting courses, and the teachers were magical. I loved my experiences at Rutgers especially, sitting around the French table in the cafeteria, and living in the French dorm, which was a floor in one wing of one of the Raritan River dormitories, and conversing in French, which was the one and only rule at the table and in the dorm. I wish they were all alive to see this book.

To conclude, I hope you, gentle readers, enjoy the tales of my travels, of my dreams come true.

PART ONE

My First Trip to Paris

CHAPTER ONE

Getting to Europe

I HAD DECIDED TO become a French major at Rutgers because I had learned at an early age to love French history, literature and philosophy, and French, music, painting, and sculpture. My parents had prints on the walls of French Impressionist paintings by Renoir, Degas, and Gauguin, and a few by Van Gogh, as well as seven watercolors my father had brought back from Paris. I loved them all, and had been fascinated by France ever since I was nine years old, when my father went on his first trip to Paris, of which you will hear more in chapter fourteen. I also loved the language, its beautiful sounds, and its interesting grammar. I spoke it quite well enough to communicate even then, but not nearly as colloquially or fluently as I do now. And as one might expect, my command of the language improved by leaps and bounds in the course of my first stay in Paris. I seldom spoke English most of the time, so this was an experience in total immersion.

I was in love with the city before I ever saw it outside of my dreams, fueled by the books of photographs that my father brought back with him, and by all I read about it. And once I did see Paris, live and in person, I loved it even more, and I have never stopped. I feel in touch with times past as I walk in its streets, and I am surrounded by beauty everywhere I go. Paris is one of the most beautiful cities I have ever been to, an architectural, cultural, and culinary paradise. But before I got there for the first time, I spent two obligatory and delightful weeks in Scheveningen.

Off I had gone on an overnight flight to Holland with my group of Carnegie Foundation fellows. We were to meet there for the last two weeks in May before proceeding to our individual main destinations. We twelve Carnegie Fellows for 1963 had all been introduced to each other in a large room in a building on the Princeton University campus, since the fellowship was given in connection with the Woodrow Wilson School of Public and International Affairs, which was part of the university, and we had a long meeting explaining exactly what we were going to do and what was expected of us. Incidentally, the name of the school was changed to the Princeton School of Public and International Affairs in 2020 by the Princeton University Board of Trustees, which voted to remove Wilson's name because of his racism and racist policies, both when he was the university president and when he was president of the United States.

Sitting there with all these strangers whom I would be getting to know, I found myself feeling rather nervous and tense, which manifested itself as a tightening of all the muscles in the back of my neck. As I said in the preface, we were each to do research at our principal destination, and then write a paper on the topic that had won us the fellowship. Mine, suggested to me by my wonderful adviser, Professor Serge Sobolevitch, was on the Tunisian and Moroccan Jewish post-World War Two immigration to France in the twentieth century, when there was a large North African influx from what had been French colonies. It had been quite recently, in March, 1955-1956 that Tunisia was officially given its independence from France, and not until March 2, 1956 that the protocol declaring Morocco independent had been signed.

During World War Two, the Jewish populations of these two North African countries, as well as those in Algeria, often impoverished to begin with and living in ghettos called mellahs, had suffered terribly and a great many had been murdered by the Nazis in Algeria and when they marched in and occupied Tunisia, establishing concentration camps with all their attendant horrors in both countries. Those Jewish people in Morocco were also in dire straits under the antisemitic Vichy French government, but afterwards, when it was possible to envision a better life in the French Republic than they could ever have in their home countries, many Tunisian and Moroccan Jewish survivors had opted to leave, often to take up residence in Paris.

Once I was awarded the fellowship, where was I going to stay in Paris? The question was answered in short order. The kindly G.

Reginald Bishop (1922-2012), then Assistant Dean of the College of Arts and Sciences of Rutgers University and a Professor of French as well, called me into his office to congratulate me on winning the fellowship, and told me he had a room in an apartment for me to stay in when I got to Paris, and he gave me all the necessary information. Somebody contacted the apartment owner, possibly Dean Bishop, or one of the Carnegie Foundation people to whom he had given the information; I no longer remember whom, but I was all set. He had stayed at the same place when he was a student, and kept in touch with the proprietor, the result being that he could find rooms for Rutgers students as necessary. Princeton students also stayed at the apartment, possibly through the Dean's good offices. Having earned his Ph.D. at Princeton, Dean Bishop had immediately been hired by the Rutgers French Department, and would have a very distinguished university career, becoming head of the department eventually and Dean of the College of Arts and Sciences.

On the plane to Holland, I sat next to an old Dutch man who spoke no English. When I asked in German if he spoke German, he looked absolutely horrified. "Nee, ik spreek geen Duits!" he practically screamed at me. He was friendly enough otherwise though, and although we could not converse, he managed to make me understand he was from Eindhoven when we flew over it the next morning by pointing to himself, then down at the city, and saying its name while nodding and smiling. And he made it very clear that he hated, no, loathed the Germans for what they had done during the Second World War. I gathered he had been in the Dutch resistance in Arnhem, which he also pointed out to me when we flew over it, saying "Duits! Nazi!" and shaking his fist and pretending to shoot a gun. I nodded and pointed at him and said "Resistance" and he nodded back. I applauded and gave him a thumbs-up.

Our group stayed in a pension with the picturesque name *Op Gouden Wieken* (On Golden Wings) in Scheveningen, the charming beach resort and fishing town near the Hague. The name is pronounced with a 'skh' sound in the first syllable and was used to catch German spies during World War Two, since they said 'sh', which is the sound the letters stand for in German, and they were not able to pronounce that first syllable in the Dutch way.

The boardwalk and beach right near the pension were great places to walk. It was fairly warm and there was a light breeze, and the fishing boats drawn up on the strand reminded me of the Van Gogh painting we had on the wall at home, *Fishing Boats at Saintes-Marie*. In fact, he had also painted fishing boats at Scheveningen, and the paintings look remarkably similar to each other.

There were food stands on the side of the beach near the buildings, but I don't recall that the food was very interesting. They sold decent French fries with mayonnaise as a dip, as opposed to the French and Belgian way, which was to dip them in mustard, or the American dip of ketchup. I was told that the thing to do was to order a whole small lightly brined raw herring, called soused herring or, in Dutch, *Hollandse Nieuwe* (Dutch New), and swallow it down whole, then eat some fried potatoes. I love herring any way it's prepared, so of course I tried it at a stand right near our pension, but I actually found it nauseating to eat it that way and I felt sick and started gagging. The people around me had expected my reaction and they laughed, including some of my fellow students, so at least somebody had a good time.

We had seminars and talks on political science at a classroom in the American School of the Hague, and very interesting lectures they were, too. I also took the time to go to the Mauritshuis to see its collection of seventeenth-century Dutch painting, including many by Gerrit Dou, also known as Gerard Douw or Dow; and superb evocative landscapes by Meindert Hobbema; as well as a number of canvases by Rembrandt, including *The Anatomy Lesson of Dr. Nicolaes Tulp*. The paintings by Vermeer include *Girl with a Pearl Earring*, and the one painting I had really gone there to see, his *View of Delft*. I had read about it in Marcel Proust's *À la recherche du temps perdu* (In Search of Lost Time) which I had started to read in French from the beginning while standing in the stacks of the Rutgers University Library. I had read parts in the two-volume translation mostly by C. K. Scott Moncrieff that my parents had, before reading *Un amour de Swann* (Swann in Love), the second part of *Swann's Way*, in my Princeton High School senior French class.

And I was lost in wonder, and in the world he had created. I quickly developed a passion for Proust that was to grow with the years. As I read his pages, I almost thought I was reading about myself, as if he had known me, known about the kaleidoscopic emotions I had gone through when I was in love. He had the art and the perception not only of tapping into the universality of human feelings and psychology, but of making his perceptions crystal clear in his writing about them. Eventually I started what I call my Proust Collection and amassed many shelves of rare books and his complete correspondence as well as first editions of collected letters exchanged with individual friends of his, biographies, and critical material. I have willed the collection to the Rutgers University Library.

In 1961, my father had rented a cabin on Lake Dunmore in Vermont for our family vacation. Shortly before we went there, I had returned from Québec, where I had been studying French for a couple of months at Laval University.

Incidentally, I got my first passport before going to Canada, and discovered when I looked at my birth certificate, that my name was not Robert L. Blumenfeld, as we all had thought it was, and that would be the name on my degrees, but simply Robert Blumenfeld without the middle initial. My parents had wanted me to have a middle name starting with L, but couldn't think of one they liked. I wanted Louis for Robert Louis Stevenson, but in any case no official name was ever selected, and of course my passport was without the L. I later officially changed my name for Social Security purposes, since my original card also included the middle initial.

At the end of the Spring semester, just before going to Laval, I had checked *Du côté de chez Swann* (Swann's Way) out of the Rutgers library, and I took it with me to Vermont. One afternoon, I rowed out onto the lake and stayed there reading until I heard my mother calling me into dinner. We had done some shopping on the way to the cabin, and my mother made a delicious beef stew with fresh green beans.

On the weekend off between our two weeks of Carnegie Foundation seminars in Scheveningen, I and some others took a trip to Amsterdam on Saturday, just for the day. We went on a boat tour of the canals, and then for a delightful walk that included the famous red-light district, and to the Rijksmuseum, with its amazing Rembrandts, Vermeers, and Hobbemas. On Sunday, we took a boat cruise to Rotterdam, a very modern port city with its skyline of skyscrapers and glass towers, because the city had been entirely rebuilt after having been bombed to bits by the Germans during World War Two.

One day the next week, when we had a free afternoon, several of us rented bicycles and took the sixteen-mile round trip to Delft. I wanted to see the city largely because of Proust's description of Vermeer's painting, which he had seen on one of his last outings at the 1921 Vermeer exhibition in Paris. His description of it and its *"petit pan de mur jaune"* (little section of yellow wall), as he called it, is exquisite. And we all wanted to see Delft in any case because of its reputation as a charming picturesque town, justly renowned for its blue and white pottery, on sale at numerous shops carrying everything from urns and vases to complete dinner services.

Despite all of these unforgettable experiences, I could hardly wait until our two weeks in Scheveningen were done, and I could go to Paris.

CHAPTER TWO

On to Paris

I WAS TWENTY THE first time I went to *La Ville Lumière* (The City of Light), so named in 1820 when Paris was the first European city to use gas lighting to illuminate most of its streets. Paris is also justly called *La Ville de l'Amour* (the City of Love), because of its associations with great art and artists, literature, poetry, and movies, and its romantic atmosphere as a setting for love stories, and as a honeymoon destination.

It was a hot day at the beginning of June, 1963 when I arrived in the majestic metropolis on the banks of the Seine, a name transformed as the French language developed and dropped certain Latin consonants, from Sequana, the Gallo-Roman goddess of the river. She is supposed to have protected the fishermen of the Parisii tribe who had lived since ancient times on what is now the île de la Cité, the island in the river where the Cathédrale Notre-Dame de Paris is located; hence obviously the name Paris.

The name of the river is also the word for a large weighted wall of netting used to trap fish. The Parisii were supposed to have used such netting, stretched from one bank to the other between the island and the mainland, to make a great haul of fish that they would both eat and sell. Once the fish had swum close to the netting, they would detach the seine on both sides and, moving in on boats, surround the fish with it, dragging it onto the island.

They had built wooden bridges to the mainland on both the north and south sides of the island, established farms, and sold their fish and agricultural products widely, using boats to ship them up and down the river. The village's central location in the province had also served to bring it into prominence.

Julius Caesar mentions the Parisii in *Comentarii de bello Gallico* (Commentaries on the Gallic War), his book about the conquest of Gaul by his invading Roman legions. As everyone who has studied Latin knows, it begins, "Gallia est omnis divisa in partes tres, quarum unam incolunt Belgae, aliam Aquitani, tertiam qui ipsorum lingua Celtae nostra Galli appellantur..." (All Gaul is divided into three parts, of which one is inhabited by the Belgae, the second by the Aquitani, the third by those who in their own language are called Celts, in ours Gauls...)

The Romans called the town on the small island Lutetia, which they adapted from the Gaulish word *lutos*, meaning swamp or muddy place. The full Latin name of the place was actually Lutetia Parisorum: the Swamp of the Parisii. The shortened name could be translated as Swampy or Muddy.

Gaulish is the ancient Celtic language of the inhabitants of Gaul whom the invaders found living in the province, divided into a number of tribes, including the Parisii. They gave the name Galli to the people and Gallia to the province that would become France. Incidentally, there are Gaulish words in modern French, since the Romans had no names for some of the trees or fish native to the area. They simply adopted the Gaulish words that remained in the language as French evolved from Latin. But our knowledge of Gaulish is sketchy, because we don't have many examples written in Gaulish aside from some rare inscriptions in Roman letters on gravestones, since the Druid priests believed writing to be evil and unlucky.

In its development from Latin, the French language, dropping some Latin consonants, eventually changed the word Lutetia to Lutèce, making it sound much like the original Gaulish word, and it appears in such names as the elegant sumptuous Paris Hôtel Lutetia in the sixth arrondissement (district); and the well-preserved Roman amphitheater, the Arènes de Lutèce, in the fifth arrondissement.

The Roman emperors found the climate so salubrious that they traveled there because of its pleasant summer weather, its vineyards, and its fruit orchards, so that from being a small well known fishing and trading village, it became an imperial vacation resort, its old buildings replaced by new ones worthy of an emperor's stay. Those buildings too are long gone, but you can see vestiges of Roman ruins two thousand years old in the Crypte Archéologique de l'Île de la Cité, a fascinating museum below the *parvis* (square) in front of Notre Dame.

As the Roman Empire was drawing to its end, the Franks, who spoke a Germanic language called Frankish, invaded from the east and conquered much of the province, which they renamed Francia. The Franks continued to call the city Lutèce until 310 CE, when fortifications were built on the island, and it was transformed into a garrison as a base from which to fight invaders, principally the Vikings, the Norsemen who succeeded in conquering what is now Normandy, to which they gave their name, and which is to the west of Paris, which they did not succeed in conquering. For reasons unknown, the establishment of the garrison also led to the change of the small city's name to Paris, shortened from the Latin *civitas Parisorum* or *urbs Parisorum* (City of the Parisii). However, the name alternated for more than a hundred and fifty years with Lutèce.

Eventually, after the collapse of the Roman Empire, the Frankish king Clovis (456-511), the first Christian king, united the Frankish tribes and founded the Merovingian dynasty, the first of the French monarchical dynasties, controlling the territory between the Loire and the Rhine. He built his fortress palace on the island, thus making it his capital, which from then on was called Paris.

At the fall of the Roman Empire, Vulgar or Colloquial Latin, which evolved from the classic version of the language with the rise of the Roman Catholic Church, remained the main language of communication among groups who spoke different tongues, as English often is today. It evolved into the French language as the vernacular of the peoples who lived in that territory, just as it did elsewhere into the Spanish, Portuguese, Romanian, and Italian languages and dialects.

Having expanded south under the Romans into what is now the fifth arrondissement of Paris, the small city the Franks took over from the Gallo-Romans gradually spread from the once muddy island onto the north bank as well, expanding outward and evolving to become the huge metropolis we know today. For centuries it was a walled city, the limits of the walls changing over time, with entry gates, several of which from the seventeenth century remain as ornate landmarks, such as the Porte St.-Denis.

I was sent on a plane to get to Paris from Schiphol Airport in Amsterdam (pronounced with that distinctive 'skh' sound, now evolving into 'sk'), instead of going by train, on which I have taken round trips on two subsequent occasions. There was no high-speed train between the two cities in those days, and I had to get to Paris as quickly as possible. I took the bus from Paris's Orly Airport to the transport hub station near the Invalides on the left (south) bank just off the Seine and in the middle of the city. I had been given very clear directions.

When I saw the cathedral of Notre Dame in the distance for the first time from the bus, I had tears in my eyes. Notre Dame is such an iconic and amazingly beautiful symbol of Paris, just as and perhaps even more iconic than the Eiffel Tower, that although I was a staunch atheist, I was deeply moved. I could hardly believe I was actually there at last.

My parents were both lifelong atheists even though they were brought up by religious parents, and from the age of seven I too have not believed that any god existed, and I have no religion. Despite my lack of religious belief, I appreciate the art, architecture, and music religions have given us as being magnificent contributions to our general culture and a foundational part of our history. My parents and I had a good laugh when I said that I loved Christmas carols and Handel's gorgeous *Messiah*, as long as I didn't pay attention to the words.

I was raised to revere science as an insightful road to the ever expanding knowledge of who and what we are and where we come from. But I should make it clear that I believe firmly that everyone has an absolute right to their beliefs, and to the peaceful and secure practice and enjoyment of whatever religion they believe in, and I have total respect for people who have different beliefs and traditions from mine, many friends and acquaintances among them. As the saying has it, whatever gets you through the day!

I was also brought up with a great knowledge of my Jewish ethnic roots, particularly those of my Eastern European Ashkenazi family with its Yiddish-speaking culture, and of more general Jewish history, about which I was given books that I found very interesting, but obviously we were totally secular and never went to synagogue. Family weddings and funerals actually took place at other venues. We did, however, observe the old folk custom of having the Passover Seder, a religious ceremony conducted in the home to celebrate the holiday, at my maternal grandparents' house when we were kids, because they wanted us to, and it was a way of teaching us children more about our roots and traditions. But there was no pious concentration on the part of my parents or aunts, uncles, and cousins on the religious aspects of the holiday, though my grandparents were believers, and my grandfather conducted the service with deep respect and reverence as he told the tale of Moses leading the Hebrews out of Egypt. For my grandparents, the story was actual history. For the rest of us in the family, it was myth or legend, and symbolic of the horrors of slavery, a rejection of it, and a celebration of liberty and freedom. The holiday also represented the fun side of having a Jewish heritage, with great holiday foods and fun games for the children after dinner. I always enjoyed myself.

The roast chicken dinner after the religious ceremony was always delicious. My grandmother was an excellent cook. She made the best latkes (potato pancakes), and I used to watch her grating the fresh potatoes and preparing them just before the Seder began. At the same time, when I was a bit older, I myself had the pleasure of making the kharoyses, as we pronounced charoses in the Galician Ashkenazic way, for the ceremony, using apples and walnuts chopped fine and blended together with sugar and sweet red kosher Manischewitz wine, which we also had sips of as part of the ceremony. Charoses represents the mortar with which the Hebrew slaves in the legend built the pyramids.

The ceremony itself was usually cut short by my grandfather because he professed to be annoyed when my parents and aunts and uncles were cracking jokes about what he read from the Haggadah, the book that sets forth the order of the Passover service. I myself was far more interested in my grandparents' true tales about their lives in the eastern Austro-Hungarian province of Galizia, anglicized as Galicia, from whence they had emigrated to America around 1900, than in the religious stories I had read.

I was very tired when I got to the apartment where I would be staying for the next two months on the rue des Saints-Pères, because I had taken the Métro from the Invalides, and then dragged my heavy suitcase through the streets from the Sèvres-Babylone stop past the Hôtel Lutetia and the square du Croix-Rouge, as I had through the airport. It wasn't that far from the Métro to the building I was going to, but it seemed a great distance because I didn't yet know the streets. There were no rolling suitcases in those days: they were invented in 1970. I have since learned to travel light, with one rolling carry-on and a shoulder bag.

So there I was, at the door of the apartment in 76 bis rue des Saints-Pères, a bit out of breath, having been admitted by the concierge, and climbed the two long flights of stairs to the apartment of Mademoiselle Marie-Louise Haumesser. I stood a few moments to catch my breath, then rang the bell. The door was answered by an old lady (she was eighty, as I later found out) in a wheelchair, her right leg in a heavy plaster cast. She was wearing oval, rose-colored glasses. She looked me up and down. Smiling and bowing my head slightly, I said in my politest manner, "Bonjour, madame... Comment allez-vous?" (Good day, Madame. How do you do?)

"Mademoiselle. Mademoiselle Haumesser, s'il vous plaît. Et vous êtes...?" (Mademoiselle. Mademoiselle Haumesser, if you please. And you are...?)

"Je suis Robert Blumenfeld. Je crois que vous m'attendez." (I am Robert Blumenfeld. I believe you are expecting me.)

She looked me up and down some more, and replied in a flat dry voice, "Ah. On m'avait dit que vous étiez américain." (Ah. They told me you were American.)

"Mais je suis américain." (But I *am* American.)

"Non. Vous êtes juif." (No. You're a Jew.)

I was taken aback.

"On peut être les deux." (One can be both.)

"Non. Si vous êtes juif, vous n'êtes pas américain (No. If you are a Jew, you are not an American)," she said pointedly, as if I had lied to her. "Eh bien, ne restez pas là comme ça sur le seuil de la porte ! Entrez ! (Well, don't stand there on the doorsill like that! Come in!)."

I was shocked. I didn't know what to say or do. And I was so angry and upset that I would have left then and there had I not been so tired and so weary, and if I had had the slightest idea where to go. So I stayed. Just like that. In an angry mood. This was beyond my ken. Nobody had ever said anything like this to me before. As far as I was concerned, I was an American, period. By the time I was a preteen, I had never thought of myself as anything else, but not in a nationalistic or even patriotic way, simply as a fact of life. I had always been taught in school that I was an American, and we recited the Pledge of Allegiance to the flag and to the nation every morning before beginning classes. And being Jewish was my ethnic background, which I already knew and enjoyed when I was a small boy, even though I had never heard the word "ethnic," and of course every American has an indelible ethnic background.

I was very young, and quite sensitive in those days. I had not yet developed the thick skin when being confronted by bigotry that I would develop later on in my life.

Of course, I was not ignorant and I knew that along with conspiracy theories and the other antisemitic claptrap and vicious stereotypes that many believed, however illogical they are, it was the case for many centuries that in the eyes of many and perhaps most of the majority European Christian populations, only Christians were actually part of the nation. Jews were a distinctive group of ethnic outsiders, despised as deicides and for not accepting Jesus Christ as their savior, and even considered to be a separate "race" although most, except for the ultra-Orthodox who preferred to live in their own communities, had long been assimilated into society. So according to the people who thought that way, French Jews were not French, Austro-Hungarian Jews were not Austro-Hungarian, Polish Jews were not Polish, Russian Jews were not Russian, English Jews were not English, and so forth, even though Jews were legal co-citizens, and had been emancipated by successive laws in nineteenth-century England, and from the ghettos of continental Western Europe since the French Revolution and Napoleonic Wars, and from the Pale of Settlement during the Russian Revolution. But I had never actually encountered such an attitude before in person, although I had certainly read about it, for instance in Marcel Proust's *Swann's Way*, where Charles Swann is considered Jewish even though he is a third-generation Catholic. And of course everyone knows what horrors such attitudes about Jews have led to historically.

As a teenager, I had only encountered antisemitism directed at me personally a few times, and it had been deeply upsetting, but nobody had ever said I wasn't an American because I was Jewish. That was a new one on me.

Jews, after all, had never been forcibly segregated in the United States, being equal citizens since the nation's founding, although largely Jewish neighborhoods existed, particularly where the ultra-Orthodox Chassidim or newly arrived immigrants dwelled, but then every arriving group settled into its own neighborhood. Nor had Jews ever lived under severe restrictive legal disabilities. Antisemitism clearly did exist however, and some antisemites were quite vocal in the outpouring of their vitriolic hatred. Among other things, prejudice against Jews meant restricted housing and not being able to be members of certain country clubs or to stay in certain hotels, a subject treated in Laura Z. Hobson's 1947 novel *Gentleman's Agreement*, made into a successful film in the same year. Antisemitism is a prejudice that seems to wax and wane according to circumstances such as the wars in the Middle East, although the Oldest Hatred is always with us.

The idea that they would be equal with other citizens was one reason for the massive emigration of Jews from Eastern Europe around 1900 to the United States, escaping the pogroms and legal disabilities that prevailed in what many came to call "the old country." Possibly unknown to them was that they were to become citizens of a profoundly racist society, woven through, for instance, with the vile murderous prejudice from which black people and Native Americans have suffered for centuries, and often still do suffer; a society that we are still in the process of trying to change for the better, but that seems sometimes to be going backwards rather than forwards.

Mademoiselle Haumesser was born in 1883, and she had absorbed those aforementioned commonly held attitudes towards Jews in her youth. She had continued to hold the same antiquated views all her life, and as far as she was concerned, being Jewish meant being a member of a separate, unassimilable ethnic group, and not simply a fellow citizen of a different religious background and a human being with faults and virtues like everybody else.

When I thought about it later that night, more calmly, I realized that she knew what she had done. She had deliberately tried to make me feel uncomfortable, to see what my reaction would be, and what she could get away with. I'm sure she meant what she said, but there was certainly no objective reason for her to have said it; to have greeted me in such a rude manner with her superfluous remarks. First of all, she obviously already knew from my name that I was Jewish. So what was that greeting all about? Why confront me in that way? Why not keep the idea she expressed to herself? She was baiting me, that's all there was to it; putting me in my place.

Needless to add, this encounter and some of what followed, about which you will hear farther on, did not destroy my love for Paris and French artistic culture, in which French Jews are active participants, after all, making notable contributions to painting, music, and literature. For decades now I have had very dear close French friends of various backgrounds, and they were appalled when I told them what had happened. At this remove in time, in fact, I just laugh at my initial welcome and shake my head at her nastiness. My French friends and I laughed together, once they were over their own surprise. "Quoi ? Mais c'est ridicule !" (What?! But that's ridiculous!"), said one astonished friend.

So, to return to 1963... I swallowed my shock and dismay, and stepped into Mlle. Haumesser's spacious, L-shaped apartment, into the large and not very well-lit reception hall. There was a door to my left that led to a tiny hallway off which were my bedroom, fronting on the street, and a small toilet room opposite the hall door, with another bedroom just across from mine, rented to another Rutgers student. I knew him slightly from college. He was there for about a month, on his first trip to Europe, and left to travel elsewhere. He was quite nice, and we had occasional conversations, but never became friends since we didn't really have much in common.

Standing in the doorway and facing into the apartment away from my bedroom, I saw ahead of me on the left wall an archway entrance to a large room full of bookshelves, and beyond the library the salon, with a grand piano. Beyond the salon, forming the third in this suite of rooms, was the dining room, also book lined. There were bedrooms along the hallway across from this suite, and a bathroom with a large tub on that same side of the corridor just to the right of the apartment door. Three of those four bedrooms were rented to students from Princeton and Rutgers—the fourth bedroom was hers. The corridor continued on, turning right to form the L, which was a shorter corridor that led to the spacious kitchen and pantry suite. The furniture in all the public rooms, and in my bedroom, was massive and very old-fashioned, and comfortable, as I was to discover.

After paying Mademoiselle Haumesser in cash for the week (I paid her every week), I was introduced to a Monsieur Paul Bouissac, who had been standing near the door, and had witnessed my arrival. He would be spending his last night in the spacious, airy, well-lit bedroom that I was to occupy by myself for the remainder of my stay. There were two beds, and a sink that I would use for my morning and evening ablutions. I could only take a bath in the bathroom; there was no shower.

Paul would be leaving the next morning to rejoin the circus. I don't remember which one, or in what capacity. No doubt he was staying in the apartment because it was less expensive than a hotel. As a circus worker he couldn't have had much money.

When I was preparing and researching this book, I decided to Google him, since I thought I might find out about his activities as a circus person, if he were well enough known, and I quickly discovered that a person of the same name had become famous as a university professor and had written books in his field of expertise: semiotics. Some of his books, in fact, had to do with semiotics and the circus, so I was pretty sure it was he. He was born in 1934, so in 1963, he would have been twenty-nine, which would be right also. And I then became certain he was the same person when I discovered a book, *The*

Pleasures of Time: Two Men, A Life by Stephen Harold Riggins, which is about Professor Bouissac, and of which I ordered a copy. Mademoiselle Haumesser, in whose apartment he stayed several times, is discussed briefly, along with her Société Internationale des Haumesseriens. Thus, our paths crossed that one time before he ever became famous in his field.

There are quite a few hotels in that area, in some of which I later stayed, and they were all excellent, and fairly expensive because the St.-Germain neighborhood is a very popular tourist destination. My fellowship money would have paid for a hotel, but the prospect of staying in an apartment seemed far more interesting as soon as Dean Bishop told me about it. Whenever I am in Paris, I always walk past 76 bis rue des Saints-Pères and gaze up at what had been my intricate wrought iron balcony, out of pure nostalgia, in spite of some of what I experienced there.

Paul was awfully nice, very friendly, and he volunteered to show me the neighborhood, including the Sorbonne, and to point out some restaurants where I might eat, out of the dozens in the neighborhood.

He had seen how upset I was by the way Mademoiselle had greeted me. "You can't take her seriously," he said. I nodded, and smiled, and said, "Hmmm…" And thus began my adventures in Paris.

CHAPTER THREE

My First Evening in Paris

PAUL AND I set out on our walk just as it was beginning to grow dark. The rue des Saints-Pères is the street that constitutes the border of the sixth and seventh arrondissements on the left (south) bank of the Seine. On the west side of the street, where 76 bis is, you are in the seventh; cross the street and you are in the sixth, going east. Cross streets usually change their names when they go into another arrondissement. For instance, the rue Jacob in the sixth, situated a couple of streets north of the boulevard St.-Germain as you go towards the Seine, becomes the rue de l'Université when it continues on the other side of the rue des Saints-Pères into the seventh. It was in a building then called the Hôtel d'York at what is now 56 rue Jacob that the 1783 peace treaty ending the American Revolution was signed by all parties, as a historical plaque on the building tells us.

Paris is divided into twenty arrondissements (roundings off; districts), that spiral round like a snail shell from the first arrondissement on the right (north) bank, where the Louvre is located, to the twentieth, also on the right bank, all the way to the east. Each arrondissement has its own mayor and its own town hall, just as each of the five boroughs of New York does. Paris also has an Hôtel de Ville (City Hall), gorgeous architecturally, standing on the place de l'Hôtel de Ville, a wide plaza in front of it in the fourth arrondissement on the right bank, and containing the offices of the mayor for the entire municipality of Paris.

Just beyond the city limits to the east is Vincennes, a beautiful wooded park surrounding a chateau and containing a small zoo. Just south of the sixth arrondissement is the fourteenth arrondissement, Montparnasse, with its superb brasseries and cafes, cinemas, theaters, train station, and famous cemetery, where Jean-Paul Sartre, Simone de Beauvoir, and Alfred Dreyfus are buried.

At the southern end of its major artery, the boulevard du Montparnasse, is the Tour Montparnasse, the skyscraper that some consider an eyesore and the ugliest building in Paris. It was built between 1969 and 1973, so it wasn't there the first time I saw Paris. The Tour was built over the old Montparnasse train station, replaced with a sprawling, bustling new station that has a couple of stories full of shops and small restaurants, and plenty of parking nearby. The Métro station, Gare Montparnasse-Bienvenüe, is one of the most complicated in the system, since many lines meet there, as they do at that other Métro station that is difficult to navigate, Châtelet-Les Halles.

Le Ciel de Paris, the restaurant near the observation deck in the Tour Montparnasse, is excellent and you dine in style while the restaurant revolves very slowly, affording a sweeping panoramic view of the city. Some Parisians joke that it's the best restaurant in Paris because it's the only one from which you can't see the Tour Montparnasse.

Paul took me north on the rue des Saints-Pères and then east into the sixth into the St.-Germain neighborhood for what seemed at the time like a long walk on the boulevard St.-Germain, to the corner of the boulevard Saint-Michel, where the medieval Cluny Museum is located. At that point we were practically in the Latin Quarter in the fifth arrondissement, where the Sorbonne is located, because the boulevard is the boundary between the sixth and fifth arrondissements. We then went north on the boulevard towards the Seine the few short blocks to the place Saint-Michel. I marveled not only at the architecture all along the way, at the church of St.-Germain-des-Prés, at the famous cafés Flore and Deux Magots, at the Cluny Museum, and also at the magnificent fountain with its statue of St. Michael on the place Saint-Michel, and at the Seine and the buildings across it on the right bank. The amazing, impressive Louvre was gray and dingy at that time, while still losing none of its majesty. With the deep cleaning of the façade that had already begun, some of the original bright beige color of the stone could be seen. Eventually, it would all be cleaned and shine forth in its full splendor.

I now learned that the usual French time for dinner is eight o'clock, referred to as *vingt heures* (twenty hours), since the French are on a twenty-four hour system of telling time, like the military. Many people do have dinner at 7:30, however.

We went down to the rue de la Harpe, to an excellent restaurant that unfortunately no longer exists. I don't remember its name. We sat at a long table, ordered a main dish, and helped ourselves to servings of mashed potatoes and vegetables, and other family style accompaniments, all quite delicious. It was also the first time I had tasted French bread, and I couldn't believe it. It was amazing, so delicious, a revelation. I had never tasted bread quite like it. I was hooked.

Monsieur Bouissac and I hit it off very well, as we talked and walked before and after we ate. We talked about Mademoiselle Haumesser, of course. Again, he dismissed Mademoiselle's prejudices as silly, and not worth taking to heart, but of course I was still unhappy about how I had been greeted. Paul—he had asked me to call him Paul, and I asked him to call me Robert—told me she was rumored to be Jewish herself. But that cannot have been true, because, as she herself later told me—did she lie? she was a mass of contradictions and dishonesty—she had hidden a Jewish friend, Madame Salomon, in her apartment during the Second World War, at the risk of her own life, of course. This was supposed to be proof, I imagine, that she was not antisemitic. I wonder if the fur coat and the jewels she said Madame Salomon gave her could have been a motive. And were they given voluntarily? In any case, had she been Jewish, she would no doubt have been arrested at some point during the Occupation.

She was a Parisienne through and through, since she had been born and brought up in the city at the turn of the century, and never lived anywhere else. She claimed to have seen Oscar Wilde in Paris—"I didn't like the way he looked, unhealthy"—and to have noticed the author Henri de Montherlant wandering about. Her family had come to Paris from Alsace, where they had owned a ribbon factory that made them a lot of money. So she was well educated and very musical and literary in her tastes, of which more later, but she had never married, and in retrospect I don't find it surprising, considering her personality.

At some point she must have used up a good deal of her inheritance, so she had decided to rent rooms in that huge apartment that was much too big for one person. She had spread the word and somehow she had also developed contacts with Princeton and Rutgers Universities, and possibly other schools as well, so she had a constant turnover of residents.

There was a club of correspondents who apparently wrote to her regularly, mostly students from Princeton and Rutgers who had stayed with her, Paul told me. It was called the Société Internationale des Haumesseriens; the Haumesseriens for short. And he laughed. At the time, my French was not good enough to get the pun right away, but I laughed, too, when he explained to me that it was called by those cynics who knew her "the 'Oh, mais c'est rien' " (oh, but it's nothing), which rhymes with Haumesserien. However, the very existence of this club showed that were there some people who appreciated her and thought enough of her to keep in touch, perhaps because at the very least she was a colorful character with pronounced old-fashioned views that she did not hesitate to express; views on society that seem to be much like those of the more snobby members of the upper economic classes as portrayed by Marcel Proust, who brought the world of pre-World War One France to life so brilliantly and often in a humorous, satirical way. Who knows what opinions on life and politics those Haumesseriens held?

We returned to the apartment and Paul removed his shoes before opening the door and gestured to me to remove mine. He was the soul of consideration, and wanted to make sure nobody would be awakened by our late entry. He opened the creaking doors as quietly as possible. And we made our way the short distance to our room across the creaking floorboards. They creaked only very slightly as we crossed them. Every time there was a creak he would stop and put a finger to his lips, as though one of us had made a sound. For the rest of my stay, although I didn't remove my shoes before entering, I followed his policy of being as completely quiet as possible when I ventured in or out.

When I awoke in the morning, after a good night's sleep, he was already gone, having performed his ablutions so silently and stripped his bed so quietly that I had heard nothing. I would never see him again.

Just after I had awakened, Mademoiselle Haumesser knocked, and wheeled herself in with my breakfast tray, with delicious strong coffee, a sliced baguette and fresh butter and jam. Everything was excellent, but a week or so later I cancelled breakfast when I found cat hairs in the butter, and I went out to cafes from then on, and discovered croissants. She had four cats, and they were spoiled rotten, allowed to do anything they wanted to do. They wandered all over the apartment.

In those days I enjoyed sleeping late, and I often did so. I don't really know why, but she had decided to take a proprietary interest in me and she took me to task about that habit. She seemed to feel that she had to take me under her bony uncomfortable wing. She told me that I should get up early and go out, that I should explore Paris and go to Versailles, and so forth, all of which I eventually did, but obviously not because she had told me to.

CHAPTER FOUR

Doing the Work and Exploring the City

P ROFESSOR SOBOLEVITCH HAD told me not to worry too much about doing the work, although certainly to do what was essential. The important thing was that I "get to know Paris," he said. I took his advice on that point seriously, and of course I also did the necessary work. My research topic, as I mentioned in chapter one, was the Jewish immigration to France from Tunisia and Morocco, not a subject I was passionate about, although I found it interesting enough. And I went eventually to see an official by appointment at the Foreign Office at the Quai d'Orsay, once I had stopped in at the front desk and explained my situation. The receptionist was very charming and obliging and made the appointment for me for a few days later, since everybody who could help me was busy.

The official was very kind and welcoming, and extremely helpful. He told me a good deal about what had happened during and after World War Two and with his permission I took notes about everything he said, including information about CRIF, the Conseil Représentatif des Institutions Juives de France (Representative Council of Jewish Institutions in France), the Jewish charity organization founded in 1944 in Montmartre that he sent me to, supplying me with its address and the names of people who worked there. A very helpful official at the organization discussed the immigration with me further—again I took notes—answered my questions, and gave me some addresses of immigrants who would allow me to interview them in Belleville, the sprawling erstwhile working-class and sometime artistic neighborhood that is spread out over four arrondissements.

A good part of it is in the nineteenth arrondissement, and some of it is in the twentieth, which is where I was sent for the interviews. At its southwest corner is the famous Père Lachaise cemetery, which I later went to visit. I got a map of the cemetery at the entrance, and a long leisurely walk took me past the elaborate mausoleums and simpler tombs to the grave of Marcel Proust and his family, interred not far from the Bizet family, including Jacques Bizet, Proust's school friend, son of the famous composer Georges Bizet and Geneviève née Halévy, later Proust's great friend, Madame Straus when she remarried. And in the same area is Oscar Wilde in a stately modernistic tomb designed by the British-American sculptor Sir Jacob Epstein. Among the other tombs of notable figures are those of Sarah Bernhardt; married couple Simone Signoret and Yves Montand in a joint tomb; writers Molière, Pierre-Augustin Caron de Beaumarchais (the author of *The Barber of Seville*), Jean de la Fontaine, Honoré de Balzac and the love of his life, Madame Ewelina Hańska, interred in one tomb; the Romantic poet Gérard de Nerval, the historian of the French Revolution Jules Michelet, for whom the hotel is named, Colette, and Guillaume Apollinaire; the Italian composers Vicenzo Bellini and Gioachino Rossini; French composer Daniel François-Esprit Auber; musicians Edith Piaf and Jim Morrison; the decipherer of hieroglyphs and Egyptologist Jean-François Champollion; the artists Delacroix, Caillebotte, Modigliani, Jacques-Louis David, and Camille Pissarro, and an amazing number of other political figures, composers, writers, and artists.

The part of Belleville that I visited was clearly a world apart from the sort of neighborhood one generally associates with Paris, of which most people see the tourist center along the Seine, Montmartre with its striking Basilica of Sacré-Coeur de Montmartre, and perhaps the famous cemetery just mentioned. But every city has its slums and insalubrious neighborhoods. I took the Métro there, and when I got out and had walked around a bit, I asked people, who were very helpful, to show me how to find the address I needed.

In those days, each Métro station had an *Indicateur d'Itinéraires* (Itinerary Indicator) just inside near the entrance. This was a huge map with a board below it with every station listed. You pressed a button next to your starting point and then one next to the ending point of your trip, and the map lit up, illuminating the line or lines of the route you had to take, with all the changes. It was easy to follow. You just had to remember where to make the changes, if any. Nowadays you have to look at a map on the wall, and search until you find your route, which can take some time.

The people I interviewed lived in poverty and in rundown buildings whose damp unpleasant corridors smelled of urine, stale food, tobacco, and other indefinable odors, all most unpleasant. The courtyards were running over with garbage, strewn all over the place. The people with whom the CRIF official had made appointments for me were expecting me so they came downstairs immediately when I rang them. We stood in the doorway of the building, and I took notes as they answered my questions and described their often unhappy experiences as newly arrived immigrants looking for jobs and places to live. They had not given up hope of bettering their lives, however, and were very gentle and very nice to me.

I also explored the Marais in the fourth arrondissement well to the southwest of Belleville, particularly the rue des Rosiers, Rosebush Street, the heart of the old Jewish quarter, which had nothing to do with my research project, really, but was certainly worth a visit, and represented a very different Jewish past with medieval roots, and later, at the end of the nineteenth century, assumed its present character with the arrival of East European immigrants of my own background. I also went to the Mémorial des Martyrs de la Déportation, reached down some steps in a small park near the Seine, and to the very moving Mémorial de la Shoah (the French Holocaust Museum), both not far from the rue des Rosiers.

All over Paris are monuments to fallen World War Two resistance fighters, with fresh flowers placed in holders on such occasions as VE Day. And there are historical plaques on building walls explaining what happened there, such as that on the wall of a school on the rue des Rosiers, which details the deportation of Jewish students and teachers. As one goes along past the school to the west, the street opens out into the Pletzl, a Yiddish word for a small central plaza, so named by the Eastern European Jews who emigrated to the medieval Jewish neighborhood, as a historical plaque on the wall tells us. Incidentally, it is also the word for a flat onion roll.

Nowadays, of course, there is no single Jewish neighborhood, and Jewish people live all over the city. The very Orthodox, such as those in the Marais, live near their synagogues, some of which date from the Middle Ages. The rue des Rosiers still retains its Jewish character, however, with Jewish bookstores, restaurants, and a wonderful bakery, Finkelsztajn, with delicious authentic Eastern European cakes, pastries, and breads including delicious pletzls, which I used to eat when I was young, but which I seldom find in New York nowadays. In 1963 there was a Jewish delicatessen on the street, Chez Jo Goldenberg, with real gefilte fish and cold cuts such as corned beef. In 1982 it was bombed by Palestinian terrorists, resulting in deaths and injuries. It has never reopened.

Not far away is the gorgeous place des Vosges, one of the most beautiful parks in Paris, with a statue of Louis XIII in the middle, under some trees, and fountains in the open spaces. The square is surrounded by red brick buildings in Louis XIII style, and trees in front of them surround the park, which is turn surrounded by galleries all around it, with shops and restaurants. Once called the place Royale, it used to be where the royal family, the court, and foreign diplomats and aristocrats gathered for special occasions. Victor Hugo lived there, and his house at the southeast corner is an excellent free museum.

A couple of very short blocks to the west of the place des Vosges is the Musée Carnavalet, the Museum of the History of the City of Paris. It's a gorgeous seventeenth-century building that was the town house of Madame de Sévigné, known for her correspondence with her married daughter, who had left Paris and lived in Provence. They exchanged letters almost every day, and present a detailed picture of what life was like in their era

The museum itself is arranged in the order of the centuries, and on a later trip, the section on the French Revolution reminded me of my visit to the museum at the Conciergerie, which had been the prison on the Île St.-Louis where those awaiting the guillotine were kept. It was very sad to see the courtyard where they waited, the cells where they were kept, and the tiny cell where Marie-Antoinette had been imprisoned before being driven in a tumbril across town to be executed at Paris's main guillotine in what is now the place de la Concorde, in front of the entrance to the Champs-Élysées.

If you go east to one of the streets bordering the Marais, the boulevard Henri IV, and turn south down the boulevard's west side in the direction of the the pont Sully, you find yourself across the street from one of the headquarters of the French National Guard, a military and police reserve force, who emerge periodically mounted on horseback, and march through the streets, making a picturesque sight in their uniforms.

Right near the headquarters, continuing south towards the bridge, is a little riverside park with a playground on the river, and right near the bridge, you can see the base of a round tower. There is a historical marker that tells you this round construction of large stones piled one upon another is all that is left of the original Bastille, which was a vast prison fortress, larger than one could have imagined, its northern end far away in the place de la Bastille, its monument clearly seen from near the park when you look north up the boulevard Henri IV.

Several weeks after my arrival, I went to interview the author Albert Memmi, whose wonderful books had inspired me and on whom I had written a class paper that no doubt suggested the research topic Professor Sobolevitch proposed to me. Albert Memmi was a very erudite philosopher and novelist, a Tunisian Jew, writing about colonialism, the colonized, racism, and the conflict of cultures. Among his books are *La statue de sel* (The Statue of Salt; 1953) and *Portrait d'un juif* (Portrait of a Jew; 1962).

He was awfully nice to me, as I sat in his apartment and took notes on what he had to say on these subjects, on the antisemitism of his native land in the newly independent Muslim state, and on how he had felt driven to leave and to take up residence in Paris. My research and the resulting paper I wrote for the Carnegie Foundation, including what Memmi had to say, perhaps served some purpose for the State Department, but I have no idea what use that information could have been. I did not pursue the subject after that summer.

One of the most useful things I learned in the course of my research into the Maghreb was a knowledge of its cuisine, a branch of Ottoman Empire cuisine, which includes Greek and Turkish dishes. Couscous is among many superb North African dishes, which one can sample in such Parisian restaurants as Le Méchoui du Prince, an excellent Moroccan restaurant on the rue Monsieur-le-Prince. The word *méchoui* means barbecue in Arabic, and refers originally to a whole spit-roasted lamb. The word couscous refers not only to the very fine steamed semolina, but also the dish of which it is the base, prepared in various succulent, delicious ways. It also serves as a Jewish Sabbath dish, prepared on Friday afternoons so it only has to be heated through on Saturday without any forbidden work, whether with just vegetables or with meats as well, just as the Ashkenazi Jews prepared the slowly simmered chulent, a bean and meat casserole, similar to the southern French cassoulet. The word undoubtedly comes from a combination of the French words *chaud* and *lent*, hot and slow.

CHAPTER FIVE

The Pleasures of
Wandering the Streets

ONE MORNING WHEN I awoke late, as usual, and opened my bedroom door to go to the bathroom, I was greeted with the pungent odor of excrement. It seems that one of the cats had taken a dump right in front of my door. I called Mlle. Haumesser, who came rolling up immediately in her wheelchair, a slight smirk on her face. I pointed to the pile of cat turds on the floor. "Ah, ils ont fait encore une sottise (Ah, they've done something stupid again)," she said, without the least apology, "ils ne font ça que quand ils n'aiment pas quelqu'un." (They only do that when they don't like someone.) And she wheeled herself away. She had the attendant who came in daily to take care of her and to perform the duties of a general maid of all work including her shopping, clean it up, while I performed my ablutions and got dressed for the day. I thought that the pile of droppings must have been there for awhile, that she knew about it, and deliberately waited for me to open the door.

The attendant would bring in clean sheets once a week, and collect laundry in a sack to be sent out. She was very pleasant, and she must have had a very even temper to be able to put up with Mademoiselle.

I proceeded to the kitchen where, since I was late, I was supposed to get my breakfast, instead of having it on a tray in my room. The four cats were all over the place, clambering up onto the table and the cabinets, eating everything they could get their paws on, including the butter. That was the moment I decided I was definitely no longer going to have breakfast in the apartment, especially since I had found those cat hairs in the butter the day before. Every once in a while, when one of them climbed onto her, she would start to purr herself, and then take the cat and put it down onto the floor. She adored those cats, more than she ever did people. The kitchen was huge, a great old room, well furnished with everything anyone could have needed. She sat at the table slicing onions. She was a fabulous cook, as I was to discover.

As I stood there patiently waiting for my coffee, she started to lecture me once again about my habit of sleeping late. She then launched into a little speech about Jews, aware no doubt of my feelings about our first meeting, and of what I must think of her. "Je distingue trois sortes de juifs : les bons juifs, les mauvais juifs, et cette crapule qui est venue de la Pologne." (I distinguish three sorts of Jews: good Jews, bad Jews, and that crap that came here from Poland.) The word *crapule* means "scoundrel" or "crook," literally, but of course it reminded me of the English word, and my translation is therefore accurate in tone, if not in literal meaning.

I looked at her astounded. Again with the antisemitic bull? And totally unprovoked. By this time I was already used to her provocations. All four of my grandparents were from a shtetl, Yiddish for small city or town, in the eastern reaches of the pre-World War One Austro-Hungarian Empire, from the province of Galicia, as I said. Nevertheless, I said to her, "Mademoiselle, I prefer to alert you to the fact (je prèfère vous avertir) that my grandparents were from Poland." In fact, the shtetl they came from was in Poland between the two world wars, and my maternal grandfather and paternal grandmother spoke excellent Polish, among other languages. I thought that warning her would make her think twice about carrying on like this, and that I would get the better of her and make her feel embarrassed, but without batting an eyelash, she said drily and disdainfully, turning her head away, "Ah, je regrette." (Ah, I'm sorry; or Ah, how regrettable.) In other words, "That's too bad." This was my dismissal. She went back to her onions and her cats. I had drunk my coffee so I put down the cup and turned and left without another word. I should have known that you can't faze an antisemite. At least this time I felt contempt rather than hurt.

Another time, when I got home one afternoon, she had invited me to listen to her play the piano, so I went and sat in the salon. In her snobby way, and while she was playing with lots of wrong notes, she was going on about how wonderful the aristocrats of France are and what a shame it is that they are no longer considered worthy of adulation as they were in the old days, as Hollywood movie stars are today. I rolled my eyes and said, "Ah, oui, les aristocrates…. Je les connais un peu, j'ai lu Marcel Proust" ! (Ah, yes, aristocrats… I know them a little. I've read Marcel Proust.) To which she replied, almost shouting, "Proust ! Un juif pédéraste ! Naturellement il écrit des saletés !" (Proust! A Jew pederast! Naturally he writes filth!)

I sat there stunned. I was very upset by this malicious remark. I couldn't believe she'd said it. This was one attempt to hurt me that actually succeeded, which it wouldn't have done nowadays, when I would have treated it with total sneering contempt.

So why in the world after all this nonsense did I continue to stay there in that old apartment? I was no longer tired and no doubt I could have gotten it together to leave, to find a hotel. I probably had enough money, just as I had enough to pay for my room in the apartment, and money for other necessary expenses: food, transport around Paris, some recreational activities such as the theater. Perhaps I could have gone to the one where another member of the group was staying at the hôtel Port-Royal. We were not supposed to have too much contact with each other, but to pursue our research and immerse ourselves in the language. Somehow, despite these incidents, which occurred at some remove in time from each other, it was easier just to be lazy and stay there, rather than contacting the people at the Carnegie Foundation and getting permission to search for another place to stay, packing my things, and moving on. Laziness, inertia, the path of least resistance—call it what you will—prevailed.

I left the apartment as quickly as possible that late afternoon to wander the streets, one of the greatest pleasures of being there, still today. Even on my first time in Paris, although I sometimes had a specific place I was going to, I was a great *flâneur*—an aimless wanderer, just enjoying exploring the city and discovering beautiful buildings and squares and parks I had never seen before, not to mention new restaurants and cafes. I was what the French call a *badaud*: an idle onlooker, sometimes with head in the clouds, who gawks or stares at the various sights, whether architectural details or pastry shop windows. And wherever I went I had a sense of being surrounded by history, partly because of the numerous plaques on buildings telling of the people who had lived there; and the historic markers in the form of brown shields on short poles on corners and in front of buildings recounting the history of the immediate surroundings, including that of buildings long gone.

I discovered the small, fairly inexpensive restaurants on the rue du Dragon not too far from the apartment and I would go there often for dinner. I explored the neighborhood, marveled at the architectural details, and discovered the delights of walking along the Seine and browsing in the stalls of the *bouquinistes* (booksellers) that line both banks of the river, still one of my great pleasures on every visit. As the Swiss-born poet and novelist Blaise Cendrars (1887-1961) said, "Paris, la seule ville au monde où coule un fleuve encadré par deux rangées de livres" (Paris, the only city in the world where there flows a river framed/bordered by two rows of books).

I walked out onto the pont des Arts, the only fully pedestrian bridge across the Seine, although bicycles use it too. Wandering out into the middle of the bridge and stopping to lean against the rails on either side or to sit on one of the benches in the center, you have a magnificent view of both the right and left banks, and all the way to the east and to the west, where you can see Paris's most famous landmark, the Eiffel Tower. I went countless times to the pont des Arts, always so wonderful. To the east on the right bank you can also see the roofs of the buildings in the place du Châtelet, including that of Sarah Bernhardt's theater. There are two theaters in the square, on either side of it, as well as a number of cafes. The place du Châtelet was originally the site of a stronghold and prison, the Grand Châtelet, where certain city officials had offices until the complex of buildings was demolished in the early nineteenth century,

Of course, I had to go to the Eiffel Tower, and I walked there from the rue des Saints-Pères, turning west on the boulevard St.-Germain and continuing on the rue Saint-Dominique. After waiting on the usual very long line, I finally got in, and I took the elevator to the top, stayed to look at the view, then climbed the flights of stairs down to the different platforms, marveling at the views from each one. The Jules Verne Restaurant on the second floor of the tower did not open until 1983, and when I did eventually eat there, I found the food exceptionally delicious and the view an amazing background for dining.

I also went to the western tip of the Île de la Cité to the little triangular park that is there next to the pont Neuf, the New Bridge, actually the oldest bridge in Paris. The park that ends in a point at the tip of the island is called the square du Vert Galant, named for King Henri IV whose sobriquet was Vert-Gallant, the Green Gallant, because of his many mistresses. His statue is on the pont Neuf just above the park, at the spot where he was assassinated. I sat there for an hour one sunset, and it was glorious and so very beautiful to look westward with the Louvre on the right bank, the pont des Arts, and the Académie Française on the left bank. Boats sailed past, including the great tourist boats filled with passengers. You could have a meal on some of those boats. I did take a river cruise with a very good informative guide, who explained the history of everything we were passing as we took a huge kind of circular path up and down the Seine. You got on the boat not far from the square du Vert Galant, just beyond the park and just below the Pont Neuf on the right bank side of the island.

In short, I was getting to know Paris, as Professor Sobolevitch had advised, and falling in love with the city.

One of my other favorite teachers at Rutgers was Professor Gerald Bertin, whose specialty was medieval French, and he and his wife and two sons were in Paris on vacation while I was there. I had gotten to know him first of all because he was a regular at the French table in the cafeteria on the days when he had classes.

In his course on medieval French literature I enjoyed learning how to pronounce medieval French, as we read one of the most famous examples of the medieval literary genre, the *chanson de geste* (song/saga of the hero; epic rhymed poem), *La Chanson de Roland* (The Song of Roland) in its original version. I loved learning to say the opening lines, "Carles li reis, nostre emperere magnes, / Set ans tuz pleins / ad estet en Espaigne..." (Charles the king, our great emperor [Charlemagne],/

for seven full years / was in Spain), pronouncing almost all the letters. In modern French the second line would be "sept ans tous pleins", and instead of the modern pronunciation, 'se tahn too plen' with both the n sounds nasalized, we said 'set ahnts toots plents'.

Professor Bertin got in touch with me and invited me to dinner. We went to a Chinese restaurant, of all things to do in Paris if one is not a full-time resident, and I was very surprised to see how French cuisine had influenced the Chinese food, which was very different from American Chinese food in some ways, and quite delicious. Red wine was used in sauces, for instance.

I met the family at their rented apartment, going up broad flights of stairs with an ornate iron balustrade. The rooms were spacious and beautifully furnished, and it was light and airy with high ceilings, quite different from Mademoiselle Haumesser's place. I learned the expression *l'esprit de l'escalier* (staircase wit) from Professor Bertin as we were going down the stairs. It means something you think of when you're on the way down that you should have said as a reply or a riposte while you were upstairs at a party or a dinner.

We had a great evening, and it was wonderful to see someone from home. Professor Bertin was a very nice man, and back in the US, during the next semester, he hired me to tutor his sons in French. "They won't listen to me," he said. I used to go out to his house in Edison, NJ and always had a delicious meal afterwards, and excellent coffee as well.

I think they were in Paris for about another week, and I didn't see them again on that trip. In the course of my wanderings I did meet other people, a couple of whom I saw several times.

CHAPTER SIX

Guy at the Polidor

ONE DAY, FAIRLY soon after my arrival in Paris, my leisurely meandering took me over to the Odéon, as I browsed in the numerous bookstores in the St.-Germain neighborhood, stores which cater not only to the general reader but to students and professors of the Sorbonne as well. Unfortunately, many of those wonderful bookstores have been replaced today, in the first quarter of the twenty-first century, by fashion boutiques—who shops there? how do they stay open? I never see anyone in them. Anyway, on my walk, I discovered a restaurant on the rue Monsieur-le-Prince, at the time a street of inexpensive restaurants, include a very good crêperie with a counter on the street where you could buy crêpes to go, just as you can at the many stands all over the city. Crêpes are the Parisian snacks par excellence, much as pizza is in New York City.

Much frequented in those days by university students, the restaurant I discovered was the Crèmerie Polidor, usually just called the Polidor, on the corner of the rue Racine, a short way from the Sorbonne on the boulevard St.-Michel. The traditional classic food was very good, with daily specials not to be missed. Their starters, including *pâté de campagne* (country-style pâté), and an *assiette de crudités* (plate of raw vegetables), with grated carrot salad, celery rémoulade, cucumber salad, beet salad, and lettuce were delicious. Their *confit de canard* (roast duck made with onions and herbs and preserved in its own fat, then sauteed to crispness in that fat), served on a bed of sauerkraut with French fries on the side was mouthwatering. And their version of *boeuf bourguignon*, beef in burgundy wine sauce, with mashed potatoes, was excellent. I was familiar with the dish already because I had had it at a restaurant in New Brunswick that served some French dishes. The classic desserts at the Polidor were superb, among them their specialty, *Tarte Tatin*, an upside-down caramelized apple tart, served with whipped cream and/or vanilla ice cream on the side.

Today, however, it is pretty much foreign tourists who eat there, often in groups, although there are plenty of French people there too. Since the early 2020s, when there was a change of management and chef, the food has gone downhill. For years afterwards, every time I went to Paris, I avoided it because of the smoking, but back then in 1963, although I detested smoking, I didn't have the sort of allergic reaction that I have developed since. I coughed a lot, but I bore with it. Once smoking had been outlawed inside Parisian restaurants, I returned, and since I have been at the same hotel, the Michelet Odéon in the place de l'Odéon across the rue Rotrou from the theater for decades, since 1992, it had become my *cantine*, and I was a well known habitué. They offered me a kir (white wine and crème de cassis) every time I went there, and kirs to everyone I was with. But the new management more or less requires reservations and caters to large groups. Nor were they welcoming, coldly asking me if I had a reservation, and when I said I hadn't made one because I didn't realize one had to, making me wait at the bar in the next room before showing me to a table, where I had a good time and a decent meal, but I stopped going there nevertheless.

The Polidor's beautiful old-fashioned décor has been preserved since its founding in 1845. Woody Allen used it in his 2011 film *Midnight in Paris*. Particularly interesting are the cabinets with small drawers against the back wall. In the days when few Paris apartments had kitchens so that everyone went to restaurants for their meals, the drawers were meant for regulars who left their *couverts* (covers) in them; that is, their cutlery and napkins. In later years, the restaurant used to have a funny, prominently displayed sign that read, "La maison n'accepte pas de cartes de crédit depuis 1845." (The house does not accept credit cards since 1845.) In 1963, I don't recall ever even having heard of credit cards. There weren't any ATMs back then or of course the bank cards to go with them until 1969. Now they are legally obliged to take credit cards, and they dislike it if you offer them cash.

Everyone sits communally at long tables with classic red and white checked tablecloths, but there is no family-style service as there was at that restaurant in the rue de la Harpe. In those days, as today, you could converse with your neighbors. In fact, you are expected to do so. I have encountered very few people who do not wish to engage in conversation. I was shown to one of the tables in the center of the room, and I sat opposite a young man with dark hair and a look of great concentration. He was about my age who seemed interested only in reading his newspaper, *L'Humanité*, the Communist newspaper, although I didn't yet know that. In fact, I didn't know much about French newspapers, but I did know that each one had a particular political stance, and that *Libération*, for instance, was a leftist, and, as I incorrectly thought, a Communist journal.

I decided to start a conversation with this person, so I said, stating the obvious, in a joking manner, "I see you are reading *L'Humanité*. I guess you're not a Communist then?"

He looked at me as if I were an idiot. "Bien sûr que je suis communiste!" (Of course, I'm a Communist!), he said.

"Oh, very interesting," I replied. I had never actually met a young person who would state so boldly and openly that he was a Communist, but in France then as today, the Communists were a respectable and respected political party; well, not respected by everybody, of course. Still, it was no crime to be a Communist, and the Communist Party was on the election lists and ballots along with so many other parties. In the United States, especially in those days, but even today, few people would dare make such a statement, especially not to a stranger. And at that time, McCarthyism had only been discredited a few years before, but the witch hunts and Hollywood blacklisting continued, so it was still a dangerous admission in the United States.

"I thought *Libération* was the Communist paper."

"No, it's Socialist. This is the Communist paper," he said, holding it up.

"Well, I am also sort of a Communist," I said. I don't think that was strictly true, because my sympathies were much more socialist and pacifist, not for any violence against anyone, and certainly not for any violent revolution, but for equality and the equal distribution of wealth, as well as full and supportive social services for people. I was opposed even to capital punishment, and in tune with worker's rights, national health care, and socialist institutions; in short, the sort of governments that prevailed in the Scandinavian countries. I would characterize myself as a democratic socialist. But I did like certain things about the Communist regimes at that time, such as their universal health care, before I found out that they came at the cost of lies, crimes, and the repression of free speech and other freedoms I took for granted, and all in the name of social justice, equality, and workers' rights.

At any rate, his face lit up. "Where are you from, that you don't know these things?" he asked, "I mean, you're from France of course, but what part of France?" Even then, my accent was very good. I did not yet speak with the colloquial Parisian accent that I was to absorb on later trips, but rather with the more cultivated accent one might associate with the stage. And of course I had lots of vocabulary and *argot* (slang) yet to learn.

"I'm an American. My name is Robert."

"I'm Guy. Nice to meet you," and he offered me his hand. "An American! Unbelievable. I mean your French is perfect. Your accent is so classic! And you're a Communist, too. But that's incredible. I've never heard of an American who's actually a Communist."

"Oh, we do exist. But underground mostly. Nobody dares to admit it. And as for my French, I am majoring in the language and literature for my university degree. I'm a student back in the United States at Rutgers University, the state university of New Jersey." And I told him something about my family, whose sympathies during the Great Depression of the thirties were far left. But back home we didn't dare talk about that openly, outside the family house. "It is still too dangerous," I explained. He had heard all about McCarthy, and he understood very well. But in Paris, I suddenly felt that I would be free to be myself, politically, and to explore the world of leftist ideas and ideals. Guy and I proceeded to have a long discussion, which continued after lunch in a walk around the neighborhood. We agreed that we didn't like the idea of a violent revolution, but of a peaceful transition to a more egalitarian system.

He invited me up to his apartment on the charming old rue des Quatre-Vents—I loved the name: the Street of the Four Winds. It had been spared destruction during Baron Haussmann's rebuilding of parts of Paris in the 1850s under Napoleon III, when he put through the boulevard St.-Germain and the boulevard St.-Michel, and tore down many of the narrow streets in their vicinity, while leaving vestiges of many others. I was very interested to see another Paris apartment, this one quite different of course from the one I was staying in. It was rather cramped, with room for a bed, a table and chairs, a small couch, and very little else, with part of one wall reserved for a stove, sink, and refrigerator; and a small bathroom.

Later on, he would introduce me to his girlfriend Jeanne and invite me to parties, and to meet his other friends. He presented me almost as a curiosity, an American Communist, or at least an American with Communist sympathies who hadn't bought into all the propaganda, although we both knew about and deplored the Stalinist crimes. He thought the system was working better after Stalin's death. I wasn't really quite so sure. But it was a great pleasure to discuss these issues openly.

CHAPTER SEVEN

Monsieur Zaki

I WOKE UP LATE one morning, around ten, as usual, this time to the rather screechy strains of a violin, and the accompanying sounds of the out-of-tune piano in the salon. After I had finished my ablutions, and as I was preparing to go out to get breakfast and for the rest of the morning, I peeked into the salon. Mlle. Haumesser, sitting in her wheelchair, was playing the piano, and a nice-looking man with a little black mustache was playing the violin.

Mademoiselle seemed sometimes to have eyes in the back of her head. She wheeled about. "Come in!" she ordered. I did so, and she introduced me to M. Zaki, an Egyptian violinist who was her protégé, as she said, using that exact word.

Sitting at the far end of the room, was a woman who was introduced to me as Madame Zaki, and their two demure little daughters, aged about six and eight, both dressed identically in adorable deep blue velvet dresses with lace collars. They actually curtseyed to me. The family was an enchanting one, friendly and smiling, and completely charming.

The violin and piano playing over, they all left, and as I was about to follow, Mademoiselle summoned me back, and launched into a tirade. "Did you see that woman? So unattractive, she doesn't know how to dress, she makes herself up in such a vulgar fashion." Madame Zaki was elegantly and simply dressed and did not use a lot of makeup. I thought she looked beautiful. I said nothing, however. "And those two dreadful little girls---they might be pretty if she dressed them well. Did you see how she dressed them? So vulgar. She has no taste..." Of course, I thought they were beautifully dressed, and looked adorable. Naturally, I gave Mademoiselle a quizzical look, but again I didn't tell her what I thought. "But he, on the other hand," she continued, "has wonderful taste. Did you hear how beautifully he played that Beethoven piece?" It was then that I realized that Mademoiselle Haumesser was madly in love with Monsieur Zaki. And she was obviously deeply jealous of his wife. I simply nodded, and said, obviously unenthusiastic, "Well, uh, yes, I heard…"

"Well, run along!" she commanded. "Here you are standing about, up late as usual. You really do yourself a disservice, getting up so late. So lazy…" I left.

She was such a mass of contradictions, nice enough to me one moment, then abrupt, dismissive, and even unkind the next, treating me to her antiquated notions about people. All of a sudden she was taking me into her confidence as if we were friends, as if she could trust me. Very odd indeed!

I never did learn how they met, or how he became attached to her. She had high hopes for him as a concert violinist with an international career in store, and told me later that day that she wanted to launch him into society with a concert in her salon. I have no idea how he actually earned a living that would have allowed him to buy those beautiful, expensive dresses for his daughters. Perhaps he was independently wealthy. He seemed, from what I heard later, to know nobody in the world of Paris music, and was pretty much a new immigrant without friends. Maybe he thought he could earn some money by teaching. And of course he was desperate to start a career as a concert violinist. I was skeptical, after the bit I had heard them play, of course. He might possibly secure a position in the string section of an orchestra, if his playing improved considerably, or he might teach the violin, but he would never be a concert soloist.

CHAPTER EIGHT

Monsieur Maximov

I DIDN'T ALWAYS GO out in the afternoon after I came back for lunch. There were times when I just wanted to stay in the apartment and read one of the new books I had gotten, and rest. Mademoiselle used to invite me occasionally to listen to her play or to meet friends of hers. I don't know why. She was so strangely inconsistent. She was a complicated character, no doubt about it. I got the impression sometimes that she actually liked me.

One day I arrived home after lunch and, as I opened the door, I was greeted with the most marvelous, quite loud lively music, with wonderful almost Offenbachian strains. I smiled and could not resist going into the salon. There sat Mademoiselle in her eternal rose-colored glasses. She beckoned me into the room. As usual she was unsmiling. In fact, as I recall, she hardly ever did smile.

I entered, and she motioned me into a chair. When the playing stopped, I applauded. "Bravo, monsieur, bravo!" Mademoiselle did not applaud, and she looked at me as if I were crazy.

"This is Monsieur Maximov. He's Russian. He was a circus pianist. A glass of wine, Monsieur Maximov?"

"Oui, merrrci beauooocoup, chèrrre Mahdmouahzyel…" he said, rolling his Rs and swallowing his words, practically licking his lips. I introduced myself, while Mademoiselle wheeled herself over to the sideboard, and poured a generous glass of wine for the pianist, who went over to retrieve it from her. He staggered very slightly, and I realized he had already had quite a few glasses of wine. And he spoke French with such a heavy Russian accent that I had some difficulty understanding him, especially as his speech was quite slurred because of the wine. As I learned later, that was what he visited her for, the wine, with which she was quite generous, and the handouts she gave him. He was nearly broke, and his old dark blue suit was quite shabby, his shirt frayed at the collar and the cuffs. His unpolished shoes looked so old that they might have had holes in the soles.

Monsieur Maximov had left Russia as soon after the Revolution as possible, like so many, and, being a trained musician, had gotten a job with a traveling French circus. He had enjoyed life on the road, but eventually he got too old and was too tired to continue such an arduous existence.

When he left, Mademoiselle said, "That awful, vulgar music. He plays so badly."

"I rather liked it," I said. "It was so lively, so vivacious. Lots of fun. And I thought he played rather well."

"You would," she said drily. One did not contradict Mademoiselle. I had discovered that she hated being contradicted, and I enjoyed doing just that. It was nice to get a bit of revenge. And she added, "You have no taste in music, like most Americans." Ah, so I was an American after all! At least when it came to musical taste.

"On the contrary. My father loved classical music, and I grew up hearing Beethoven's Violin Concerto played by Jascha Heifetz, one of his favorites, and symphonies by Mozart, Beethoven, and Brahms. I love that kind of music, both the eighteenth-century classical, and the later Romantic school. Ah, Schubert…I do like folk music and jazz too though, but not rock and roll."

"Très bien, très bien," she said dismissively, with a downward motion of her hand. And she wheeled herself over to the piano, where she proceeded to play a Beethoven sonata with so many wrong notes and stumbling passages, as usual, that I had all I could do not to burst out laughing. The fact that the piano was out of tune had been less noticeable when Monsieur Maximov had been pounding out his rousing circus marches.

Eventually she finished. She waited for my applause. After a pause I applauded, not very enthusiastically. "Well…I find your playing… absolutely astonishing…"

"Of course. I was professionally trained. I could have been a concert pianist. But the war intervened." She meant the First World War, but since she was born in 1883, she was thirty-one by the time the war broke out, a bit late in life not to have started on such a career, especially with her prestigious professional training. Needless to say, I refrained from mentioning this obvious fact.

"Nadia Boulanger, you know, thought I was very promising," she said.

"Did she really? That's nice."

"That's all you have to say? 'Nice'?" she said disgustedly. And she wheeled herself away, as I smiled broadly to myself. I bet she never knew Boulanger at all. Maybe she saw her walking around, as she claimed to have seen Oscar Wilde.

CHAPTER NINE

The Algerian Colonel

ONE NIGHT, I was invited to a party by Guy, and he warned me to be careful when talking with the "Algerian colonel," whom I was sure to meet.

"C'est un type difficile (He's a rough customer)," Guy informed me. "He thought nothing of killing Algerians during the war and would take potshots at them. And he has a vile temper. Once, his wife bought a hat after he had forbidden her to do so, and then he hated the hat too, and he tore it off her head and stomped on it. Then he drove into town and threw it at the milliner and demanded his money back. And he got it, right away, I am sure. Another time, a local farmer, a Frenchman, came into his office to complain about Algerian poachers and thieves who had stolen things from him. Apparently, he berated the colonel roundly for not doing his job, for being lax in the performance of his duty. ' "Tournez-vous et sortez !" (Turn around and get out!),' he said. The man turned to go, and the colonel shot him in the back, and had his men drag the body out. Obviously, he was never punished for that vile murder! So be careful. He's capable of anything."

"Wow!" I said. "I certainly will be." I was intrigued at the prospect of meeting this brute, whether or not the stories were true, which I doubted slightly, especially the one about the murder. I had never met anyone remotely like him. And I was rather scared too.

When I arrived at the party, I saw the colonel. He was not in uniform, but there was no mistaking him. He was tall and ramrod thin, scowling at everyone through narrowed eyes. And he was drinking shot glass after shot glass of cognac, I believe it was.

I was introduced to everybody, all smiling and friendly. And then I was introduced to the colonel, who shook my hand with an iron grip and looked me straight in the eye in a rather challenging way. I bowed my head to him in a respectful way. Then I joined this terribly forbidding man, this murderer if he was one, in a glass of cognac at his insistence. And later I had some wine to drink. Our conversation was very brief. He was happy to welcome an American, and had nothing much else to say, but was glad to meet someone whom he probably thought was a fanatical anti-Communist. I don't know whom he knew to get invited to the party, but he cannot have known about Guy and his politics. I moved on, and I noticed that nobody talked to him very much. Why would they really? What could they say to each other? He left soon after our brief conversation, and the party grew more relaxed.

The evening was amusing, the usual sort of thing, lots of conversation, lots of drinking. I stuck to Guy and his girlfriend, and we talked a lot about politics. They told me about the bodies found hanging in the Bois de Boulogne, the lynched Algerians. Nobody was ever punished for those crimes. And Guy and his girlfriend Jeanne were very anti-De Gaulle; that is, the De Gaulle of the present day, not the one who had led the French Resistance from London in World War Two. In fact, the party stopped while everybody gathered around the record player to listen to a parody of De Gaulle. Somebody did a speech called "Piétons de Paris" (Pedestrians of Paris), a takeoff on his speech about what was expected of citizens by the new regime, "Citoyens de Paris" (Citizens of Paris). The parody was all about crossing the street, observing the red and green lights, and it was very authoritarian in tone, providing one laugh after another. I used to be able to do some of the routine myself, but I have long ago forgotten it.

The evening was terrific, light-hearted and frivolous and fun, and I and Guy and Jeanne walked back from wherever it was on the right bank to his apartment on the rue des Quatre-Vents, and I proceeded back to the rue des Saints-Pères for a good night's sleep.

CHAPTER TEN

My Week in Copenhagen

IN THE MIDDLE of the sweltering summer, I decided to take a week off and go to Copenhagen, where a college friend of mine, Alan, was staying for a couple of months in an international student dormitory, where Danish and students mostly from other Scandinavian countries rented rooms. He had invited me, if I had the time, to visit him there, and he secured a room for me.

He was a fellow French major, and as such, we had many of the same classes and became good friends at Rutgers, and even lived in the French dorm one year. The dorm was one floor of one of the large dormitory buildings on the banks of the Raritan, Frelinghuysen.

Alan lived in Summit, NJ, where I had been invited to visit him and his family. His father was a wonderful artist, and his charming mother was Danish. I could see where Alan got his interest in French from. His father had studied in Paris and was bilingual. His conversation was a mixture of French and English, and he would switch from one language to another without any warning. Alan had already graduated, being a year or so ahead of me at Rutgers, but we had remained in touch, which unfortunately we no longer are. He was in Denmark to study the Danish language, to take courses at the University of Copenhagen, and to visit his grandparents.

When the day came, I left the Gare du Nord on the overnight train to Hamburg, where I was to change trains in the morning for Copenhagen, taking the ferry across the Baltic Sea. The train was extremely crowded. I sat in a compartment with three older French ladies, and the corridors quickly filled with groups of German students who were quite loud and unruly, leaning out the windows and yelling to the vendors who wheeled their food carts up to the train, selling snacks and drinks.

One of the French women couldn't stand it. She said quite loudly, "Cette sale graisse, ça vient encore nous emmerder!" (That filthy grease, they've come to shit all over us again!) It was only eighteen years after the end of World War Two, and memories of the horrors of the Occupation were still fresh.

The ride through France and Germany was spectacular. Night was falling when we crossed the Elbe, and I could see Köln (Cologne) all lit up, with its beautiful cathedral standing out in the moonlight.

Eventually we reached Hamburg. Not having been able to get much sleep all night, I was rather tired. And I had no idea where to go to get the train to Denmark. I approached an official on the platform and asked him in German what I should do. He pointed at the track across the platform I was already on, and said, "Bleiben Sie da. Der Zug kommt bald." (Stay there. The train will be along soon.)

Almost two hours went by, and I started to wonder what was going on, whether the train was late, or what. So I approached the official again and asked him about the train. He shouted at me, "Was wollen Sie? Ich hab' Ihnen gesagt! Bleiben Sie da!" (What do you want? I told you! Stay there!") From the way he shouted, I immediately saw pictures of Nazi guards in my mind's eye, and I wondered what he had done during the war. He was certainly old enough to have been in the armed forces. Of course, I simply thanked him, and stayed put. The train arrived within another half hour.

We arrived at the ferry at Lübeck in short order. The trip across the Baltic was a delight, calm and under sunny skies. The sea was full of seaweed, there were few waves, and the crowded ferry moved very slowly. There was a superb buffet with what I am sure were many wonderful herring preparations, but unfortunately I had no marks, only travelers' checks, which is how one traveled in those days, so I couldn't get anything to eat, because I hadn't cashed them for German currency, and they wouldn't take French francs. Of course, there was no euro in those days, and each country had its own colorful banknotes and coins.

I cashed some checks for Danish kroner (the currency still used today, pegged to the euro), when I arrived at the station. I had a city plan, and I asked in English at the information desk for directions. Everybody seemed to speak English. I was directed to a tramway that would let me off near the dormitory. On the tram, I was looking at the map, and a gentleman interrupted me and asked me in English if I needed help, which I was happy to accept, thanking him profusely. How wonderful, I thought, that a perfect stranger asks another perfect stranger if he needs help, and so politely and kindly too.

So I readily found my way to the dormitory and was warmly welcomed by my friend. After I had settled in, we went for a walk. In the days after my arrival, Alan and I walked around the port and the royal castle, all so beautiful. Of course I loved the statue of H. C. Andersen's Little Mermaid, and all the boats. What a splendid place! And I attended a couple of very interesting university lectures with him, one about the Danish language; and one a detailed account of the now well known Danish Resistance in World War Two, about how they sabotaged factories, and rescued almost the entire Danish Jewish population, many of whom were ferried by fisherman across the water to safety in Sweden. The general history was recounted, with a slide show, as well as individual stories.

Alan introduced me to his grandmother, who was Jewish, the daughter of the deceased rabbi, and we went to synagogue services on Friday evening. Afterwards, she introduced me to the cantor, who had survived the Holocaust, and we had a conversation in German, ironically enough, because he spoke no English and I spoke no Danish. He told me that during World War Two King Christian X used to go sometimes to Friday night services, to flout the Germans. He was a revered, beloved monarch, and a national symbol of the Danish Resistance to the Occupation. It's a myth that he ever wore the yellow star, because Danish Jews were not required to do so, possibly as a result of the king's intervention with the German authorities, threatening to wear the star if they should impose it on the Jewish population.

That evening she took us to a cafeteria for some delicious *smørrebrød*, open-faced sandwiches, a Danish specialty. The word actually means buttered bread, and the sandwich, which can be quite elaborate, always begins with a thick layer of butter smeared on whatever kind of bread is used.

Danish eating hours include early dinner, around five o'clock; and late last snack at ten, including the absolutely delicious *rødgrød med fløde* (red pudding with cream), a summertime red berry pudding with heavy cream on top, served regularly every night at the dormitory after we had returned from evening activities. Everyone helped themselves from big bowls on the side buffet. The Danish students who were there taught me to pronounce the name: The barred 'o' is pronounced like the German umlauted 'o' and the 'r' is very guttural, while the 'd' sounds are 'th'. They were surprised that I could pronounce it, and very pleased. To pronounce Danish requires a mastery of the glottal stop, which occurs regularly, as it does in the Danish name for Copenhagen: København (pronounced k'øbm haw'n; the apostrophes are glottal stops).

Soon after I arrived, Alan introduced me to his grandfather. He was the soul of courtesy and gentility, friendly and smiling, a true gentleman, very well dressed, in his wheelchair in an excellent retirement residence within walking distance of the dormitory. He would not have been out of place at a royal reception. As Alan informed me, good manners in Denmark require that one not refuse something to eat when it is offered, and his grandfather would be sure to offer us something, so although I was quite full from a delicious breakfast of coffee, cold cuts, cheeses, fruits, and juices at the dormitory, I accepted and ate the chocolates he offered me from a box. He spoke English quite well.

Alan, his grandmother, and I went to the Tivoli Gardens, with its marvelous selection of carnival rides, including an antique roller coaster, none of which we were interested in taking; and its food stands and live entertainment. In fact, I found some of those rides rather intimidating, even to look at.

We saw a simply wonderful ballet when the gorgeous peacock curtain lifted on the Tivoli Theater stage. The music played by the small orchestra seated below the stage must have been by the Romantic Danish nationalist J. P. E. Hartmann, some of whose delightful ballets are available on YouTube, and when I was doing some research to refresh my memory, reminded me immediately of what I had seen at the Tivoli.

We then strolled over to have tea at one of the outdoor restaurants, joined by a friend of hers and her friend's mother. At one point, he said to her in Danish, "Mere te, mor?" (More tea, mother?), which sounded so like English with an accent that I was startled for a moment. In fact, he spoke English beautifully with a perfect Oxford accent. We talked of opera, and the wonderful Swedish tenor Jussi Bjoerling, one of our very greatest favorites. He made just one mistake in English, when he said, "His singing was an absolute miracle," pronouncing the word 'miracle' with the diphthong used in the first-person pronoun 'I'.

There were two things I wanted to do that there was no time for, but that I would accomplish twelve years later when I was in Copenhagen again. I was on tour in Norway, Sweden, and Denmark, with the Little Theater of the Deaf, the children's division of the National Theater of the Deaf. In Copenhagen we made a television show for Danish TV. We had plenty of time off in all three places, so I had time to do those two things: to eat at Ida Davidsen's, the renowned restaurant where open-faced sandwiches were a specialty, and one could make a meal of them or have one simply as a snack with a beverage. I had a lunch, and I remember that for an appetizer I had a sandwich with piles of tiny shrimp in rows with a lemon wedge; called in Danish *rejer i traengsel* (shrimp in trouble), in imitation of a rush hour tramway car. I had a truly delicious sandwich of roast duck with red cabbage for my main course. The restaurant was on one of the bridges overlooking the city's central canal, so I also had a superb view.

The second thing I had wanted to do was to visit the museum in the charming well wooded Rosenborg Park, the Rosenborg Slot (Castle), a beautiful Renaissance fairytale castle housing the Royal Danish Art Collection. I was not disappointed.

Finally, of course, it was time for me to go, so I took a fond farewell of Alan. I retraced the same route, of course, and returned on the train from Hamburg to Paris, having had a wonderful time, and vowing to return one day.

CHAPTER ELEVEN

Mademoiselle Invites Me to Lunch

MADEMOISELLE WELCOMED ME back to her apartment with her customary frosty demeanor, this time with a cold half smile. Well, you couldn't call it a welcome exactly, but she was not uncordial at least.

She decided a few days later to give a luncheon party, and, to my surprise, she invited me, perhaps because I was the only one of her *locataires* (renters) to speak fluent French, and the others might have been at a loss to understand the conversation.

I got up late as usual on the day of the informal lunch and took a nice hot bath before going to the library. There were two other guests: Monsieur Maximov and Docteur Dupont. Actually I have forgotten his name, so Dupont will do.

The good doctor was from the "provinces," which was a mark against him in the eyes of some Parisians in those days. I never found out which one he was actually from. He dressed rather sloppily in a baggy jacket and baggy trousers. He had what seemed to be a perpetual smile playing on his lips, and he looked down a great deal. He seemed a bit shifty to me. I don't know how he met Mademoiselle Haumesser. Most probably he had had occasion to serve her as a doctor, and they became fast friends, so much so that he hoped to inherit her extensive library from her, as he confided in me when he saw me admiring the books on her shelves. She had promised it to him, he said. Indeed, it was a wonderful library of French literature, full of first editions purchased when they appeared.

We were all ushered into the dining room, and Mademoiselle, who said she needed no help, went out to the kitchen to get the lunch she had prepared. The main dish was a blanquette de veau—a creamy veal stew with mushrooms and lemon. It was the first time I had ever had it, and it was truly delicious, savory and flavorful. I ate fairly slowly, contrary to my frequent habit of eating quickly. I remembered my mother's remark, "How can you eat such delicious food so quickly?" I was fulsome in my compliments. Monsieur Maximov, leaning low over his plate, almost guzzled his food, and the doctor ate decorously. Mademoiselle was very pleased at the result.

Conversation ranged over various topics, from the weather to the Algerian situation, to the Indochinese situation. France had suffered a humiliating defeat at the battle of Dien Bien Phu in 1954 and had been decisively driven out of what is now Vietnam. Saigon still remains a French-influenced capital, as I understand it, with the colonial buildings and French restaurants, but the Vietnamese wanted their independence, and they got it, for a while. Dien Bien Phu was the climactic battle between the French expeditionary army and the Viet Minh, the Communists, and effectively ended French domination in the region.

Mademoiselle had nothing but scorn for the defeatist French army, and unutterable contempt for the "Indochinois" people. They were scarcely human, she said. In fact, according to her, they were actually not human. "Les indochinois sont des singes!" (The Indochinese are monkeys!)

I couldn't believe she meant it. I laughed.

"What are you laughing at?"

"I thought you were joking. I mean, you can't really mean that. The Indochinese are human beings, just like you and me."

She snorted. "How stupid! A lot you know. They are not human. They are monkeys." So she had meant it!

I stared at her. "What? That is complete nonsense. I know you can't mean it. Of course they are human!" She pursed her lips in contempt. I appealed to the doctor. "Doctor, you, who are after all a biologist, who know biology, you know they are human. Tell her!" But he mumbled something I could not hear and leaned over his plate.

"But this is outrageous!" I pursued. "Is no one going to back me up? Surely you don't agree with this ridiculous nonsense!"

Nobody said a word. Finally, Mademoiselle said, "Si vous n'aimez pas ce que je dis, vous n'avez qu'à aller dans votre chambre !" (If you don't like what I say, you can just go to your room!) And she wheeled herself out as majestically as she could. I just sat there, thinking of…I don't remember what. Possibly I thought that here was grist for the entertainment mill, another anecdote I could regale my friends and family with when I got back to America.

I remonstrated with the doctor, who shrugged and said, "Well, you know, that's how she is…"

Monsieur Maximov pointed at him with his fork. "He wants to inherit her library," he said, in slurred, heavily accented speech, as always.

"Well, why didn't *you* say anything?"

"He wants her red wine, and the handouts," chortled the doctor.

Monsieur Maximov looked as if he would hit him, but he took a sip of wine instead.

Soon Mademoiselle returned, with a Basque cake filled with pastry cream, in the classic manner, that she had baked herself. It was the first time I had tasted such a cake, which I later learned to bake for myself, and it was just delicious. There wasn't much conversation over dessert. The Indochinese incident seemed to have placed a pall over everything. When the meal was over, everyone thanked her profusely for such a delicious lunch, and left a bit hurriedly, I thought, while I went to my room to take a nap.

CHAPTER TWELVE

In and Around Paris and A Visit to the Loire Valley

AS A RESULT of my being a Carnegie Foundation fellow, I received an invitation in the mail that served as my entry ticket to the annual graduation ceremony at the Sorbonne in the main building off the boulevard St.-Michel. I walked over along the boulevard St.-Germain and away from the Seine past the Cluny Museum and on up the boulevard St.-Michel. Joining the throng entering the building, I was directed all the way upstairs to the balcony.

There were several speeches that I listened to with interest at the time, and have no recollection of now. The place was completely filled, and it was a pleasure to look around and see all the eager faces and the lively interest they showed. Afterwards, I walked all around the building, looking in the classrooms, something usually not allowed to the public except on the two *Journées du Patrimoine* (Days of the Patrimony) a year, when buildings normally closed to the unauthorized public are open to everyone, such as the Senate in the Luxembourg Palace or the École des Beaux-Arts, both very much worth standing on the long entrance lines you have to endure in order to see the marvelous interiors and collections of artworks.

The Jardin du Luxembourg, the Luxembourg Gardens as it is usually called in English, though the French name actually means the garden of the Luxembourg Palace, is one of my very favorite parks. Its spacious open area centers around a large round bassin, a pool where children accompanied by adults sail small mechanical sailboats that they either rent or bring with them, particularly on weekends, when the area is very crowded.

I couldn't help but be delighted as I remembered the scene in Alexandre Dumas' *The Three Musketeers* in which D'Artagnan meets Porthos, Athos, and Aramis behind the Luxembourg Palace to fight a duel with each of them. They are interrupted by the Cardinal's guards who come running down the nearby hill from the direction of what is now the boulevard St.-Michel, from across the river where you can still see the old Musketeers' barracks. The garden and much of what surrounds it was a royal hunting ground in those days, all forest and meadow, and without any of the city streets that were built up subsequently.

Nearby is the wonderfully sculpted Fontaine Médicis, built for Queen Marie de Médicis, with the statues at one end and the rectangular basin stretching in front of them towards the palace. People sit on metal chairs on either side of it, and there are carp and ducks swimming in it. If you go up the stairs to the right of the fountain, as you are facing it, you can see the Panthéon, where some of the many of France's most illustrious citizens are interred, in the distance. It looks a lot closer than it is, as does the Basilica of Sacré-Coeur de Montmartre when seen from the Tuileries Gardens.

I enjoyed visiting both impressive buildings, each magnificent in its own way. And I loved walking around the place du Tertre in Montmartre after seeing Sacré-Coeur, listening to the violinists and accordionists, and looking at all the artists' work. They surround the place, with its snack bars and restaurants, and some of them draw people's portraits for pay.

The nearby Montmartre Cemetery was also worth visiting. There you can see the tombs of Jacques Offenbach with his bust on top of a plinth surrounded by flowers; of his librettists Henri Meilhac and Ludovic Halévy; of the author Alexandre Dumas fils; of the German poet and writer Heinrich Heine, his tomb destroyed by the Germans as soon as they occupied Paris in 1940, because Heine was Jewish—it was rebuilt after the war; and of composers Léo Delibes and Hector Berlioz. The novelist and social activist Émile Zola had been buried there, but his remains were transferred to the Panthéon, where they repose along with those of Victor Hugo and Alexandre Dumas père, Jean-Jacques Rousseau, and Voltaire.

Walking along past the Luxembourg Palace, with the Fontaine Médicis at your back, you arrive through the wooded alley at the Musée du Luxembourg, which only has traveling exhibits. I enjoyed them so much. On later trips, for instance, there was an exhibit of works by Mucha, who is famous for his posters of Sarah Bernhardt's productions, and one devoted to the brilliant Hungarian Impressionists.

If you go back in the other direction along the rue de Vaugirard, you arrive at the back of the Théâtre de l'Odéon, and you can take the narrow, short rue Rotrou into the place de l'Odéon, where the hotel I have stayed in for such a long time is located. Across from the theater on the semicircular place is a magnificent seafood restaurant, La Méditéranée, where my father had dinner back in 1952. The menus and dishes were designed by Jean Cocteau.

The theater is the third one on the place, the first two having been burned down and rebuilt. It was the site of a famous street fight between the partisans of Classicism and Romanticism on the occasion of the premier of Victor Hugo's 1830 Romantic drama *Hernani*.

The place itself was the courtyard of a huge palace built in 1612 belonging to the Prince de Condé, son of Marie de Médicis, who had the nearby Palais du Luxembourg built subsequently starting in 1615, because she felt her son needed his own place to live. Its outer walls are where the rue de Condé now is on the west and the rue Monsieur-le-Prince on the east. In the eighteenth century, when the royal family needed money, they sold the palace to real estate developers, who tore it down, and built apartment buildings surrounding the place, which once had a beautiful fountain in the middle. So what you see today is pure eighteenth-century urban architecture, if you look up. The ground floors are all different from what they were back then.

At the east side of the rue de l'Odéon, which leads north out of the place towards the Seine, is a historical brown shield in front of a building that used to house the Café Voltaire, where leaders of the French Revolution met in the back room to plan the rebellion. That room is the scene of the first chapter of Victor Hugo's 1874 novel *Quatrevingt-Treize*

(Ninety-Three), which refers to what is often considered the first year of the Reign of Terror, and is the year of the royalist insurrection opposing the revolution in the Vendée in western France.

Thomas Paine, who supported both the American and French Revolutions, and opposed capital punishment, lived at 10 rue de l'Odéon starting in 1797, as a historical plaque on the building informs us. A plaque on the building at 22 rue de l'Odéon tells us that the great revolutionary orator Camille Desmoulins and his wife Lucille Desmoulins lived there, on the corner where the place de l'Odéon leads into the street of the same name, across the street from the building in which is La Méditerranée restaurant is now located.

Going away from the Seine through the Luxembourg, you arrive at the Montparnasse area, with its incredible restaurants on either side of the boulevard du Montparnasse. They include La Coupole, frequented by writers and musicians. Jean-Paul Sartre and Simone de Beauvoir had a regular table there.

On the right bank, I went several times to the Louvre. I just had to see the Mona Lisa! It is behind a protective bullet-proof glass structure, and surrounded by such crowds that one has to push one's way through in order to get a good view.

Beyond the Louvre is the Tuileries Gardens, where I went any number of times. I far preferred the Luxembourg to the open spaces with their sandy walks of the Tuileries. The park is so named because it used to be the vast fields where *tuiles* (tiles), the huge stones that were used for facing such buildings as the Louvre were hewn and shaped. The royal family decided to make it into a park where they and the court could walk at leisure. At the other end, there are two more museums, the Jeu de Paume, which used to be the indoor tennis court, as its name indicates; and the Orangerie, where oranges and other fruits were once grown. At that point, you have reached the majestic place de la Concorde, with its Egyptian obelisk, stolen by Napoleon, and its splendid fountains. On the other side, you get to the Champs-Élysées, the Elysian Fields, now a shopping mecca, although it used to be an area of aristocratic estates. Ledoyen, now a three-star Michelin restaurant, near where the Champs-Élysées debouches onto the place de la Concorde, is the one mansion that remains, on a broad tree-lined plot of land. In Alexandre Dumas' novel, the Count of Monte-Cristo has his mansion farther along on the avenue.

I have strolled up and down the Champs-Élysées countless times, and one day in 2005 I went to the famous monumental Arc de Triomphe with its traffic circle, and went to the top to see the splendid panoramic view of Paris on all sides. I took the elevator going up, and the long staircase going down after I had been there gazing out at the city for about a half hour.

The year 1963 was the only year that I was in Paris in July and the weather was often stiflingly hot, but a lot cooler at night. On July 14, Bastille Day, I decided to brave the crowded streets, which were swarming with celebrants. I made my way to one of the crowded bridges over the Seine, not to far from where I was staying. People were shouting and screaming and singing the "Marseillaise" while waiting for the fireworks display. When they started a great shout went up from the crowd. It soon subsided to a murmur of oohs and ahs as the splendidly colorful show brought forth wonder after wonder in all kinds of shapes and combinations from exploding stars to straight lines that then curved upwards and outwards. I was tired when I got back to my room, entering as quietly as I could so as not to disturb anybody, and I slept late the next day.

I made three trips to Versailles, easy to get to by train from the St.-Michel station near the river: once to see the palace, and a second time for the gardens. The third time was in the evening for the magnificent *Son et Lumière* (Sound and Light Show), which described and depicted a history of the palace. We were given programs listing the music by Lully and other seventeenth-century composers and explaining the rest of the dramatization in order. Sound effects and the occasional trumpet accompanied horses with soldiers dressed in seventeenth-century uniforms, galloping in the distance beyond the Grand Bassin, near which we sat on one side. There was an excellent voiceover narration explaining everything, all so beautifully done.

The moon shone above the majestic old trees, and all was otherwise in darkness, so that when the light came on to illuminate the horses, the effect was superb, and the recreation stirring and exciting.

The first time I went to Versailles, following the directions to the palace from the train station, I suddenly came across a crowd behind a barrier, beyond which nobody was allowed to proceed. All of a sudden, two great gates in a wall to our right opened up, and a huge crowd together with carts and horses and soldiers, all in eighteenth-century costume, spilled noisily out into the street. They were making a film about the French Revolution! Once the scene was over, we were allowed to proceed.

The breathtaking palace interior, with its famous Hall of Mirrors, is beyond superb, absolutely gorgeous and splendid almost beyond imagining, with its royal bedrooms and salons ornately decorated with great and delicate intricacy, and the stunning throne room, and all the magnificent paintings and sculptures.

The splendid, huge and spacious gardens are eminently worth a day's visit. Fortunately, the trees had not been blown down in a terrible storm, as they were to be in the devastating storm on Christmas, 1999, so I saw them in all their majesty. Among other sites in the gardens are the *Hameau de la Reine* (the Queen's Hamlet), a little peasant village with cows and chickens and little houses, constructed for Marie Antoinette, who would play with her ladies at being a peasant, milking cows and feeding chickens, and dressed inn peasant costume. Farther on are two small palaces, the Petit and the Grand Trianon, where the king used to go for assignations or with small groups of his favorite courtiers just to relax from the sometimes-stultifying formalities of court life.

A few weeks after my return from Copenhagen, I left for another short trip to visit the châteaux of the Loire valley, found not only on the Loire River but also on the Indre and the Cher Rivers. I went with Roger, the other Carnegie Fellow whose destination was Paris, and whom I saw a couple of times at his hotel, the Port-Royal, near the boulevard du Montparnasse, even though Fellows were not supposed to have contact with each other except at the beginning and end of our stay in Europe. But we both felt there was no harm in seeing each other once or twice, and we both missed home despite having a wonderful time.

His brother and sister-in-law were visiting him, and they had rented a car, and invited me to come along. I met them at Roger's hotel and we drove out of Paris through the beautiful farmlands. Although it was tourist season, so the out of the way auberge where we stopped on the chance that they might have rooms, did have two rooms available. Roger and I shared one, and his brother and sister-in-law shared the other. We returned after each day's trip for a couple of nights. The food at the auberge was excellent. There was no menu in the hotel dining room, and they served whatever they were making that day, including freshly baked bread and fruit culled from the orchards just outside the auberge, which were also owned by the hoteliers. And we had delicious Loire wines.

The chateaux we visited were each gorgeous and unique both outside and in, their vast halls and rooms breathtakingly decorated. Of course, they constituted a mere fraction of the three hundred or so chateaux in the area, dating from the Middle Ages to centuries later.

The first one we saw was the fifteenth-century Château d'Amboise, located in the town of Amboise on the hills above the Loire River in the département of Indre-et-Loire. The chateau was seized as a royal residence by Charles VII in 1431 after he had pardoned Louis d'Amboise, Vicomte de Thours, its owner, accused of attempting to assassinate King Louis XI. The chateau is of incredible grandeur, yet with a feeling of hollow emptiness and cold vastness inside. It was built in the Middle Ages, then expanded amazingly by Charles VIII beginning in 1492. He invited Leonardo da Vinci to be his guest, and Da Vinci's tomb is there.

We next went to the village of Chenonceaux with its extraordinary picturesque Château de Chenonceau. The chateau's amazing and elegant gallery bridge, its arches below spanning the Cher river, and its sixty rooms furnished in Renaissance style, together with its extensive gardens in different styles, from Japanese to English and French, make the grandest of impressions. It was the favorite residence of some very powerful women, including Diane de Poitiers and Marie de Médicis.

My favorite of all the ones we visited was Azay-le Rideau, the smallest of the chateaux we saw, set on an island in the Indre River and surrounded with colorful water lilies. Having been built between 1518 and 1527, the chateau is a perfect example of Renaissance architecture. The very beautiful gardens, however, were redesigned in the nineteenth century.

We next went on to Villandry known especially for its splendid, extensive, and varied kinds of gardens, which you can see from above on a terrace overlooking them. When you walk down the steps into the gardens, you are in the midst of superb flower and vegetable gardens, as well as a water garden with a marvelous elaborate fountain. Originally a medieval chateau, it was purchased by Jean Breton, Finance Minister to King François I in 1532, and he immediately set about transforming it into the superb Renaissance chateau we saw.

Perhaps the most impressive of all, seen from a great distance away as one approaches it along winding roads, is the amazingly ornate and enormous French Renaissance Château de Chambord, with its incredible number of intricate small and large turrets, and its blended mixture of Medieval and Renaissance architectures. Originally built as a relatively modest hunting lodge for King Henry I, it is now the largest of all the Loire chateaux, the most complex I have ever seen in pictures or in real life, and it took more than twenty-eight years to construct, expand, and elaborate from 1519-1547. Inside one of the main halls is pure white, with an incredibly elaborate staircase leading all the way up. I stood looking at it in awe.

The last chateau we visited was the Château Royal de Blois, a favorite royal residence dating from medieval times. It is situated on the heights overlooking the Loire River and the view is splendid. Architecturally it is eclectic, and each of its four wings is from a different period from Gothic through Classical, yet the chateau has a unified feeling to it. It is home to a wonderful art museum, as well as fantastic halls and royal apartments. We were there in time for sunset and for the brilliant *Son et Lumière* show, which recounts among many other things the assassination of Henri, duc de Guise on the grand spiral staircase on the outside of the chateau on December 23, 1588. Founder of the

Catholic League, the duc was the arch-enemy of King Henri III, who was forced to flee Paris during the Wars of Religion, on the *Journée des barricades* (Day of the Barricades), when the staunchly conservative religious Parisian population rose up against the tolerant policies of the king. The king took refuge in the chateau, and the League controlled France and public policy. The king summoned de Guise to attend him so that they could discuss matters and come to an agreement, and as soon as he entered the throne room, from which the king was absent, the King's guard, the Forty-Five as they were known, went after him, and he fled out of the throne room and down the staircase, where the assassination took place. During the show we were seated with a view of the staircase, and there were sound effects of footsteps, shouts, and a final scream, as well as the lights of torches going up and down the staircase. Incidentally, *Les Quarante-Cinq* (The Forty-Five Guardsmen) is the third volume of a brilliant absorbing trilogy on the period by Alexandre Dumas.

What a magnificent, superb trip that was! I returned to Paris in a happy satisfied mood, and they dropped me off at 76 bis rue des Saints-Pères early in the evening. I'm sure I slept well and had pleasant dreams.

CHAPTER THIRTEEN

Adventures in Gastronomy: 1963 and Beyond

O NE CAN HARDLY talk about a trip to Paris without discussing the epicurean delights of a city famous for its varied gastronomic experiences, from pastry shops and bakeries and traiteurs, which is what they call stores where you can buy excellent prepared dishes to take away, to restaurants, both French and international, brasseries, and bistros, salons de thé (tearooms), cafés, crêpe stands that dot the landscape the way large and small pizza restaurants do in New York, and snack and ice cream stands in the parks. Indeed, all my trips to Paris were gastronomic delights.

I learned early in my first trip that working hours for eating establishments are regulated by a law that says the establishment must declare those hours publicly. Those in the restaurant category have specific opening hours for lunch and dinner. They are closed in between those two meals, and are very strict about observing the hours. I've had the occasion to arrive at 1:30 when the closing time for lunch was 2, and they would not seat me, although of course those who were already eating would have been allowed to stay and finish their meal even at a little past two. And I have arrived at around 7:30 at a restaurant and had to wait outside for the doors to open at 8. If you get to one of the three-star Michelin deluxe haute cuisine restaurants early, they usually have a comfortable waiting salon, from which they will conduct you to your table as soon as the doors open.

Many restaurants serve classic gourmet and haute cuisine food with the sauces for which French cuisine is known, or are devoted to a specific regional cuisine, and many serve what have become traditional classic dishes like those prepared at home, such as *boeuf bourguigon* (beef Burgundy, in red wine sauce), *canard à l'orange* (duck with orange sauce), *boeuf à la mode* (a beef pot roast stuffed with carrots and threaded with long strips of pork fat, and braised in red wine and beef stock, and served hot or cold), and other dishes from the various regions that have been incorporated into general French traditional cuisine. Some are seafood restaurants only, with the occasional choice of a meat or poultry dish as well. They all have extensive wine menus, with a choice of Bordeaux, Burgundy, Loire, and Rhone wines. Reservations are required, and usually have to be confirmed a day or two before.

It is customary in all kinds of eating establishments to have lunch or dinner in three courses: the *entrée*, which is what the French call the starter; the *plat* (main dish with its accompaniments), and dessert followed or accompanied by coffee. An optional cheese course before dessert is always offered. You can order from the "carte," the large menu; or order the "menu," a prix fixe meal with more limited choices, often served only at lunch. I also learned that the waiter's tip of fifteen per cent is always included in *l'addition* (the check), which often arrives with the abbreviation *SC* for the phrase *service compris* (service included) on it. It is customary especially in deluxe establishments to leave a little extra beyond the fifteen per cent, or at least it was until prices went way up in recent years.

In the deluxe restaurants, all kinds of extras are served, including hors d'oeuvres called *amuse-bouche* (entertain-mouth; mouth amuser), which is a one- or two-bite appetizer preceding the first course; extra little dishes of some kind between courses, such as a sorbet between the entrée and the plat to cleanse the palate; a sweet pre-dessert dish after the plat and before the cheese course; and *petits fours* (little pastry treats cooked in the oven), also known as *friandises*, with or without a plate of chocolates after dessert, with coffee. Meals usually last at least two and often three hours of leisurely dining, with a long time between courses.

It has been my great privilege and pleasure over the decades to eat in nearly all the three-star and two-star Michelin restaurants in Paris. Of the two-star restaurants my favorite remains Le Relais Louis XII, which not only has marvelous service, food and wines, but is also interesting historically, because, as a plaque on the wall of the building informs us, it is the house in which the Dauphin Louis XIII was informed that he was king shortly after his father, King Henri IV, had been assassinated nearby on the Pont Neuf, where an equestrian statue of the king marks the spot. The simple interior is well preserved, with beamed ceilings and fireplaces.

To name three of the other starred restaurants that I enjoyed the most and dined at a number of times, there were several restaurants belonging to brilliant star chef Joël Robuchon (1945-2018), whom I had the pleasure of meeting and whose traditions have been carried on by his successors; the Epicure restaurant at the Bristol Hotel, notable for its superb chariots of cheeses and desserts; and the newer Le Clarence, located in an elegant nineteenth-century private mansion, where you dine on the amazingly inventive, vibrant, very modern cuisine of Christoph Pelé, who serves many small courses of whatever he has decided to prepare that day, depending on what is in the market. There is no menu, and you tell the server if you have any food allergies, so nothing will be served that you can't eat. And you can enjoy wines from the proprietor's vineyard, Château Haut-Brion in Bordeaux, or others on the extensive wine list. It would require a book twice as long as this one to describe all those memorable meals, and those at the many bistros and brasseries where I have eaten.

A brasserie remains open the entire time between its opening and closing hours, for *service continu* (continual service). Its food is often what is called traditional bourgeois cuisine: appetizers such as herring and potatoes, pâté, or a selection of charcuterie, salads, soups, stews, casseroles, and pork dishes such as *jarret de porc aux lentilles* (pork thigh with lentils). The bill of fare often includes some foods that are native to the various regions and are also cooked and served in the home. Large and small seafood platters, shrimp, langoustines, lobsters, oysters, fish, and elaborate salads are usual, as are marvelous desserts, including a variety of fruit tarts, chocolate mousse, and everybody's favorite: crème brûlée. Brasseries usually do not take reservations. You can arrive at any time, although many customers still observe the usual 12 or 12:30 hour for lunch, and the 7:30 or 8 o'clock time for dinner, so if you want to be sure to get a table, you arrive outside those hours.

Bistros, also spelled bistrots, are restaurants that are on small premises and provide relatively simple, inexpensive meals in a relaxed, convivial, intimate setting, as opposed to the grander setting of the de luxe establishments, where diners usually remain aloof from each other. They have specific times for lunch and dinner, and are closed in between those meals. The food is usually like that served in brasseries, but can be more specialized, from various provincial cuisines such as Alsatian or Provençale, or national such as Greek, Italian, Japanese or Chinese, to seafood or vegetarian.

Cafes, like brasseries, are open continuously from opening to closing times, and you can go to a café just for a cup of coffee at any time, perhaps with a pastry or tart, or to have a light lunch or dinner of as many or as few courses as you wish. You can sit there writing for as long as you like for a cup of coffee, as I have done on occasion at the Café Rostand, which is not usually too crowded in the middle of the afternoon. Cafes usually open early for breakfast, which often consists simply of a croissant or pain au chocolat and coffee, and sometimes a "tartine": a buttered baguette with jam. If you want an orange juice, you don't ask for a *jus d'orange*, which comes in a small bottle, but for an *orange pressée* (squeezed orange), which is fresh, served with sugar and water on the side so you can make orangeade to your taste. You will find excellent cooking in cafes, from different kinds of omelets to a great variety of salads, as well as charcuterie, meat and poultry dishes, and excellent desserts.

The term haute cuisine, the food generally served to the upper classes through the ages, means a highly refined style of cooking, full of flavor and with exquisite subtle sauces, with plates of food artistically designed for an appetizing presentation, and with such expensive ingredients as truffles and caviar. The chef uses only the best ingredients, the freshest fruits and vegetables, and brings out rather than disguises the flavors.

The origin of French haute cuisine is actually Italian, since Marie de Médicis, originally Maria de'Medici, Queen of France and Navarre, and the second wife of King Henri IV, and the mother of King Louis

XIII, not trusting that French chefs would be able to cook food to her liking, brought her battery of cooks and pastry chefs with her when she moved from Florence to France to assume the throne. They taught the French chefs their techniques and recipes, and thenceforward the French cooks refined and added to the cuisine, their methods and incomparable recipes becoming classic and unsurpassed, especially with the invention of sauces, many of which are begun by preparing a *roux*, which is a mixture of butter and flour whisked or stirred together to form a thickening agent for the ingredients that are then added to it, the sauce being continually stirred as it cooks gently over low heat. It was at Versailles in the time of Louis XIV that haute cuisine began to assume its modern form, with multi-course meals, the courses being served in a certain order, and accompanied by wines and champagne.

The phrase is associated since the late nineteenth century with one of the very greatest of chef-restaurateurs, Georges Auguste Escoffier (1846-1935) of the Ritz Hotel in Paris and the Savoy Hotel in London. He established the kitchens at the Ritz Hotel at the invitation of the Swiss hotelier César Ritz (1850-1918), and at the Savoy at the invitation of Richard D'Oyly Carte, producer of the Gilbert and Sullivan comic operas. Escoffier's major cookbook among eleven that he wrote, still used today, is *Le Guide Culinaire*, which codifies and categorizes food, and sets forth classic cooking techniques. He invented several famous desserts that we still enjoy today, including Pêche Melba, a poached peach half on a scoop of vanilla ice cream, with a raspberry coulis poured over it. Dame Nellie Melba, the Australian lyric coloratura soprano, had sung one of her few Wagnerian roles, Elsa von Brabant in *Lohengrin* in 1892 at Covent Garden, and was dining the next evening at the Savoy, where she had often eaten. She had sent Escoffier tickets to the performance, and he invented the dessert to honor her, placing the portions in a huge swan carved out of ice. Thus a classic dessert was born, and there would be later variations, including the addition of whipped cream.

My favorite restaurant for many years was Taillevent, which had three Michelin stars, and an extraordinary, huge wine cellar. It is located not far from the Champs-Élysées in a gorgeous, tasteful mansion which used to belong to the statesman Charles Auguste, duc de Morny, Napoleon III's half-brother, who also wrote several libretti for Offenbach, the most notable and hilarious being *M. Choufleuri restera chez lui le...* (M. Choufleuri [Cauliflower] Will Be at Home on the...), for which he contributed to the libretto.

The haute cuisine when I first dined there was that of the magnificent Claude Deligne, chef de cuisine from 1970 to 1991, who published an excellent cookbook, *Le bien manger* (Eating Well; 1984), co-authored with Gilbert Jouanin, another master chef and fellow *Meilleur Ouvrier de France* (Best Worker of France). Under M. Deligne, with his magic touch, the restaurant earned its third Michelin star.

He also adopted certain Nouvelle Cuisine ideas, such as lighter sauces and some unusual combinations of ingredients. The house cocktail is champagne with raspberry puree and Triple Sec, and it is just delicious. Freshly baked *gougères de fromage* (cheese puff pastries) are always placed on the table almost as soon as one sits down, sometimes after drinks are ordered. Mineral water, sparkling or plain, is not unusual at any eating establishment. One can always order free tap water, sometimes jokingly called "la cuvée de la mairesse; or du maire" (the Mayoress's or Mayor's vintage). One of the greatest starters I have ever had was Asparagus *au jus de truffe* (with truffle butter sauce). Another delicious starter consisted of three eggshells filled with scrambled eggs, one flavored with chives and other herbs, one with mushrooms, and the third with truffles. It may not sound like much but it was out of this world. Inventive main dishes were so amazing that I would roll my eyes with pleasure after the first taste. Among them was duck prepared two ways, the breast sauteed and the thighs grilled, with sauces made from the duck juices and reduced meat stock, and with crispy potatoes on the side; and another was duck with black olives and tender baby turnips in a savory brown sauce made with the duck juices. Creative, absolutely delicious desserts with unexpected combinations of flavors included poached peaches with *verveine* (verbena) ice cream and a *fondant de chocolat* (an individual chocolate cake with a melting chocolate center) with thyme ice cream. M. Deligne was succeeded by the excellent Philippe Legendre, who later went to Le Cinq, another superb restaurant, in the

Hôtel George V, where he continued devising dishes such as the dessert of carrots prepared several different ways, unusual and delicious.

Every time I went to Taillevent, I had conversations with the gracious host and owner M. Jean-Claude Vrinat, who always received guests cordially in the lobby before diners went upstairs to the restaurant. I had a fantastic meal with my mother's brother, Uncle Seymour Korn, whom we called Uncle Sy. His wife, my Aunt Shirley, no longer wanted to travel, although they had made several trips to France, and on one of them they had retraced his steps during the war, using the list that he had made at the time of every place he had been in France on the way to Germany. So this time he came to Paris alone for a short time, because I was there, and of course we got together all the time, and he was kind enough to insist on paying for my meals at the best places.

As a young soldier, he had participated in the Normandy landing, and once the beaches were secured, he was stationed with his artillery intelligence unit in a village not far from the landing site, until they were moved out. The people were so happy to see them that they gave all the soldiers free Calvados, the apple brandy they manufactured there. Unfortunately it needs to ripen in the barrel, and it was too new and raw, so almost everyone got sick. But my uncle never drank any alcoholic beverage in his life, not even fine French wines or champagne in the restaurants, so he didn't have any and he was fine.

After participating in the Battle of the Bulge, his unit moved on to the liberation of Paris, and he was there on the day the city was freed, in a truck going down the Champs-Élysées, but he was not allowed to descend, because they were pursuing the Germans back across the border.

I told M. Vrinat, who was only nine years old when the war ended, what my uncle had done, and he thanked him profusely for his service in World War Two, and for helping to free France. Uncle Sy also met my great friend, Jean-Frédéric Guidoni, the maître d' whose knowledge of wine is extensive and incredible. His recommendations were always perfect, and when I am invited to dinner at his family apartment, he always has a wonderful wine to share, while his wife Delphine always makes an excellent, delicious meal.

In the 1960s, a new movement, Nouvelle Cuisine, was started to reform the heavier aspects of haute cuisine, its hallmarks being fresh ingredients, and clear flavors that stand out in light dishes. It gave chefs free rein in being creative, in making unusual combinations and juxtapositions of ingredients, and it thus saw the invention of new dishes. The movement was spearheaded by chef-restaurateur Paul Bocuse (1926-2018). Nouvelle Cuisine chefs also quickly developed the reputation of serving very small portions, which was often the case, so that people didn't feel they were getting good value for their money. In other words, *le rapport qualité prix* (the relationship of quality to price), a common French phrase when discussing restaurants, was lacking. Of course, it was not always the case that portions were small.

One of the most well known chefs to serve Nouvelle Cuisine exclusively is Pierre Gagnaire, who serves large meals in his eponymous restaurant on the rue Balzac, where I ate several times. The leisurely meals of a succession of small portions were very filling, with the occasionally jarring combinations of ingredients quite unexpected, sometimes delicious, sometimes not very successful. For instance, in a lunch of seven courses plus desserts, he served a preliminary course of three amuse-bouches at the same time: a tartlet of blue cheese and chives; a somewhat peculiar plate of a small piece of spiced pumpernickel with water chestnuts and melted butter; and a marshmallow with Asian spices on a toothpick. One main course consisted of miniature lamb steaks with celery puree, accompanied by a watercress puree with snails. For one dessert among several there was a puree of oranges and red bell pepper. For another there was an individual luscious, rich chocolate cake surmounted by a crackling chocolate biscuit with lentils on top of it! M. Gagnaire also spearheaded the fusion movement, combining European and Asian ingredients and ideas for dishes.

Not only do I appreciate French haute cuisine and fine food generally, but I also know how the dishes are cooked. I was brought up on my mother's and grandmothers' cooking. My taste buds were well trained so that I could distinguish one herb and spice from another, and distinguish the tastes of the components of sauces. I especially love French, Italian and Hungarian food, as well as the Austro-Hungarian

Jewish food of my forebears; and I enjoy and appreciate all world cuisines, Asian, European, African, and South American.

A great favorite when I was growing up was my grandmother's chicken soup (a whole bunch of fresh dill was her secret), and matzo brei, a kind of matzo omelet, both of which I still make today. I sat in their kitchens and watched my mother and her mother cook those dishes and so many others, and I remembered the recipes later on when I was living on my own and cooking for myself.

My mother, from whom I actually learned the art of cooking beginning with the breakfasts she taught me and my brothers to make when we were old enough, was a marvelous cook, and we ate superbly when I was living home, and of course when I visited after I had left the nest: veal cutlets, dredged in sour cream, breaded, and sautéed in butter—great for the cholesterol, I know—but so delicious; she didn't cook this dish often. The spareribs she made in sweet and sour raisin sauce or pan-cooked with sauerkraut were alike irresistible. So were the baked chicken in white wine, garlic-stuffed pork rib roast with apple sauce, classic rib roast of beef, canard à l'orange, spaghetti with tomato sauce, lasagna (the best I've ever had), and so forth. Her pecan pie, chocolate-walnut pie, brownies, and chocolate chip cookies were also the best ever. She cut the sugar in half in those pies and in the brownies, so the sweetness was perfect, and not overwhelming, as it can be in American bakeries. And when I was in elementary school in Roosevelt, NJ, where we lived before moving to Princeton, I had extracurricular cooking lessons paid for by my parents and taught by a young lady in her house after school so she could earn some extra money. I remember learning to make biscuits.

My father also cooked occasionally, and very well too. He used to make breakfast sometimes on the weekends. His specialties were delicious puffy jam or cheese omelets. To this day I don't know how he made them, how he got them to be so puffy. He also made scrambled eggs, onions and lox, which was another old Jewish favorite that my mother's father used to make on weekends, take outside, and allow the odor to waft up through the children's bedroom windows in order to wake them up. And the charcoal grilled steaks and hamburgers my father made outside during the summers were delicious, perfectly crusty on the outside and juicy within.

My mother told me that when he proposed to her, she said, "Okay, but I'm not doing dishes!" My father agreed, and indeed he always did the dishes after dinner.

New Brunswick was home to a large Hungarian population, which had fled the country after 1956, and one of the best restaurant in New Brunswick—indeed, one of the best I have ever eaten in in my life—was called simply the Hungarian Restaurant, noted for its marvelous goulashes, its roast duck and chicken, its soups (*gombaleves*: mushroom soup), its pastries and cakes (I've never had better rum cake), and its superb coffee. There was always rye bread on the table, excellent salty sour pickles were placed there as soon as we sat down, and there were the usual salt and pepper shakers, with a paprika shaker as well. I ate there often when I was a Rutgers student.

But it was Julia Child's first cookbook that revealed another world to me. I borrowed it from my mother the year it came out, when I had my own off-campus one story cottage on George Street near the Douglass campus, and taught myself French cooking, and trained my palate. That was actually the year after my trip to Paris, when of course I had learned a lot about French food, but now I was actually learning how to cook it, and how to refine my cooking.

In 1963 I was able to begin exploring the world of French restaurants, and to learn the different types of restaurants, as described above. At that point, of course, I did not go to the expensive, Michelin two- and three-starred deluxe houses that I would learn about and eat at on later trips, such as the splendid La Tour d'Argent (it now has one star), at the top of a building on the quai de la Tournelle with a spectacular view of Notre Dame down below, and on the site of the oldest restaurant in Paris. It is famous for its exceptionally delicious, succulent *Canard à la Presse* (Pressed Duck), made at tableside using a special machine that crushes the duck so it yields its juices. The duck is served in two courses: first the *magret* (breast) is braised in a sauce of port, cognac, and the juices from the carcass, then the thighs and legs are grilled and served in a heavier version of the same sauce. Since 1890, when the dish was first prepared and served by the restaurant's owner, Frédéric Delair, each duck has been numbered, and the diner receives a postcard with the number and a picture of Monsieur Delair preparing the restaurant's signature dish. My duck was numbered 1,150,136 at lunch on Wednesday, September 23, 2000. I was there with my Uncle Sy, who treated me to lunch.

We had been to see Notre Dame, and, seeing the restaurant in the distance across the river, he decided that we should go there for lunch. So we walked across the pont de la Tournelle and entered the restaurant. Although we had no reservations, we were allowed in and got a wonderful table. We had been seated for about five minutes when the owner, Claude Terrail, burst forth from the elevator and immediately berated the service personnel near it in a loud voice. "Il y a un monsieur en bas qui attend son taxi ! Qu'est-ce qui se passe ?" (There is a gentleman below who is waiting for his taxi! What's going on?) The question was apparently settled, and someone went downstairs. By that time everyone was looking at him. Assuming the air of a courtly gentleman, he put on an affable smile and approached the tables. When he got to ours, I nodded and said, "Monsieur Terrail, je suis ravi de vous voir et de faire votre…" (Monsieur Terrail, I am delighted to see you and to make your…) He looked at me, astonished, and interrupted me. "On se connaît ?" (Do we know each other?) "Non, monsieur, mais je sais qui vous êtes." (No, monsieur, but I know who you are.) "Ah, très bien (ah, very good)," he said indifferently, and turned away to continue making his way to the other tables.

I have eaten there several times, and only a bit more than a decade earlier, at dinner with two friends on Sunday, June 18, 1989, I had another Pressed Duck, numbered 919,869. The view at sunset was breathtaking.

The next day, June 19, I went for lunch to a small restaurant called Chez La Vieille (At the Old Lady's House), which closed in 2012, although it has since been revived and reopened. It was run by the chef-owner Adrienne Biasin, who had her own television program, and had published two superb cookbooks: *La Table d'Adrienne* in 1983, written in collaboration with Jacqueline Saulnier; and *Les Carnets d'Adrienne*

(Adrienne's Notebooks) in 1987, with recipes that I had at the restaurant and some I have made at home.

She was quite a character, as I discovered from her gruff manner when I called to make a reservation and was grilled as to who I was. I explained that I had heard so much about her restaurant, that I was conversant with French cuisine, and that I was an American on vacation in Paris for a few weeks, and really wanted to have lunch at her restaurant. She complimented me on my French, and gave me a reservation. When I arrived, there she was, standing at the entrance to the restaurant on the tiny rue Bailleul at the corner of the rue de l'Arbre Sec near the Samaritaine on the right bank, while her sister and assistant chef Madeleine continued to work in the kitchen just off to the right as you faced into the restaurant. Even if you had made a reservation, you had to pass inspection as she looked you up and down. If she took a dislike to you, you didn't get in. I told her who I was, and she let me in, so obviously I had passed muster.

There was a buffet against one wall of the dining room with platters of prepared dishes and desserts, and thirty tables. The meal was fantastic, one of the best I have had anywhere. I had a kir, a glass of red Bordeaux, and sparkling mineral water. There was a *farandole* (originally a Provençal dance, with the extended meaning of a selection) of starters, beautifully arrayed on a small platter: succulent melon and prosciutto; and superb terrine, a pâté of meat; cold tomatoes stuffed with ground meats, egg, breadcrumbs, shallots, the flesh of the tomatoes, and fresh thyme, baked in a heavy covered casserole on a bed of rice with butter, just like the recipe that I have made from her book *La Table d'Adrienne*; a marvelous ratatouille, of eggplant and peppers; and a small piece of grilled tuna steak with olive oil and peppers. The main dish was a sauteed lamb steak, rare and tender, very simply prepared with parsley and black pepper, and French fried potatoes. I didn't have a cheese course for a change, but went right on to an elegantly arranged *farandole* of desserts: a *clafoutis* (fruit baked in a thick batter, usually in a pie crust) with two kinds of cherries; a chocolate cream mousse with oranges; a slice of chocolate cake; *oeufs à la neige* (snow eggs) meringues floating in a custard sauce; delicious fresh strawberries with sugar; and excellent expresso and a snifter of Armagnac to complete the meal. Madame Biasin ran around the place dishing out and serving the food and with pursed lips, looking as if butter wouldn't melt in her mouth, but it was all an act. Afterwards, I said to her, "C'était superbe, le bonheur même ! (It was superb, happiness itself!)" "Il ne faut pas exagérer. (One mustn't exaggerate.)," she said, but I could see that she was very pleased.

I had other amazing memorable lunches and dinners at Lasserre, one of the greatest restaurants, once considered the greatest in fact, with a retractable ceiling that opens to the sky in nice weather, and a marvelous elegant décor, with the tables on several levels. Their canard à l'orange is the best I have ever had, with the exception of my mother's; and it was fascinating to see the waiter prepare the delicious Crêpes Suzette, crêpes with an orange-butter sauce to which he added Grand Marnier orange liqueur that he flambéed.

The oldest surviving Paris restaurant is called Le Procope, with the words Café Restaurant on its awning on the street, and it opened in 1686. It is actually mainly a restaurant, although some people go in for just coffee in the afternoon. They can sit inside or outside in back at the open-air tables in the Cours du Commerce St.-André, a covered passage between the rue St.-André des Arts and the boulevard St. Germain, with the words Brasserie and Salon de Thé on two signs on the Cours side. The recipes for some of their dishes are historical, such as the Revolutionaries' Beef Tenderloin with a bordelaise sauce, dating back to the French Revolution, when the establishment was much frequented by the revolutionary leaders. The elegant décor is also in the eighteenth-century style. I ate there on later trips, and the food is delicious.

In 1963 I was delighted to go to the less expensive cafes, bistros, and brasseries that I could afford, and where no reservations were necessary. As a world cultural capital, Paris was and is home to world cuisines, but when I am there, I prefer to eat in French restaurants. I enjoy those other cuisines immensely in New York.

When I was staying at Mademoiselle Haumesser's, there was a restaurant called the Restaurant des Saints-Pères, an excellent place known for its classic cuisine on the southeast corner of the rue des Saints-Pères and the boulevard St.-Germain. Unfortunately, it is long gone, having been successively replaced by a number of fashion boutiques. This restaurant was the first place where I ate the much-vaunted *Chateaubriand,* a tenderloin cut that was excellent, serve quite rare. I had heard that beef in the United States was superior to that in France, and while I found French beef to be quite good, depending on the restaurant and the cut, I thought American beef products better, from the sirloin, porterhouse, to the prime rib roasts and rib steaks that we had at home, beautifully prepared by my mother or father.

Another superb establishment on the boulevard St.-Germain not far from the rue des Saints-Pères was the Brasserie Lipp, with its gorgeous historic décor and classic brasserie cuisine. It has daily specials, worth exploring, including boiled beef with carrots, cassoulet (a casserole of southwestern origin, consisting of beans, meats, and duck), and for starters their famous Bismarck herring served with crème fraîche, very much like sour cream but without a sour taste, on the side. The Brasserie Lipp, which opened in 1880, has had its ups and downs, and in 1963, it was clearly in one of its up times, and much frequented by celebrities, film and theater artists and politicians alike. Over the years, I have seen many. Once, I sat next to Jacques Chirac's bodyguards, who were quite friendly, facing a table next to the door sat Monsieur Chirac himself with his family. When he entered after the bodyguards, I nodded to him and put my hand on my heart as a further salutation, because I appreciated the fact that he had refused to participate in the Vietnam War.

Monsieur Chirac had their famous *choucroute garnie,* a succulent mouthwatering dish of Alsatian origin found in almost all brasseries, consisting of rib pork chops, ham steaks, pork belly, and sausages on a bed of sauerkraut in which the meats have been simmered for hours with white wine, often Riesling, and juniper berries, and with mustard on the side. Some of the meats are browned first before they go into the sauerkraut, and others, such as the frankfurter sausages, are added later, depending on the cooking time needed. There are endless combinations of meats possible, and innumerable recipes. The Lipp version is excellent.

Actually, the original *choucroute garnie* was from Normandy, and was a *choucroute de la mer* (of the sea), with a combination of fish and crustaceans, including lobster, as well as raw oysters and/or clams, all prepared separately from the bed of buttered sauerkraut, cooked in white wine, on which they are served. The Brasserie Bofinger, opened in 1864, another great historic restaurant with a superb décor, serves an excellent version.

Like so many Americans, one of the first things I noticed was how delicious the French bread was, as I said, as well as how much tastier the butter was than American butter. As I later learned, French flour has less gluten than American flour, which is part of what distinguishes the famous French baguette—a word that means several things, including a rod, a magic wand, a conductor's baton, and chopstick(s), in the plural: baguettes.

A lunch I had regularly at various cafes was a glass of red wine, usually Beaujolais, and a ham sandwich on well-buttered baguette. The French *jambon de Paris* (Parisian-style ham) is mild and flavorful and not too salty, and the lunch was ideal. It was excellent at the Danton in the Carrefour (crossroads) de l'Odéon just off the boulevard St.-Germain. I sat outdoors, despite the traffic noise on the streets that all crossed: the rue de l'Odéon, the rue Monsieur-le-Prince, and the rue de Condé. They also had a superb selection of salads, including a Salade Lyonnaise, with frisée lettuce, charcuterie, Cantal cheese, hard-boiled eggs, and boiled potatoes. I learned that there was lettuce beyond iceberg lettuce, which was all we had at home along with occasional romaine lettuce. I particularly loved the delicate frisée, with its light feathery fronds. And I appreciated the perfect vinaigrette, made in house. The building is still there, but the Danton was replaced by a number of other restaurants with new managements. Currently it is Le Hibou, not a bad place.

Excellent, but somewhat noisy, is the Café Danton, a bit farther down and actually on a short feeder road where taxis park off the boulevard St. Germain, wonderful for breakfast with their perfect café au lait, which is colloquially called a *Crème*, although there is no cream in it, and excellent flaky croissants and pain au chocolat, a croissant stuffed with chocolate. Their salads and roast chicken for lunch are the best.

One evening I went to see the huge covered wholesale food market called Les Halles on the right bank, now paved over and transformed into an underground shopping center. In the old days, stores and restaurants bought their food supplies there, and it was fascinating to see the men carrying great sides of beef and lamb on their shoulders, the stalls with a great variety of fresh fish, and the men unloading the trucks full of fruit and vegetables from the countryside. The wholesale food market is now just outside the southern city limits at Rungis.

Afterwards, I went to have onion soup at the nearby brasserie Le Pied de Cochon, which I had been told was the thing to do. It did not disappoint, and was very crowded. The delivery men went there too, and the waiters were running around. The place was quite noisy.

Usually, French eating establishments are not noisy, because French children are taught restaurant manners, which means speaking in hushed tones so that only people at the table can hear you. One used to be able to tell American tourists by how loud they were. That situation is changing, and French diners are often no longer as quiet as they were back in 1963, and for the first couple of decades after my regular return. Restaurants also never used to play music, but that too has changed with American influence. You can always ask them to turn the music down, which they are usually happy to do.

French pastries are world renowned for their elegance, sophistication, and delicious tastes, and with good reason. In those days I could scarcely pass by a *Pâtisserie* (Pastry Shop) without walking in and getting something to munch on the street, or at one of the tables just outside. French pastries and cakes have less sugar than American products do, which is also what made my mother's baking so superb, since she would cut the amount of sugar called for in a recipe, as I said.

When you walk past an American bakery, everything looks good, sometimes amazing, but it doesn't always taste good. The cakes are much too sweet, and the texture too thick or fluffy without being agreeably moist, as French cakes are. The texture of French pastry recipes yields different textures according to a delicate, meticulously measured balance of flour, water (when called for), eggs, and butter that give you flaky, làyered dough or fluffy or more dense dough. For instance, I make a French one-layer chocolate cake that balances melted butter, chocolate, eggs, and sugar, and a minimal amount of flour. The cake is dense and moist, and I cover it with a simple *glaçage* (icing; glaze) of melted chocolate and butter.

Decades after that first trip in 1963, my dear friends Jean-Frédéric and Delphine Guidoni had a marvelous Michelin-starred restaurant called Jean on the rue St.-Lazare, where I ate regularly for years until they closed their doors, regrettably. At one lunch, after I had finished my peach dessert, Jean-Frédéric asked me what I thought of it. "Be honest!" he said.

"Of course," I chuckled, "well, frankly, it was just a bit too sweet. This is a taste I associate with American baking, not with French."

It turned out that he had just hired a new American pastry chef recommended by his friend Danny Meyer, the New York restaurateur. "You're not the first person to have told me that," he said. smiling. He took me back to the kitchen to meet her. She was charming and spoke excellent French.

The next time I had lunch there, the dessert was better and less *sucré* (sugary; sweet). Monsieur Guidoni had had a talk with her, and now the amount of sugar was less than it had been. Incidentally, Alexandre, the second of their three sons, is an expert pâtissier, still studying, and undergoing quite an apprenticeship at various bakeries in different cities. Among his courses was one specially devoted to chocolate, and he also makes an excellent baguette, which he has brought to his parents' apartment, where I have often had the great pleasure of being invited to dinner. Madame Delphine Guidoni is such an excellent cook that I told her she could have been the cook at the restaurant, had she wanted to be, but it is not a life that appealed to her. She preferred to be the restaurant's business manager and accountant.

An inexpensive restaurant with copious portions where I ate a few times was the Café des Beaux-Arts, at the corner of the rue Bonaparte and the rue des Beaux-Arts. A lot of students from the gorgeous École des Beaux-Arts ate there, and I had many conversations over steaming bowls of stew, the sauce lapped up with slices of baguette. It was another of those restaurants like the Polidor where one sat at long tables, although there were also some individual tables along the walls.

On the same street between the rue Bonaparte and the rue de Seine is a hotel simply called L'Hôtel, where Oscar Wilde had a suite of rooms on the ground floor. An excellent restaurant is now located where his sitting room was. He had a small garden with a fountain out back, too small to sit in but lovely to see. His bedroom, where he died, is to the right as you enter, in the area where the hotel reception desk is now to be found. The receptionist was kind enough to give me all this information when I went to have lunch there for the first time, on a later trip to Paris.

I went one day to have lunch at one of the student cafeterias in the Cité internationale universitaire de Paris, in the southern part of the fourteenth arrondissement on the boulevard Jourdain near the surrounding highway that circles much of Paris. I'd been told it was a place worth visiting, so I made my way down there on the Métro, which has a stop right near the CIUP. I'm afraid the food was not very good. It was the first place I had *lapin à la moutarde* (rabbit with mustard sauce), which tasted like chicken, so the experience was interesting at least. I have since had excellent versions of that dish.

The Cité internationale universitaire de Paris (CIUP) was established in 1925 as a private foundation meant to provide general and public services, including residences for visiting academics and students. André Honnorat, rector of the Sorbonne, wanted to establish a meeting place where international academics and students could freely exchange ideas in a spirit of cooperation and peace. The CIUP was actually built under the auspices of the University of Paris, which still maintains and sponsors it. The main building is the impressive, chateau-like Maison Internationale, and there are a number of restaurants and cafeterias on the campus. So it was worth a visit, especially since one could freely engage in conversations on the spacious lawns with other students.

Later on in my visit, I had the great pleasure of a home-cooked dinner at the apartment of one of my father's chemist acquaintances and his wife, a superb cook.

CHAPTER FOURTEEN

Monsieur Courtieu
and the Petit Bleu

M Y INTEREST IN France and in things French began with
my father's first trip to France when I was nine, as I said in
chapter one. Because of his expertise in the production of penicillin, he
went to France in January 1952 as part of a team of scientists to help the
chemical company SIFA set up its first penicillin factory in Levallois-
Perret, one of the suburbs just outside of Paris. SIFA is a Swiss company,
but it had a factory outside Paris at the time nevertheless. During World
War Two, my father was not drafted into the armed services, because
the civilian job he had as a chemist was considered essential for defense:
he worked on developing antibiotics and developed a method for the
quick production of penicillin, relatively new as a widespread treatment
at the time, so that it could be gotten quickly to the troops.

We all went into New York from New Brunswick, NJ, where we
were living then, to see him off on the *Île de France* (he returned on
the *Liberté*) at the French Line Pier 88 at 48th Street. It was fantastic.
It wasn't too cold, and I was allowed to run freely all over the deck.
Afterward, my mother's sister, my Aunt Bertha Friedman, who lived
in New York City, met us there to see my father off and support my
mother, and we all went for hot dogs at a diner near the docks before
we took the train back to New Brunswick.

The food on those great ocean liners was amazing, and my father
saved some of the menus, which I still have, and which make for
glorious reading. He enjoyed the feasts partly because he was one of the
few members of the team who did not get seasick.

Upon their arrival in Paris, they were taken to stay at the deluxe Hôtel Louvois, set back from the street in its own garden. I went specially to take a look at it when I was walking around exploring that neighborhood in the first arrondissement. The hotel is now the Résidence Louvois, across the street from the old Bibliothèque Nationale de France, the original branch of the National Library of France, on the rue Vivienne behind the Jardin du Palais Royal. Its amazing collections include the Proust papers donated by his niece, Suzanne Adrienne "Suzy" Mante-Proust. She said, "Mon oncle Marcel Proust était fascinant, il avait un charme extraordinaire." (My uncle Marcel Proust was fascinating, he had an extraordinary charm.) And the Salle Richelieu is the most beautiful library reading room anywhere.

We laughed when he told us about the daily greetings in Paris when the team arrived at the SIFA factory in the mornings. Everyone, of course, asked the usual question, "Ça va?" (That/It goes [well]; how are things; how are you?)

And the invariable reply was, "Ça va. Ça va?" (That goes; things are fine. How goes it?)

There was a sort of chorus set up—Ça va? Ça va. Ça va? Ça va. —until everybody had been properly greeted.

When I was about twelve, living in Roosevelt, NJ, Monsieur Courtieu, a French chemist with whom my father had been friendly during his stay in Paris, and his wife came to the United States. We went to meet them at the Princeton train station, about fifteen miles away. My father had taught me to say, "Bonjour. Comment allez-vous?" (Hello. How go/are you?), and to count from one to ten in French. I demonstrated my ability to Monsieur and Madame Courtieu, who were suitably impressed.

I also remember that my father sometimes said, "Qu'est-ce que vous faites là? (What are you doing there? What are you up to?)" Of course, I didn't understand, but he did translate. However, until I learned French, I always heard the last two words as *fetlock*. My father didn't speak much French but he could read it, as his résumé states.

Later, when I went to Paris for that first time in 1963, Monsieur and Madame Courtieu invited me to their apartment in Levallois-Perret for dinner with some of their friends, fellow chemists and their wives. I took the Métro, and he met me there and conducted me to his apartment not too far away.

My father had written to Monsieur Courtieu with my address, and Monsieur Courtieu sent me a *petit bleu* (little blue) with the invitation. The citywide system of subterranean pneumatic tubes going from post office to post office is no longer used. The customer would write a letter on a piece of blue paper that was then sealed, stamped, and given to the clerk to be dispatched. The postman found me and delivered the *petit bleu* even though my father had sent the address without barring the seven, the usual French way of writing it. Thinking it was a sixteen, Monsieur Courtieu had written the address as 16 bis rue des Saints-Pères. But the clever mailman, when he couldn't find me there, somehow knew right away to go to 76 bis, in plenty of time. I was able to telephone and accept the invitation.

It was great to see them again, and to meet the friends they had invited. And the dinner was delicious, with the main course a superb *poulet basquaise* (Basque-style chicken) that Madame Courtieu prepared. The chicken is browned in butter, flamed in cognac, and then cooked in white wine in a heavy covered casserole in the oven with tomatoes, red and green peppers, onions, garlic, salt and pepper, and pieces of ham. Much to the surprise of my hosts, I had heard of the dish and I actually knew the recipe from books, since I had long enjoyed reading cookbooks. But this was the first time I had had the dish.

During our dinner conversation, the subject of Louis XIV came up, and his finance minister Colbert was mentioned. They were very surprised that I knew who he was. When I was a kid watching *The Early Show* on CBS with my mother just after dinner and before finishing my homework, I had seen a Hollywood film I loved, *The Man in the Iron Mask* (1939), based on the novel by Alexandre Dumas, in which Colbert was a character, the arch-rival of the villain, Fouquet. The astonished Monsieur Courtieu turned to his guests and said, "Je savais que Max aurait des enfants sérieux." (I knew Max would have serious children.) After dinner, they played an LP of part of the soundtrack of the film *Marius* by Marcel Pagnol and found my incomprehension amusing.

At the time, I didn't understand some of the dialogue because of the Marseilles accent, which I loved, and have since learned to understand. And Pagnol's trilogy of plays made into films, *Marius* (1931), *Fanny* (1932), and *César* (1936), became some of my favorites.

After a delightful evening, and slightly tipsy on the excellent wine served at dinner, I took the Métro back to Sèvres-Babylone in a dreamy contented state.

CHAPTER FIFTEEN

The Bald Soprano and The Coach with the Six Insides

I HAVE LOVED THE theater since I was a child and was taken to see plays and shows, from children's theater to Shakespeare, mostly by my mother, since my father was at work. And when I was a high school student, I ushered for three seasons for the Princeton Players, a summer theater group on the campus of Princeton University. The pay was the equivalent of a ticket to the show, one show a week for ten weeks. It was quite a theatrical education, like taking a course in theater literature.

When I was a junior in Princeton High School, we read Corneille's *Le Cid* in class, and then went as a class to the McCarter Theater to see the memorable production of the play mounted by the TNP, the Théâtre National Populaire, which was on tour in the US in 1958. The play was directed by the TNP's artistic director Jean Vilar, who also acted in the very moving tragedy, and I can see him now as Don Diègue, father of Le Cid, Don Rodrigue, kneeling on the stage of the McCarter Theater and intoning, "Ô rage, ô désespoir, ô viellesse ennemie… (Oh, rage, oh despair, oh old age enemy…)" The production starred Gérard Philippe in the title role and Maria Casarès as Chimène, both marvelous. He died young, in 1959, shortly after the tour, and there is a brown historical shield telling us about him on the street in front of his house at 17 rue de Tournon, right around the corner from the Hôtel Michelet Odéon and near the Palais du Luxembourg.

I was pleased to go to the theater in Paris a number of times on that first trip, and many times to the opera and to plays on later trips, and my diverse theatrical experiences included modern plays as well as productions of the classics. Paris has no single theater district equivalent to Broadway in New York. The theaters are all over the city, many the only one on a street, many of them, such as the Opéra Comique, off the Grands Boulevards on the right bank,. And in the Montparnasse area, the rue de la Gaîté is home to a number of theaters as well as brasseries and cafes.

In 1963, we were still in the era of the Theater of the Absurd. That post-World War Two movement virtually began with Samuel Beckett's *En attendant Godot* (Waiting for Godot) and Ionesco's *La Cantatrice chauve* (The Bald Soprano), both produced in 1950. Decades later, when I was recording audiobooks, I had the great pleasure of recording a bilingual edition of *Waiting for Godot*, with Beckett's original French and his own English translation on facing pages. And I had loved the play when I saw it on PBS's Play of the Week broadcast in 1961, excellently played with a cast that included Burgess Meredith, Zero Mostel, Jack Gilford, Kurt Kaszner, and Alvin Epstein, whom I had the great pleasure of meeting decades later when I did a play reading in which he was one of the actors. I was able to tell him how much I had loved his performance. He and Kurt Kaszner were the only two actors in the Play of the Week program to have done the original 1956 Broadway production. Play of the Week was one of my favorite programs. They showed a play every evening for a week, and I was sometimes allowed to watch a play more than once, if I had finished my homework.

The Theater of the Absurd portrayed new and original situations in the midst of the familiar everyday life that was their background, dismissing the realistic or well-made play almost as a passé genre; and was based on the philosophical ideas of Albert Camus and on Jean-Paul Sartre's existentialism. In his 1942 essay "The Myth of Sisyphus," Camus had said that life is basically meaningless and absurd, and Sartre maintained that life, which is basically absurd, has the meaning you give it, which you do by engaging in whatever you choose to involve yourself in, on both the personal and societal level. Its theatrical precursors included Luigi Pirandello, among whose plays is *Sei personaggi in cerca d'autore* (Six Characters in Search of an Author; 1921); and Alfred Jarry, with his famous and hilarious play *Ubu roi* (Ubu King; 1896), of which I have heard a recording that kept me in stitches. Absurdism's literary forebears included Franz Kafka and the philosophical Austro-Hungarian writer Robert Musil, with his unfinished novel in three volumes and a number of drafts for more sections, *Der Mann ohne Eigenschaften* (The Man without Qualities; 1930—1943). The Theater of the Absurd set out to attack religious and political orthodoxy, and, with its broad comedy, succeeded in doing so while being highly entertaining.

For all its seemingly realistic elements, Edward Albee's deeply sad and highly funny *Who's Afraid of Virginia Woolf* (1962) partakes of the genre. I had the pleasure of seeing the original Broadway production, which had caused quite a sensation as being daring in its treatment of sexuality and covering ground about college life that nobody had explored before, certainly not in quite the same way. Rutgers University bought a block of tickets and rented a bus to take us to and from New York. I had an excellent seat in the first row of the balcony at the Billy Rose Theatre. The direction was wonderful, everyone's acting was amazing, and the brilliant Uta Hagen as Martha gave the most extraordinary performance I had ever seen. Years later, that performance inspired me to want to study acting with her, and having auditioned for her and been accepted as a student, I was thrilled to do so, and even just to meet her. And I was so happy be able to tell her how much I had loved her performance, how deeply it had impressed and amazed me.

"L'enfer c'est les autres" (Hell is other people), Sartre's character Joseph Garcin concludes in *Huis clos* (No Exit; 1944), which one might consider an early absurdist play, before the movement took off after the war. The play was a hit in New York in 1946, when it was first produced. I had seen *No Exit* presented one summer by the Princeton Players, and just loved it.

The original productions of *La Cantatrice chauve* (The Bald Soprano) and *La Leçon* (The Lesson) are still playing at the Théâtre de la Huchette on the rue de la Huchette in the fifth arrondissement, perhaps because the postage-stamp theater only has eighty-five seats, which are on a first come, first served basis. *The Bald Soprano* opened in 1950 at the Théâtre des Noctambules and moved to the Huchette in

1957. I would love to have seen the original cast, replaced by an excellent group of actors long before I saw the show.

I had seen *The Bald Soprano* and *The Lesson* in an evening of three Ionesco one-acts at the Princeton Players, with *The Chairs* being the third play—all of them amazing, and a perfect evening in the theater. They were so unusual, such eye-openers, like nothing I had ever seen before, and so hilarious. I was in stitches.

Ionesco was inspired to write *La Cantatrice chauve* when he listened to Assimil language teaching records for English, with the absurd phrases that often seemed disconnected from sentences one would actually need or use when speaking the language. When you read the play, which Ionesco called an "anti-play" on the title page, you find that even the stage directions are a riot. The scene is "A middle-class English interior, with English armchairs... A long moment of English silence. The English clock strikes 17 English strokes..." The word 'English' is used seventeen times in these opening stage directions!

I was very taken with a catch phrase in *The Bald Soprano* spoken by Mr. Martin, and that sent everyone into gales of laughter. I still use it when I think it is appropriate: "Comme c'est curieux ! Comme c'est bizarre ! Et quelle coïncidence !" (How curious! How bizarre! And what a coincidence) Mr. Martin would say that whenever anything struck him as strange, such as when a person was kneeling at an Underground entrance (the play takes place in London) to tie his shoelaces, which had become undone.

Many years later, in 1994, I went to see a delightful award-winning show by Roger Défossez, *Offenbach, tu connais?* (Offenbach, You Know? / Do You Know Offenbach?), in which the actors are in their dressing rooms preparing for the evening's performance of *La Cantatrice chauve*, which they are sick of doing. They would rather be performing Offenbach's *La Vie parisienne* (Parisian Life), from which they sing excerpts to piano accompaniment, along with pieces from *Pomme d'api* (Lady Apple), *La Grande Duchesse de Gérolstein*, and *La Périchole*. The play is thus very much in the mode and tradition of the Theater of the Absurd.

So was another hilarious and poignant play called *La Madeleine Proust en Franche-Comté*, written by and starring the immensely talented Laurence also known as Lola Sémenin, which I saw in September, 2008. The play is about a country woman in a rural area who receives endless telephone calls from those who love Proust, and are sure she has some connection with him, and want to meet her. She has never heard of the celebrated author and has no idea what Proust's madeleine is, much less that, dipped in a spoonful of tea, the pastry arouses the Narrator's childhood memories. She speaks in a fantastic country dialect, and we laugh with her, not at her during the course of her monologue as a very affecting and even moving, much put-upon character, who tells us her life story and talks about the difficulties of life on her isolated farm.

Jean Erdman's dramatization of James Joyce's *Finnegan's Wake*, which she adapted as *The Coach with the Six Insides* into a multi-performance of dance, music, spoken word over loudspeakers, partakes of surrealism as well as the absurd. I had not seen it in New York where it was highly successful 1962 Off-Broadway production, so I was quite happy to see it when it was on tour in Paris. Incidentally, you will remember that Samuel Beckett was James Joyce's secretary, and his influence on Beckett is obvious. Joyce was among the iconoclastic literary precursors of Absurdism. Joyce and the city of Paris are intimately connected: Sylvia Beach's bookstore Shakespeare and Company at 7 rue de l'Odéon in the sixth arrondissement—not to be confused with the English-language bookstore that adopted the same name on the quai across from Notre Dame—received visits from numerous litterateurs and authors, and she published Joyce's *Ulysses* when nobody else would touch it because of supposedly obscene passages. Sylvia Beach had a Princeton connection too: she spent some of her youth there and is buried in the cemetery on Wiggins Street.

The Coach with the Six Insides was an exciting, mystifying, absorbing, and sometimes hard to comprehend evening in the theater, particularly since the loudspeakers were a bit muffled and the lines were not spoken very clearly. My fall semester courses after the European trip included one in twentieth-century English literature, and we read all of James Joyce's works in the order of his writing them, including *Ulysses*. We never got to *Finnegan's Wake*, which I tried on my own and never finished.

I also had the immense pleasure of going to the Comédie Française, which performed from September through July at their wonderful theater on the right bank, the Théâtre Français, built in 1799, with its impressive marble staircases, and red plush velvet and gold braid auditorium, where I had the pleasure of seeing many other productions on later trips. They had done a highly acclaimed production in 1958 of Molière's hilarious *Le bourgeois gentilhomme* (The Middle-Class Gentleman) and revived it in 1963. The presentation was splendid with its gorgeous, elegant period costumes, and the complete ballet by Lully. The brilliant, hilarious Louis Seignier played the title role, and his equally magnificent colleague Jacques Charon played the Dancing Master. There is a wonderful 1958 film of the production that was thought so brilliant that it was well worth preserving. I also saw that film at the Garden Theater in Princeton when it was released in 1960. It is the first film that the Comédie Française ever made, so it was a very big deal at the time. Fortunately, the film is still available, dear reader, so you can enjoy it to too.

CHAPTER SIXTEEN

Un Concert Chez Mademoiselle

ONE NIGHT I arrived home late to find Mademoiselle Haumesser standing at the piano, reading a postcard that was obviously not addressed to her, as I could tell from her startled look, and from the fact that she immediately put it down. In fact, it was addressed to me!

I was astonished to see her out of her wheelchair. She hurriedly hobbled back to it, sat down heavily, and then handed the postcard to me. It was from a college friend, who was also traveling in Europe, but not on a fellowship, and simply wanted to get in touch. As I already knew, he had developed leukemia, so this was a last trip to see the world, and sadly he died perhaps a year afterwards.

I looked pointedly at her when she gave me the postcard, but said nothing. I had seen Mademoiselle Haumesser in the kitchen soon after I arrived steaming open a letter, reading it, and then resealing it. I hadn't said anything, but I had learned from watching her about steaming open letters and concealing the fact that one had done so. Very good if one wanted to be a spy! She had paid no attention to me while steaming the envelope open, as if it mattered not a whit. Indeed, it didn't matter to me. And that evening, I learned not only that she was indeed quite a busybody, of which the postcard incident was simply one more confirmation, but also that she was shamming about her leg. She probably didn't need to continue wearing the cast at all, but she wore it for her own purposes, so people would have sympathy for her and not suspect that she was capable of spying. What a character!

Soon after that, she decided to present a concert in her salon in order to promote Monsieur Zaki and help launch the career she thought he deserved. She sent out invitations and expected all her acquaintances and friends to be there. She also invited the Egyptian consul, who accepted. The consulate was not far away from the rue des Saints-Pères, so it was easy for him to get there.

The concert was well attended, and the part of the salon near the dining room had every chair full. I and the other three renters had to stay in the dining room, with the double doors closed. Mademoiselle did not consider us fit company for her exalted guests. It was just as well, since we couldn't help but laugh as Mademoiselle played the random wrong note, as usual, and Monsieur Zaki played squeakily on his violin, with an occasional smooth tone. We tried to stifle our laughter behind our hands, I don't know with how much success. We couldn't look at each other. I have no idea what the Egyptian consul and his wife thought. There was a reception afterwards with refreshments, to which we were not invited, I am happy to say. It must have been rather glum. I don't remember what I said to Mademoiselle the next day. The concert was certainly a memorable experience.

CHAPTER SEVENTEEN

Farewell to Paris

THE DAY ARRIVED at last. It was time to leave Paris for that year. I was satisfied that I had done all the necessary research for my paper and that I would have no problem writing it, and also that I had taken Professor Sobolevitch's advice and gotten to know Paris a bit on this first visit. I was off to Oxford on a plane from Orly. There were only two ways to get to London from Paris in those days before the Eurostar train: 1) a regular slow train to Boulogne and the ferry across the Channel, then a slow train from Dover up to London, or 2) a plane from Orly. Well, there was a third, if you wanted to swim the Channel. Montgolfier balloons had not been a viable option for at least a century or more, though they were used for recreational purposes out in the countryside. On a much later trip I did take the ferry and the train from Dover to London, and I enjoyed the voyage thoroughly, which was not the case with the hovercraft, which I also took back and forth before the Eurostar existed, and in which I experienced seasickness.

In short, I was given a plane ticket, and I took a train from Heathrow into London, and changed for the train to Oxford, where I proceeded to Wadham College through charming old streets with memorable unique buildings that stand out in the open spaces that surround them.

Had I taken the ferry, the trip would have taken most of the day, and we had to be there fairly quickly, in plenty of time for an evening meal and to settle in, and even walk around the beautiful city of Oxford. Unfortunately, the food at the stately majestic refectory with its high ceilings—I learned the word there—was abysmal. I don't remember that first meal, but I do remember being impressed by how unappetizing and nearly inedible it was. At one dinner they served half a veal heart swimming in watery gravy, and it was like looking at an anatomy lesson.

I nearly gagged and couldn't eat even one bite of it. I made do with the "chips" (French fries), which were like little sticks of chips off an old block, and with the green peas that were like hard little pebbles. At least the water was potable.

One night some of us went to a local tavern not too far away, and the food, while not great, was much better than that served at the college. On the other hand, they served a great afternoon tea in the Wadham main lounge, every day at 4. The tea was excellent, and I was later reminded of it when I was in graduate school and used to go to the weekly teas at Columbia University, where the tea was served from a great urn by volunteer graduate faculty wives. At Wadham, the scones and biscuits were excellent along with delicious marmalade, and so were the tea sandwiches, including the tasty cucumber sandwiches that Oscar Wilde famously has a scene about at the opening of *The Importance of Being Earnest: A trivial Comedy for Serious People* (1895), but the cakes were much too sweet with awful textures, as one could tell just by looking at them. At Columbia, by the way, all the food, including the cakes, was delicious.

During the mornings, we all met in a lounge, and each in turn reported on his research and on the trip in general. When I got back, I would turn my notes not only into the paper that I sent to the Carnegie Foundation, and but also use them for my Henry Rutgers paper, since I was a Henry Rutgers Scholar.

At Wadham, I discovered how well the National Health Service worked. Even foreigners were treated for a minimal fee, and I heartily wished we had the same kind of universal health care system in the U.S. One of the Carnegie Fellows developed an eye infection, conjunctivitis I think, and the treatment was almost gratis. He had to pay a small fee for a doctor's visit at a nearby walk-in clinic he was sent to, and the prescribed ointment cost only a shilling.

On another free afternoon, I and two other Fellows took the bus to Stratford, a beautiful scenic ride that included a splendid view of Blenheim and its palace. We had purchased tickets to *The Tempest* at the Royal Shakespeare Theatre, and we had plenty of time to walk around the town, most intriguing. We went to Anne Hathaway's cottage and had an interesting and informative guided tour of that museum. In the evening, we went to the theater to see the excellent, indeed fascinating production at the magnificent theater. Ian Holm played Ariel; Roy Dotrice was Caliban; David Warner, Trinculo; Donald Sinden, Sebastian; and Roy Marsden, Francisco—all people not yet well known to Americans and whom I saw many years later in film and on television. Tom Fleming, the excellent Prospero and Philipa Urquhart, the beautiful Miranda were well known in Great Britain, less so in the United States, although later she did do some Masterpiece Theater productions. Peter Brook and Clifford Williams were directors of this innovative production, during which entire back walls would fall away to reveal other sets, creating a magical experience.

It was too late to get public transportation back to Oxford, so we set out to hitch, and we were soon rewarded when a car pulled up, and a very kind gentleman and his daughter inquired what we wanted and where we were going, and we told him about ourselves and the Carnegie Foundation. They took us back to Oxford, to Wadham, where the porter let us in. And the gentleman invited us for dinner the following week, which we were happy to accept. He picked us up and took us to the historic Bear Hotel in Woodstock, one of the oldest in England, and we had a wonderful evening with our charming, cultured hosts.

On the weekend following, I and another Carnegie Fellow went to London. We found an inexpensive hotel near the train station, and after settling in we proceeded to explore. It was magnificent to see the extraordinary center of the city with the Houses of Parliament, Westminster Abbey, the London Bridge, and the Tower, all of which we toured. We also went to the National Gallery and the National Portrait Gallery. The Victoria and Albert Museum, the Courtauld, the Wallace, and the Tate would wait for later trips, when I was on my own, as would Petticoat Lane. We took a bus up Fleet Street, where the ruins wrought during the Blitz could still be seen, a shocking sight that told us a slight bit of what Londoners had lived through.

We had lunch at the old Cheshire Cheese Tavern, where I sat in the seat marked with a plaque that said it had been Samuel Johnson's. I had very good roast beef and a roasted onion. After lunch, we proceeded to

Samuel Johnson's House, an excellent museum. And by that time, after walking around some more, it was time to return to Oxford.

On a much later trip to London (one of seven), I dined with a friend at Simpson's in the Strand, where I had previously had a superb roast beef meal. The personnel this time were all French, which I didn't remember to have been the case formerly. Great covered carts were wheeled around to the tables and the roast beef was carved and served from them. A great show was made of the carving, but the roast beef was not as good as I had remembered. Our waiter was in London to study the restaurant business, because it was easier for him to be hired in England instead of in the overcrowded French market, and referring to the dessert cart, I asked him, "Qu'est que vous pensez, monsieur ? Qu'est-ce que je dois prendre ?" (What do you think, monsieur? What should I have?) "Rien" (Nothing)," he replied, looking surreptitiously around. We had a good life. And I took him at his word!

Our group returned to the United States at the end of those active, eventful two weeks at Wadham College, with its beautiful inner courtyard, in the midst of the superb old streets and gorgeous architecture of Oxford that I have enjoyed so much when seeing them again in the British police procedurals *Endeavour*, *Morse*, and *Lewis*. Weary from the flight, but ecstatic, I greeted my parents in Princeton with warm hugs, so happy to see them and my two brothers again. I had had the greatest time in the world, but it was truly good to be home once more.

PART TWO

My Return to Paris and Other Trips

CHAPTER EIGHTEEN

The Next Times I Saw Paris

WHAT A MARVELOUS experience those first two months in Paris were, and what colorful characters I met there. But I didn't keep in touch with even one of them, or with the other Carnegie Foundation fellows. And I no longer have any of their addresses or phone numbers. I've no idea what became of them. I regret not having maintained contact with all those people. I had vowed when I left that I would return to Paris every year, but I didn't get back there again until 1973, ten long eventful years later, during which I had been to graduate school and pursued my career as an actor. And unfortunately I was only in Paris for a long weekend.

I had completed my first season at the Rochester Shakespeare Theater (it no longer exists) in Rochester, NY and signed an Actors' Equity contract to return for a second season. One of the actors, Gavin Cameron-Webb and his wife, who were English, were house-sitting in Norwood Junction for a stage director friend of his who was away for the summer working at the Pitlochry Theatre Festival in Scotland. Norwood Junction is an area to the south of London near Wimbledon, and not north as its name implies, and Gavin and his wife invited me to stay rent-free along with our lighting designer and his wife, so I only had to pay the airfare and personal expenses. I stayed for three months, and took the train up to London every day, making sure to carry an umbrella, because it rained for at least twenty minutes each day, in the midst of a reasonably warm summer. It was rather chilly at night, and there was no central heating, which had generally not been installed anywhere at that time, so we sat in the parlor conversing while huddled near an electric heater before going up to bed.

I loved London and loved being there, seeing Buckingham Palace in the distance, going to all the great museums, large and small, and taking long walks through the streets and parks and along the Strand, to see the Gilbert and Sullivan monuments near Waterloo Bridge on the west bank of the Thames, and seeing the Savoy Theater where so many of their comic operas had been produced, as well as the Savoy Hotel, with its delightful bar and restaurant.

I found the food generally less than inspiring, to say the least, although I did discover pub lunches, and they were excellent. With the delicious bitter (pale ale, served warm), I had Scotch eggs, tomato salad, bread, cheshire or some other cheese, and pickled onions, which I had never had before, and loved. An apple for dessert completed the meal.

I also had the pleasure of seeing Maggie Smith on stage in Noël Coward's *Private Lives*, so hilarious, and we were all in stitches the whole time. I had loved her as well in the 1969 film of *The Prime of Miss Jean Brodie*.

When I told Gavin I wanted to go to Paris for a long weekend, he decided to accompany me. We took the hovercraft from Dover, and the train from Boulogne. I didn't enjoy the Hovercraft, partly because we had tickets on the bottom of two floors, and the trip was very turbulent and somewhat sick-making since we couldn't see the waves, which would have helped us maintain our equilibrium.

Walking around the boulevard St.-Germain neighborhood after the train ride to Paris and the Métro to the St.-Michel stop, we found a reasonably priced hotel on the boulevard St.-Michel near the Seine and had a great time strolling around the city. I even went over to the rue des Saints-Pères to see where I had stayed in 1963. And again, I vowed to go back every year for a long stay.

However, once again I didn't manage to get back there for many years, not until 1981 when I spent a happy week there after a trip to the Highlands of Scotland. I didn't get back to Paris again until 1983 for a short time, after a trip to Italy, and then again in 1985. At least I have managed to go there every year since then except for two years during the Covid pandemic, when US citizens were not allowed into France.

In late 1984, I had been cast in the film *Une Femme ou deux* (One Woman or Two; 1985) directed by Daniel Vigne, who auditioned me in his New York hotel room at the Meridien Hotel, on 57th Street near Carnegie Hall. I had to speak French, and he was well satisfied with my command of the language, which I had assiduously kept up all those years by reading books, watching French films without looking at the subtitles, and conversing with whomever I could.

In order to do the film, I had to break my Equity contract with the McCarter Theater in Princeton, where I had done the usual limited regional run of *Under Milk Wood* in late 1984. After a hiatus, we were contracted to move the show to the Richmond Museum Theater in Richmond, VA for a two-week run in the spring of 1985 in exchange for one of their shows going to the McCarter, but I had to leave at the end of the first week to go to Paris, and to pay a fine to the union, which I happily did. I thought making the film too exciting an opportunity to turn down.

The movie starred Gérard Depardieu and Sigourney Weaver, with each of whom I had scenes; and Dr. Ruth Westheimer in a hilarious supporting role. Monsieur Depardieu was quite wary of me at first. I was only an ignorant American, or so he thought, even though I obviously spoke French, but he warmed up a bit when I happened to quote from Molière's *Tartuffe*, and he realized I was conversant with French culture and knew he was a big star in France, so his ego was satisfied.

We made the film in April, 1985—yes, April in Paris, and pretty rainy it was, too—and then did some location work in New York many months later. I flew to Paris on April 7, and when I arrived on April 8, I was taken straight to a shoot before going to my hotel. I was put up at the Hôtel San Régis, near the pont d'Iéna. It was a beautiful place, furnished with antiques and being in my bedroom was like going back in time. The hotel has since been renovated, and though still splendid, the interior looks nothing like what it did in 1963.

Every morning I was picked up at the San Régis and driven out to the Mairie de Puteaux, the city hall of a suburb to the west of Paris beyond the Défense, with its modern skyscrapers. We went for makeup and wardrobe first in a side room off the central hall, and by the time we had finished, instead of shooting a scene, we went to lunch at different nearby restaurants, making sure to cover up our costumes with large napkins. On the restaurant tables there were always baskets of delicious French sliced baguette and abundant platters of charcuterie as well as main dishes, all copiously washed down with wine. One day lunch was at an Irish pub with long tables, and delicious smoked salmon and Irish stew among other excellent dishes.

After lunch, we would go back to the Mairie, whose main hall was meant to be the Art Deco interior of a Rockefeller Center reception hall, to shoot scenes. I don't know how we got anything done! Because I would have to perform after lunch, I didn't have wine—well, maybe one glass—but the crew certainly indulged themselves with bottle after bottle.

There was a snack table in the room where we were shooting, just as there is on American shoots, but with very little on it except coffee and some pastries. M. Depardieu wore a heavy parka to conceal the fact that he was considerably overweight, and he had a bodyguard with him whose sole function was to prevent him from eating anything on that snack table. Every time he reached for something, the bodyguard would slap his hand away!

I went to visit Sigourney Weaver at the Bristol, the luxurious hotel with a Michelin three-star restaurant where I had lunch years later. I was playing her boss in the film, and since I also knew a friend of hers, the playwright Christopher Durang slightly, having met him at the Eugene O'Neill Theater Festival where I was performing and he had a play done, I felt I could visit her. She was awfully nice, and we got along famously. She even entrusted me with a letter to mail to her husband once I returned to New York. Her French tutor was there, so I met her. She had also taught Jeremy Irons to speak the French he needed for the film *Un amour de Swann* (Swann in Love; 1984), with its beautiful sets and costumes, and a script I didn't think was well adapted from Proust's book. I made the mistake of telling her I didn't think Jeremy Irons' performance was very good. She bristled, but the fact is that his lines had to be subtitled in French when the film was shown in France, and I didn't think he captured the character at all. Still, I would have done better to have kept quiet.

On days off, I explored the area of the Champs-Élysées and went to the Louvre, where one can famously spend weeks and not see everything. There was no Musée d'Orsay in those days. It opened in December, 1986, and quickly became one of my favorite museums. But I did see the collections of Impressionists and special exhibits at the Jeu de Paume and the Orangerie in the Tuileries.

One Woman or Two opened late in 1985 and played at the Paris cinema near the Plaza hotel in New York. We had a celebratory party at a restaurant after the opening, and I met Dr. Ruth Westheimer for the first and only time. She was a riot! Daniel was thinking of moving to New York for part of the year and was looking for an apartment. Dr. Ruth asked if anybody could help him find one. After a while, I said I could always call my landlord and see if anything were available. Dr. Ruth called for silence, and said loudly in her inimitable accent, "There we are! Daniel has an apartment! All settled!" Daniel and I looked at each other and almost laughed.

In September, 1986 I returned to Paris to visit friends I had made on the film set, and I stayed at the hôtel La Louisiane on the rue de Seine, where I also stayed on a couple of subsequent trips. The location was perfect, right near the river in the heart of the St.-Germain neighborhood where I have stayed on nearly all my Paris trips, just as I had in 1963; and it was inexpensive with a good buffet breakfast included in the price. I would visit those friends on every subsequent trip, so that eventually we became good friends and not just acquaintances. Some of them moved away from Paris, and we lost touch. With certain others, and with some whom I met later, we drifted out of each other's lives for various reasons, as one does. I have no regrets, however. I have remained close friends with a number of people I met on later trips as the decades have flown by.

That month of September was notable for a number of terrorist attacks in Paris, including one in a Métro station at rush hour and another at a café on the Champs-Élysées, so I and everyone I knew avoided the Métro and walked everywhere. I felt generally safe despite the attacks. And I was happy to eat in various cafes and brasseries, and to browse in bookstores. I also went to the Delacroix Museum in the charming Place Furstenberg off the rue Jacob for the first time, and afterwards to La Palette, a café on the rue de Seine, frequented in the past by artists, hence the name. The interior still has the very old décor, with elaborately painted ceilings and walls.

On September 17 I went to Lyon to have one of the great meals of my life at star chef Paul Bocuse's restaurant. I took a taxi to the Gare de Lyon, and the TGV to Lyon for a spectacular ride through rolling hills, past little villages, farms, and great manses. The taxi driver in Lyon took me directly to Paul Bocuse's restaurant at Collonges-au-Mont d'Or on the Sâone River. I had a beautiful view of the Rhône on the way. I said to the driver that I was glad to be out of Paris for a bit, because of the terrorist attacks. He said I shouldn't be too glad, because Lyon was under very tight security, since the terrorists whom they had arrested were in prison in Lyon, and demonstrations and perhaps even attacks were expected. They appeared to be Syrian-backed Lebanese terrorists, who, among other things wanted all trace of the French presence out of Lebanon, which had long been independent, but was still under French political influence.

Eventually, we arrived at the restaurant. The charming maître d' ushered me into the dining room through majestic vestibules. Everything was superbly decorated, with lovely flowers on the tables, and gleaming crystal and silver on the elegant napery, and the service was perfect. After I was seated, Paul Bocuse himself appeared and said hello to everyone, going from table to table, before returning to the kitchen to finish preparing the lunch. He was back and forth several times.

The sommelier was very charming, and had the most extraordinary huge ringed mustaches. He recommended a Châteauneuf-du-Pape Mt. Redon 1978, a superb red wine, not too heavy, but mellow and with a great body and fruitiness, the perfect accompaniment for the entire meal.

I had the prix fix menu for 465 francs, about $75—worth about $678 in today's dollars (!)—very expensive back then, yet very reasonable considering what one got for this once in a lifetime gastronomic experience. Not only was the food creative and original, but also the portions were generous.

The amuse-bouche was a delicately seasoned Lyon sausage in a small brioche. Next came the Soupe aux Truffes Valéry Giscard d'Estaing, who had been President of France from 1974 to 1981. Bocuse created the soup in his honor when the president awarded him the Legion of Honor for his services to French cuisine, including his launching of the Nouvelle Cuisine movement, so the headwaiter informed me. The soup is surmounted with a delicate flaky pastry crust that one breaks into it. At first the soup tastes deliciously and slightly tart, with little pieces of meat and truffle, but as one eats the soup, one reaches a thick layer of truffles for a delicious finish.

The soup was followed by a Turbot à la Viennoise (Viennese), in a wonderful delicate tarragon-flavored sauce with fresh chives. The fish was served under a lightly souffléed topping, under which are finely chopped well-cooked vegetables and herbs. The dish was exquisitely delicate.

As a palate cleanser, a Beaujolais sorbet was served.

Then came three pan-fried small rib lamb chops, perfectly done, with watercress leaves and a dish of buttered bone marrow with a puree of potatoes.

A cheese course was next. I had three, as is customary: a marvelous bleu, a creamy St. Lambert in its orange rind, and a Tomme de Savoie.

After that the desserts were served. And what desserts! I tasted just about everything. Chariots were wheeled in of bowls of fruits, cakes, petits fours—I had a pear tartlet and a chocolate opera slice, one mouthful each—a floating island with caramel sauce and English-style custard; a plate of sweet raspberries served with a scoop of vanilla ice cream and a raspberry coulis. An espresso coffee with a plate of chocolates was the last course of all.

The meal lasted more than three hours. After photographing the dining room, I left, wholly thrilled and really full, and took a taxi back to the station and the TGV back to Paris, to hear the news that there had been another terrorist attack, a particularly heartless and revolting one, this time by Palestinian terrorists. Tati, a small branch of a department store on the rue de Rennes, had been bombed, the bombs thrown in from the street. This store is one where poorer people, including many Arab and African immigrants, shop for clothing and other necessities.

I went back to my hotel for a short nap, wrote postcards, and mailed them on the way to visit a friend. As usual on all my trips, I took lots of walks and ate in wonderful restaurants, usually with friends but sometimes alone.

One of my friends who had been in the movie was a wine merchant as well as an actor, and invited me and others for wine tastings in his cellar. He sold wines to the great restaurants. On display was a bottle of 1840s Hungarian Tokaji (Tokay), and other rare wines. All the wines were extraordinary, of course, and he served excellent food with them. At the first one, he had a chicken, mozzarella, and tomato salad with fresh basil, a selection of cheeses and country bread, grapes, a tarte aux quetschs (purple prune plums), brownies, and coffee from the Arab café across the street. In order of tasting, the wines were a 1981 Brane-Cantenac (Margaux); a 1984 St.-Émilion, Château Canon; a 1964 Château La Mission Haut Brion; a 1952 Château La Mission Haut Brion.

On September 21 I went to London for a few days to visit American friends who were there, crossing the Channel on the ferry and taking the boat train to Victoria Station from Dover. We had a great time. The food was pretty bad the whole time though, and I didn't have good meals except for a couple of pub lunches. We saw Alan Ayckbourn's new play *Woman in Mind*, which was very interesting but rather woodenly done, with the actors very mannered and quite obviously not organic in their performances.

On my own, I saw *Les Misérables* at the Palace Theater, which I really wanted to see because it is where Sir Arthur Sullivan's only opera *Ivanhoe* was first performed in 1891, inaugurating the opera house that Richard D'Oyly Carte had had built, and which he named the Royal English Opera House. The interior did not disappoint, but I am in the minority in not being crazy about the show, although I love Victor Hugo's book.

Quite marvelous was Jonathan Miller's updated version of Gilbert and Sullivan's *The Mikado* at the English National Opera, with Eric Idle as Ko-Ko. The comic opera was set in Edwardian England, and worked beautifully. There is a television version as well, but unfortunately, you don't see most of the background chorus, whose comic bits were extremely funny on stage. As we all know, the Japanese setting is simply a front for Gilbert's satire of English Victorian manners and mores. *Topsy-Turvy* (1999), Mike Leigh's excellent film about the making of *The Mikado*, does show the racist and imperialist context of the era, and the terrible, bigoted attitudes of many of those involved in putting the comic opera together.

Also excellent was a production of J. B. Priestley's *When We Are Married* at the Whitehall Theatre. And the hit musical *Starlight Express*, which I didn't care for that much, was very well done and spectacularly presented. I went shopping at Harrod's, and I visited some wonderful museums once again. I was especially moved by Sigmund Freud's House in St. John's Wood. Many of his collection of antiquities were on display in the large salon, where you can see the couch his patients regularly used. The house is in a beautiful neighborhood too. The War Cabinet and underground office of Winston Churchill were also fascinating. Finally, after a jam-packed week, it was time to go home, and I had a very good flight on September 27. I was so pleased to have gone to Europe again, an amazing getaway from life in America.

When I was in Paris in 1988 I stayed at the Hôtel des Saints-Pères on the rue des Saints-Pères in a room that only had space for a double bed that I had to sidle around. Still, it was a charming place with a nice bar and lobby and a garden off it. Imagine my surprise when I returned to the hotel after a superb lunch at Taillevent to see Nobel Prize winner Anthony Burgess, the English author of the 1962 novel *A Clockwork Orange*, made into a film I had seen in 1971, sitting in the little garden reading a newspaper. I recognized him immediately because just before going to France, I had read an article about him in The New York Times. I dared to speak to him, and told him how much I admired his work and how much I loved the film. He was awfully nice to me. He was in Paris to be a guest on Bernard Pivot's television show *Apostrophes*, a literary talk show that I used to watch on the City University channel back home in New York. I had to miss this episode because I was going to the Salle Favart to see the Opéra Comique's production of Jules Massenet's *Thaïs*, which was gorgeously sung and beautifully acted. I told him I had just read the article about him, and that it said that he lived in Lugano in the Italian-speaking part of southern Switzerland, and he said it was perfect for writing, so nice and quiet. He looked me up and down and said, "You're an actor. A stage actor." I was astonished, but he told me it was the way I carried myself and my good diction that gave me away. I was very flattered.

In the course of my visit ten years later in 1998, I was fascinated to see scene workers transforming the place de l'Odéon into a film set, changing it so that it looked as it had been in 1833-1835 for the movie *Les enfants du siècle* (The Children of the Century; 1999), about the doomed love affair between the brilliant writer George Sand, played by Juliette Binoche, and the poet Alfred de Musset, played by Benoît Magimel. The workers repaved the semicircle in front of the huge theater, and put a flat of an archway in front of the entrance to the Michelet Odéon, the hotel where I have stayed most often, so that the surrounding area on that side looked as it does in old prints. Room 44, my usual room, is at the very top of the hotel overlooking the place, as you can see in the front cover photo, and I could see over the false archway. The filming took place at night, and there was a crowd of extras in period costume and the steps leading up to the huge theater columns were surrounded by horses and carriages. I sat at my window and watched some of the filming. And I saw Juliette Binoche and Benoît Magimel emerging from the theater and standing between two of the columns, but I couldn't hear what they said. The next morning, the place had been restored to what it had been, with all the false paving removed.

Another wonderful experience was a private guided tour of the new Bibliothèque Nationale on the left bank of the Seine not far from the Gare d'Austerlitz on the very last full day of my trip in 1999. It came about in this way: Earlier in the trip I went for a brief visit to Amsterdam, where I saw the Anne Frank House and the Rijksmusum, among other landmark sights. On the train going there, I had a window seat, and a woman got on and approached me. She was very charming and explained that I must be in the wrong seat, because she had a ticket for that seat, which she showed me. We called the conductor over, and he inspected our tickets. Hers was indeed for the same seat, but for the next day! The aisle seat next to mine was empty and was not booked, so I invited her to sit there, and the conductor agreed.

The elegantly dressed lady was one of the librarians at the new Bibliothèque Nationale, and she invited me to visit it, and promised me a guided tour. We exchanged contact information, and she got off at Rotterdam. I called her when I returned to Paris, and on the appointed day I met her in the lobby, and we proceeded on our visit. I saw fascinating rare book collections that visitors are not usually allowed to see without special permission, given to researchers and scholars; and then I took her to lunch in the library's canteen, with very good food, before returning to the hotel for a nap, strolling in the Luxembourg, saying goodbye to my friends, including my very dear friend Madame Blanche Buffet at her bookstore near the place de l'Odéon, and then going to dinner at Taillevent, where I had a splendid meal, as always, with a charming reception from Monsieur Vrinat and perfect service.

The next day, October 7, after I got to the airport, there was a brief wildcat strike by the air controllers, so my flight was delayed for two hours. But at last we took off and I had a nice smooth flight. I saw *Les enfants du siècle* on the plane home to New York, and I didn't think it was very good, although the performances were fine. And I had to laugh, because the scene I had seen being shot was all in close-up of the two stars between the theater columns. Nothing at all of the extras and carriages and redone place was to be seen. I wondered why they had bothered. But the filmmakers had provided a great experience for me.

CHAPTER NINETEEN

Scotland: Following in the Footsteps of David Balfour

ONE OF MY childhood dreams was to take a trip to Scotland. As a boy, I had read and loved Robert Louis Stevenson's *Kidnapped*, his 1886 historical novel, first serialized as a boy's book in the magazine *Young Folks* before being published in one volume, and I dreamed of someday following in the footsteps of its hero, David Balfour, the intrepid young man who is kidnapped in 1751 by henchmen hired by his wicked Uncle Ebenezer so that he can deprive David of his rightful inheritance, and his title as Laird of Shaws. He is held prisoner in the hold of a ship, the *Covenant* of Dysart, on its way to America where he is to be sold as an indentured servant. When the ship is wrecked off the Isle of Mull, David escapes and is saved from that fate partly due to the good offices of a character based on the historical person of Allan Breck Stewart, a condemned Jacobite rebel who fought the English in the 1745 Highland uprising, known as "The Forty-Five," and who is now fleeing the British.

Anyone reading the novel and wanting to understand the politics involved should know the following information: The word "Jacobite" is derived from the Latin *Jacobus*, meaning James, since they supported the cause of the deposed King James II, the Stuart monarch of Scottish origin, and his descendants in their claims to the throne, calling for the overthrow of the Hanoverian dynasty, in the person of King George II. Parliament had decreed the Hanoverians the legitimate heirs to the throne, since George I was a descendant of Charles I's elder sister, Elizabeth Stuart, who could not inherit the throne since she had a brother. In any case, by the time she could have inherited the throne, she had become Queen of Bohemia. English law allowed women to succeed to the crown, but only if they did not have a brother; and also would not allow a Catholic to sit on the throne. George I was a staunch Protestant, while the exiled Stuarts were Catholic, so after the reigns of William and Marry and of the childless Queen Anne, the last of the reigning Stuarts, Parliament invited George I to be king.

Allan Breck Stewart has managed to get onto the *Covenant* from a small boat that has capsized during the terrible storm, and helps to free David and to fight off the crew and captain who attack them. They both manage to swim to shore, but are separated, and eventually reunited. Theirs is an unlikely friendship, because David is a Lowlander, and a supporter of the English king. He has known little of what happened in the Highlands until he meets Allan Breck. They make their way back south, and David is able to reclaim his inheritance with his new friend's help. As a wanted rebel, Stewart manages to hide with David's help, and the swashbuckling novel ends without our knowing if he has managed to make his escape from the British Isles.

David Balfour also helps Allan Breck Stewart in the novel's 1893 sequel *David Balfour*, known in the UK as *Catriona*. The title character is David Balfour's love and they marry. After more adventures, Allan Breck Stewart finally flees for his life to France.

The incidents in both novels are based on historical events, including the trial of Allan Breck's relative, James Stewart of the Glens, falsely convicted and hanged at Balachulish Ferry for the murder of the king's factor, Colin Roy Campbell of Glenure, an incident in *Kidnapped* witnessed from afar by David and Allan, as they are making their way through the woods on their journey south.

The Master of Ballantrae (1889) is another of Stevenson's superb historical novels with the1745 rebellion as its background. This book too inspired my desire to visit the land poetically called Caledonia.

As a boy learning about the persecution of Jewish people throughout history, I identified with the persecuted Scots, many killed, many more severely punished, many driven from their homes, and with the attempt made to destroy their culture after 1745, a rebellion preceded by one in

1715, to replace the Stuarts on the throne and overthrow the Hanoverian dynasty. The books really spoke to me, and I was deeply moved.

Later, when I learned the true history of what the Stuarts were trying to achieve, I had no sympathy for the cause of the reactionary Stuart claimants to the throne, but I still empathized completely with the Scottish people, whose culture, livelihood, and often their very lives were under attack once The Forty-Five was put down, so that many fled Scotland for the New World for their very lives, with their homes demolished by the army commanded by William, Duke of Cumberland, the third and youngest son of King George II. A brutal, pitiless destroyer, he was known to the Scots as "Butcher Billy."

An official ban known as the Act of Proscription, which included the Dress Act, was passed in 1746 forbidding such identifying Scottish cultural phenomena as clan tartans, the wearing of the kilt, and the playing of the bagpipes. The act was meant to punish the Scottish people and to destroy the authority of the clan chiefs. When the threat of another rebellion was considered nonexistent, the act was finally repealed by royal assent in 1782, at the urging of the Scottish aristocracy, and the beautiful aspects of Scottish culture, such as the wearing of the kilt, fully and freely revived. However, it would not be until 1822 that a British monarch would visit Scotland again, when George IV decided to attend a Highland Pageant organized by Sir Walter Scott. In *Kidnapped* the Dress Act is still in force.

The immediate aftermath of the rebellion is over by the time *Kidnapped* takes place. The novel is set in 1751, and the so-called pacification of the Highlands is almost compete, but we still see the rumblings, the discontent, and the fear of the conqueror, which reminded me of the 1950s McCarthy Era in American politics with its underground conversations by victims who were still afraid of the consequences of their beliefs, and dared not talk about them publicly, and the terrible, destructive Hollywood blacklist that ruined so many people's careers and lives.

The saga of the Highland uprisings gave rise to many beautiful folk songs that I dearly love; and the Stuarts and their tragic history retained a certain sentimental interest for me, despite the reactionary political principles they espoused. When I went to Rome many years later, I visited the awe-inspiring, incredibly majestic and gorgeous Vatican, and the amazing newly restored Sistine Chapel, Michelangelo's masterpiece that one could gaze at for hours.

Out of pure romantic sentimentality, when I was inside the Vatican, I went to look especially for the family mausoleum of the Stuarts, and I was very moved when I saw the tomb of the unhappy, lonely Bonnie Prince Charlie, as Charles Stuart, the claimant to the English throne was known. His life was so devastated and so sad. Once he was safely back on the continent, he spent part of the rest of his life in France, from which he was banished to keep the peace with England, then most of the rest of it in Florence and Rome, and his alcoholism took over. He let himself go, and drank himself to death by 1788.

Scottish culture and rights were later espoused and supported by the great Romantic novelist, poet, and historian Sir Walter Scott, an advocate and legal administrator by profession. His twenty-six novels were so popular in Great Britain and indeed the world that he made Scottish culture widely known and appreciated. With his wonderful ear for Scottish accents and dialects and the Scots language, he wrote many tales of the Highlands, among them *The Bride of Lammermoor*, adapted for the libretto of Gaetano Donizetti's gorgeous Romantic opera *Lucia di Lammermoor*; *Rob Roy*, based on historical events; and *Guy Mannering*, with a plot that has some similarities to *Kidnapped* and may likewise be based loosely on the true story of one James Annesley, whose uncle, the Irish peer Richard Annesley, 6th Earl of Anglesey and governor of Wexford, tried to rob him of his inheritance and titles, and had him sent as an indentured servant to America, from which he eventually escaped and made his way back to Scotland. Neither Stevenson nor Scott acknowledged Annesley's stories as the origin of their own, and there may well be other sources for the tales. Sir Walter Scott also wrote of something else he understood perfectly: antisemitic prejudice and persecution, in what is possibly his most famous book, *Ivanhoe*.

Finally, in 1981, I brought my dream to life and began my trip to the idyllic Highlands. I arrived first in London after a short, pleasant overnight flight, and stayed there for a couple of days before taking an afternoon train to Edinburgh so that I could enjoy the incredibly beautiful scenery, including a grand view of the great city of York and its superb cathedral. When I arrived at night, I went looking for a hotel, since I didn't always make reservations in those days, trusting to chance and fate, except for a couple of hotels, as you will see. That is something I would never do today. Indeed, I found a small hotel not too far from the train station, having stopped in at a couple of other hotels without any luck. The night porter checked me in, and said that if I was hungry, he could make up some sandwiches for me in the kitchen. He brought a tray of them and a pot of tea up to my room, and very good they were too. I stayed for a few days, enjoying the splendors of this gorgeous city. I admired the architecture as I walked the Royal Mile, so wonderful, and I climbed slowly down the hill from the castle. After a brief rest, I walked along Princes Street. I had lunch at Henderson's Salad Table, an excellent vegetarian restaurant recommended by my mother's brother and sister-in-law, Uncle Seymour Korn, whom we called Sy, and Aunt Shirley, widely traveled and sophisticated gourmets. Henderson's had cafeteria service, and the dishes included not only excellent salads and cooked vegetable dishes, but also cheese dishes, and luxurious desserts.

I don't drive, but the British government puts out a very convenient book with the schedules of trains, busses, and boats in Scotland, so that one can coordinate a trip. I knew I wouldn't be following in David's exact footsteps, taking the exact route he follows in the novel, but I would definitely be able to follow a lot of his route in order.

I went first to Oban on the train and passing by Glasgow, beautiful and stirring in the distance, and which I would visit briefly on a second trip to Scotland.

I never did go south of Edinburgh to the area where the orphaned David's fictitious hometown of Essendean is supposed to be located, from which he sets forth with a letter from his late father to see his Uncle Ebenezer at the House of Shaws, actually his rightful inheritance. The House of Shaws is a fictitious mansion based loosely on the Georgian villa Glassingall House, where Stevenson was a guest. It was the home of Thomas Stewart's descendants, and his real life story is similar to that of David's.

Before I left Edinburgh for Oban, I did enjoy the view of the bridge across the Firth of Forth and the beautiful scenery generally when I took a half-day tourist trip to the Hawes Inn, a seventeenth-century hotel at Queen's Ferry just outside of Edinburgh, to see the place where Robert Louis Stevenson was inspired to write *Kidnapped*. The inn is also the place in the novel where David's Uncle Ebenezer meets with Captain Hoseason of the brig *Covenant* to arrange David's kidnapping. Queen's Ferry was an active port at the time, and there was lots for David to see while his uncle was negotiating with the captain.

There was a group of German students with their teacher on the bus, and they could not understand the bus driver, who was our tourist guide, because of his heavy accent, so I volunteered to translate for them. I had lots of fun, and they appreciated my help.

I purchased several of the British government ordnance surveys, originally for the military, I believe, but available to the general public, and I got those for Ben Nevis and Fort William, for Morvern and Loch Aline, for Western Scotland, for Glen Coe and Glen Etive, for the Isle of Mull East, and for Inverness, Loch Ness and Culloden, the sight of the last battle of The Forty-Five, which I visited one day. The maps were very detailed, and easy to use, and proved very useful on any number of occasions.

The train arrived in Oban well before the departure time for the ferry to Mull, so I sat on a bench gazing at the splendid port and boats until it was time to board. The ride over slightly rough seas was exhilarating. We passed the tidal islet of Earraid, where David comes to land, then steps to the mainland of Mull over stones at low tide.

I crossed the island in a bus that waited for ferry passengers to the ferry on the other side of Mull, and took it to Kinlochaline. The name means the place at the head of Loch Aline, and it is now a popular tourist destination for salmon fishermen, salmon being abundant in the area. I found a hotel on the main street with an available room.

After settling in, I went to the hotel bar to have a scotch and got into conversation with a man who turned out to be a professional fisherman.

He was English but loved living there. His boat was in drydock, and his daughter in school during the day. When I told him why I was there, he was quite amused, and volunteered to drive me all the way up through Morvern, where we saw the land denuded of grass and low vegetation, because of the sheep who had been brought in to replace the cows, and we saw ruined houses and farmhouses dating from the 1745 rebellion. Eventually we arrived at the broad body of water called the Linnhe Loch and took the ferry across. So far I had been able to follow David Balfour's route exactly.

We drove to Glen Coe, where I treated him to lunch at my hotel, where I had actually made a reservation for a change. I found the food better in Scotland than I found it to be in England. For lunch I had Cullen Skink, a creamy chowder of finnan haddie (smoked haddock), potatoes, and onions, and for breakfast the next morning, I had delicious kippers. I paid my amiable driver the agreed price, and he went back to Kinlochaline. That afternoon, ordnance survey in hand and with the helpful advice of the hotel receptionist, I went for a long hike through Glen Coe, impressive in its varied landscapes.

Next day took I boarded the bus to Fort William, where I had a hotel reservation, and drove past Loch Lomond. Of course, I thought of the famous song, *The Bonnie Banks o' Loch Lomond*: "O, ye'll tak the high road and I'll tak the low road, and I'll be in Scotland afore ye, But me and my true love will never meet again, On the bonnie, bonnie banks o' Loch Lomond...."

That evening, I had a glass or two of Glen Morangie, a superb single malt scotch at the hotel bar, and got into conversation with someone who turned out to be from Glasgow. His accent was the most difficult accent of English that I had ever heard, but I managed to understand him, with his occasional guttural Rs and swallowed vowels.

The hotel was centrally located on the main street of Fort William, and within easy walking distance of the bus and train stations. One day, I took bus trip north to Inverness past the length of Loch Ness and spent the day walking around the impressive, beautiful city. I sat on the loch side of the bus, and among other sights, I saw the ruins of Eilean Donan Castle.

Next day I took a train up the coast, got off at Arisaig, and tramped over the low moors, seeing the beautiful beach, the white sands of Ardgour. I was hungry by the time I got there, and I tramped over the land to a distant inn I saw that was just opening for lunch. In fact, they were just typing up the menu. The man on duty recommended freshly smoked herring, just in from up the coast, so I had a nice portion of that with boiled potato. It was just delicious, and well fortified, I set off again on my walk.

From Mallaig, another day, I took the ferry to Skye, and a post and passenger bus around the island and back. A postman was let off to do his rounds. Several people in front of me were speaking Gaelic. Two British tourists sitting behind me expressed astonishment. One said, "I thought it was a dead language." They had no idea that the Celtic language Gaelic is still spoken in parts of the Highlands, while in the Lowlands, Standard Scottish English (SSE) and sometimes Scots, the Germanic language closest to English, is also heard. Robert Burns wrote his poetry in a modified version of Scots, which includes some words derived from French because of the closeness of the Stuarts with their Bourbon cousins, and the close relationship between France and Scotland, no doubt. "Dinnae fash yoursel" (Do not anger yourself/get angry) is one common phrase, adapted from the French reflexive verb *se fâcher* (to get angry). Another word is *ashet* (plate), from French *assiette*. And two famous phrases are "It's a bra bricht moonlicht nicht the nicht" (It's a good bright moonlit night tonight) and "Mony a mickle maks a muckle" (Many a small quantity makes a large quantity).

The bus returned to the ferry and I took it to the mainland and got the train back to Fort William. I had a pleasant evening, dining in town on haggis and potatoes, and having a Scotch at the hotel bar.

I took another bus back towards the south. Then I had a meal at an inn near the shores of Loch Leven, another of the places David Balfour passes by in *Kidnapped*, before returning again to Fort William.

In pursuit of another historical site, I decided to go tramping across the moors to find Loch Nan Uamh, the Lake of the Cave, where Bonnie Prince Charlie supposedly hid before escaping to the ship that would take him to France to the court of his cousin, King Louis XV. It is near the coast, so it may be the actual cave, although there are a number of such caverns in the area. Perhaps he hid in all of them. Late at night, he made his way overland to the sea and was rowed to the ship.

The stationmaster at Fort William train station told me how to get there, and told me the correct pronunciation of the cave in Gaelic— pronounced "Gallic" as opposed to Irish Gaelic, pronounced GAY lick. I got off at Arisaig once again and tramped over the moors, consulting the ordnance survey every step of the way, until I found a historical marker in front of the cave entrance explaining its history.

I signed on for a boat trip to visit Iona and Fingal's Cave, but we never got there. There was a storm off Mull where the *Covenant* would have been wrecked in the novel. But we had to go north to get out of danger, and we put in at Portree, a very charming fishing port village on Skye. We were able to walk around in the rain, until it was time to go back to Fort William. Everyone was hoping that the storm would let up enough for us to continue on to Iona, but it never did.

I left Fort William to return home, and took the rain to Edinburgh over the long, low-lying, sloping Rannoch Moor, in pouring rain, just like in the book. And I saw Sterling Castle on the way as well. I had dinner in the dining car, and the waiter asked me if I would like vegetables with my lamb chops. "We have two vegetables," he said, "baked potatoes and mashed potatoes." I had both. The meal was, shall we say, indifferent good.

Back to London, I stayed overnight then took the train to Dover and the ferry to Boulogne, altogether a beautiful, impressive journey. There was no Eurostar in those days. It didn't start until 1994, or of course I would have taken it, which I later did, traveling first class. It goes from city center to city center, leaving from the Gare du Nord and arriving at St. Pancras Station. At first it went to Waterloo Station, but the route was later extended.

The slow train to Paris from Boulogne was a beautiful ride through the countryside of verdant farms and picturesque villages. When I arrived in Paris, once again I had no hotel reservations, and I decided to take the Métro to the Marais, where I found a hotel near the river after wandering through the streets. I tried several that were all full up, but I finally got lucky. I was in Paris for almost a full week, going to museums and eating superb meals before I took the train to le Havre, and again boarded the ferry to Dover, with the memorable sight of the famous white cliffs, truly magnificent as one approaches them. Then there was a repeat of the train ride to London through the wonderful countryside, and finally back to New York on a plane from Heathrow. I had had a magnificent memorable trip, and I am only sorry in retrospect that I didn't keep a journal of this voyage.

CHAPTER TWENTY

Three Weeks in the USSR

ABOUT TEN DAYS after my return to New York in 1985 after filming in Paris, and before we completed the film in New York in the summer, I left on an American group tour of the USSR, from April 28 to May 19, accompanied by an American guide. Nicolai Gorbachev was in power, and the Cold War had begun to thaw under his policies of "perestroika," restructuring, and "glasnost," which means transparency.

I actually saw him and his wife on the evening of May 16 near the end of our trip when we went to the ballet at the Kirov Theater in Leningrad, now once again St. Petersburg as it had been since its founding, until its name was changed during the Russian Revolution. The Kirov Theater, named to honor the Bolshevik revolutionary and friend of Stalin Sergei Kirov, is also once again under its original Czarist name, the Mariinsky.

The theater was crawling with secret service, and we soon found out why when we saw the Gorbachevs in what had been the Royal Box. Just before the start of the program of excerpts from major ballets, including a magnificent performance of act one of *Swan Lake*, the audience turned and applauded, and he stood and applauded the audience, in true Russian manner in which actors taking curtain calls applaud the audience who are applauding them. Then he gestured that we should all sit, and let the evening begin. It struck me as so different from the way the president is greeted in the United States, with "Hail to the Chief" played, and the president royally waving to the crowd. The Soviet leader was supposed to be a man of the people, an equal among equals, a fiction reinforced by what I had just seen.

There is an eight-hour time difference between New York and Moscow, and the trip to the USSR lasted about one and a half days all told. I left my apartment at 4 p.m. and finally arrived in Moscow at 5:30 p.m. the next evening; that is, 9:30 a.m. New York time.

We flew on Finnair from John F. Kennedy International Airport in New York to the Helsinki Airport on April 29, then transferred to a rinky-dink Aeroflot propeller plane for the flight to Moscow after a two-hour wait. At that time, American policy did not allow Soviet planes to fly to and from American airports, let alone anywhere over American airspace. Ronald Reagan was the president of the United States, and he was reactionary and anti-Soviet, to say the least, so that the Cold War was freezing, and the Soviets were rather afraid of him and the possibility of a nuclear war. I thought his presidency a disaster altogether. But not caring about personal consequences and the possibility of the kind of trouble with the government that we had experienced in the McCarthy era, or being detained upon my return to be interviewed by government authorities, I decided to take that tour.

The entire trip through the USSR was altogether memorable, a real eye-opener, and also showed me that the anti-Soviet propaganda was in part true, when it came to the ubiquitous poverty, the lack of ordinary everyday necessities, the poor food distribution and even the lack of food in some places. We were told by our local guides everyplace we went how much people earned, and it was not much. On the other hand, health care was free, and houses and apartments inexpensive, and you could buy a small house for a fraction of what it cost in the United States, and pay it off over fifteen years. The terrible conditions and legal disabilities in which most people had lived before the 1917 Russian Revolution had been changed for the better in many ways, but the revolution had led to a one-party dictatorial state, where one dared not criticize the government openly, and the revolution's ideals of being a worker's paradise with full equality and justice for all had been betrayed after Nicolai Lenin's death in 1924, when Stalin took over. In short, the worker's paradise was a propagandistic fiction, and contradicting that fiction publicly led to dire consequences.

We were also confronted immediately by the ubiquitous presence of the military wherever we went. For instance, in Moscow's Sheremetyevo airport when we arrived, there were squads of soldiers lined up on the tarmac to see us as we landed, and we had to walk between two ranks of them into the airport, where we underwent the bureaucratic procedures to make sure our visas were in good order. The official checking my visa stared at me, looked back at my visa photo, started again for a very long time and finally stamped the visa and waved me on, not quite like passport control in the United States or France, which is thorough but quick and not unfriendly. The baggage inspection was also thorough and took a long time, and of course the inspector insisted on looking through my suitcase, mussing up my clothing, and naturally she found absolutely nothing and waved me on, so that I could join our group to begin our visit. It was an hour and a half before everyone had gotten through the procedures and could reassemble. It was now 12 noon New York time, and I had been on the way for twenty hours, so I was very jet-lagged.

I enjoyed observing the bustling crowd at the airport, and the many plainclothes security personnel with their walkie-talkies and a great many burly baggage handlers, supervised by a thin, unmuscular, limp-wristed man who flirted with some of them outrageously while directing them where to take the luggage carts.

Under leaden skies, we went by bus into Moscow, past large housing complexes, many of which were in a state of disrepair, with huge long cracks in the walls so that they looked as if they might crumble at any moment, and almost all of which were surrounded by mud flats instead of lawns, with only a few trees and no sign of a garden or park anywhere until we got well past the city limits. The depressive atmosphere was bleak and dreary, although there were lots of pedestrians scurrying about their business, and public transport was much in evidence. There were a great many buses going past streets filled with post offices, drugstores, and food shops. We also passed one ramshackle sort of little village of wooden farmhouses and wooden fences that were falling apart, between two of the large housing complexes. In one field, despite the mud, there were kids playing soccer. Students were walking around with schoolbooks under their arms, and young parents with children were out for a stroll.

As we got into the city, I saw people from our bus window who had come in from the countryside with cartons of tomatoes and zucchini that they were selling on street corners, with customers lined up. Everyone was bundled up in heavy parkas and fur hats with ear flaps. They all kept a wary eye out for the authorities, because what they were doing was illegal, as our guides informed us. In the Soviet Union, the food distribution system was quite different from what it is in the United States, where vegetables and fruits are shipped year round from warmer states to colder in winter, so that people can eat strawberries and asparagus in wintertime in the northeast, when they are technically not in season. I actually prefer not to do so, and to eat produce during the proper season, as in the old days before refrigerated shipping that enabled national distribution existed.

In the Soviet Union, however, each Republic was discreet, and no such system was in place, so although fresh produce was available all year in the hot Central Asian republics and in Georgia, it was not shipped to the freezing north during the famously cold Russian winters that saw the defeats of Napoleon when he invaded in 1812 and of the Germans in World War Two.

We were in the Soviet Union for three weeks of still freezing weather from shortly before the big May 1 holiday, which we spent in Irkutsk in Siberia because Moscow was too full of tourists to accommodate us. We were accompanied the entire time not only by Kevin, our expert American guide, with whom I got along famously and had very informative conversations; but also by Vera, an official Russian Intourist guide; and then by a local Intourist guide at every stop.

We arrived at length at the huge semicircular Cosmos Hotel on one of the central arterial avenues of Moscow, Prospect Mira, about three miles from Red Square, and settled into our rooms on the fifteenth floor, with a spectacular view of the city.

The hotel was filled with international tourists, all milling about the crowded lobby when we arrived. I heard French, Spanish, German, and Serbo-Croatian, among other languages. We were a heterogeneous group that included mostly middle-class elderly married couples from various parts of the United States, and a lady from El Salvador who only spoke Spanish, and had wound up in our group by mistake, nobody knew how. I was happy to be able to help her with my limited Spanish, just as I was to be able to communicate in my limited Russian as necessary.

We had dinner at 8:30 in one of the huge hotel dining rooms. My first full meal in the USSR was anything but impressive. The cucumber salad had no taste and the cucumber was limp, and the dry chicken cutlet was tasteless and hard to chew. Everything was as bland as it could be. The bread was all right, and there was some kind of chocolate pudding for dessert, glop in a dish. On the other hand, the sodas, which they called "limonade," were quite good, with such flavors as apricot and pear, but not as good as the American soft drinks I used to have in those years. Armand Hammer's Pepsi-Cola was readily available, made by a company called "Russki Pepsi," with the same logo as in the US.

Our American guide offered to take those of us who weren't too tired for an evening walk through the nearby streets of Moscow and on the Metro to Red Square. I was very excited, and went with five others who were up to it and not too tired. He explained that the reason we didn't see heavy automobile traffic was that private cars were not as common as in the United States, and everyone relied on the excellent inexpensive public transportation. He took us through to the right and around the hotel to the Prospect Mira underpass to the other side of the avenue, to the Moscow Metro, which opened in 1935, and we walked down the huge flights of stairs to the beautifully decorated station of VDNKh (pronounced veh-deh-EHN-khah). The curving arches on either side of the train platforms were hung with beautiful chandeliers the entire length of the corridor, as elegant as the hall of a French chateau. There were crowds of drably dressed workmanlike people even at that late hour, and I was immediately reminded of the New York Subway at rush hour. The Metro was totally clean, however, and nobody threw anything onto the platforms. I was quite surprised to see an obviously gay male couple madly kissing quite openly under one of the arches as train after train went by. There were also several heterosexual couples engaged in the same activity. People were minding their own business, but if one Muscovite happened to bump into another, a filthy stare was the reaction, even if the person who had accidentally done the bumping said, "Izvinitye pazhalsta!" (Excuse, please!)

Each station is a work of art devoted to a particular subject, historical, scientific, or a depiction of a particular kind of work, all portrayed in paintings, sculpture and mosaics. The VDNKh station was one of the simpler ones. I also noticed that trains arrived and departed every couple of minutes, and seemed nevertheless always to be crowded.

We exited the Metro and went for our walk in Red Square, impressively decorated for the May Day parade, the gigantic Kremlin festooned with banners, and with the gorgeous St. Basil's Cathedral all lit up, each dome with lights in its own color. When we returned to Moscow, I went inside the cathedral, which is honeycombed with small rooms, each beautifully decorated. There were uniformed personnel everywhere in and around Red Square, police, army and navy officers, of whom the civilian populace, also out in great numbers, appeared to take no notice.

On our way out of Red Square, a young man approached us, offering to buy any sport shirts or jeans we might have. We had to tell him that we had nothing to sell or to give. Then a drunk came up to us, staggering slightly and waving his arms. He turned out to be American, and shouted in a slurred voice, "We must have peace!" We agreed, of course, so he left us in peace. Our guide explained that it was actually safe to walk around the city at any hour despite the appearance of these rather unsavory people because there was no mugging or street crime, generally speaking.

Finally, we returned on the Metro to our hotel. We had to check in with a guard who sat at a desk just outside the elevator on our floor, another part of the Soviet system that was totally unexpected. Clearly, an eye was kept on us, and on all the guests at the hotel. Apparently, bureaucratic procedures are a way of life. You had to leave your key and take a card, which you presented to the floor guard at the desk on coming back to the hotel, so you could retrieve your key. There were lines of returning guests waiting for their keys. Each guest was thoroughly checked and you had to show your ID as well as to hand in the card.

I used bottled water to brush my teeth, because of the US State Department warning not to drink the water anywhere in the USSR, since it was unsafe. I slept well in the huge bed and got up early to take my shower. After an unmemorable breakfast, we went back out to the airport and boarded our flight to Siberia. The flight was memorable for its discomfort: we flew in a World War Two-vintage propeller plane that bobbed up and down with every gust of wind. At least it flew pretty low, which was great for having a view of the country, mostly desert as we flew on past the green fields. We had a stop to refuel in Omsk airport, in the middle of no place, with a huge number of ICBM missile silos reportedly strategically placed in the desert surroundings.

Being there reminded me of one of Tom Lehrer's funniest songs, *Lobachevsky*, a 1953 satirical patter number, itself a parody of Danny Kaye's song about Stanislavsky and method acting. The song centers around the famous Russian mathematician Nicolai Ivanovich Lobachevsky, with whom the narrator has a distant connection: "I had a friend in Minsk, who had a friend in Pinsk, whose friend in Omsk has friend in Tomsk..."

Despite the fact that the remote airport was almost empty, our group and an elderly couple who were following the same route under the obligatory auspices of Intourist, had to stay in the Mezhdunarodnoy Sektsii (International Section) waiting room, so as not to mingle with the Soviet citizens. There were uniformed guards to ensure that we remained where we were supposed to be. There were pro-Communist and anti-American propaganda pamphlets displayed on shelves around the room, as well as anti-Israel booklets. One of the pamphlets maintained that the Soviet Union had actually won World War Two since they had entered Berlin before American forces, thus ignoring the Normandy invasion almost completely. I collected some of these pamphlets, as we were meant to do. And we were able to have some coffee.

As we continued on our flight, we were served a meal, but the food was horrible: ancient chicken wings with almost no meat on the bones, and little else. Who knows when they had been cooked? Not recently, I thought. The rather tough stewardess came by and barked, "Tchai?" (Tea?) I replied, "Nyet, spasebo, kaffee, pazhalsta." (No, thanks, coffee, please.) She practically shouted, "Nye kaffee! tchai!" (No coffee! tea!) I thanked her, and accepted the watery, almost tasteless lukewarm tea.

At length we landed in Irkutsk, which is a beautiful city, largely built up by the aristocrats exiled there during the 1825 Decembrist Revolution. They built majestic mansions, and since Irkutsk was the center of the fur trade, there were also mansions that had belonged to fur millionaires. All the mansions had long ago been appropriated by the Soviet government as headquarters for such organizations as the Komsomol, the Communist youth organization.

Our hotel was right on the Angara River, and I had a great view of it, still frozen over. We arrived late at night and went straight up to bed. I was startled awake next morning by a loud announcement on the radio that nobody had turned off and that I hadn't know was on: "Moskovski vremya, tri chisav." (Moscow time, three o'clock.) It was eight o'clock where we were! So strange. It was as if one were awakened in San Francisco by an announcement that said, "The time in Washington, DC is eleven o'clock." This announcement was followed by patriotic music. It was May Day, and announcements of congratulations from all the nations of the world followed: "narod yevroepeiskii stran pozdravyaiut..." (people of the European countries congratulate...) the Soviet Union on the May First holiday, etc., followed by the people of the countries of other parts of the world. I finally turned the radio off and got up and showered. I turned it on again, and listened to the endless anti-US and anti-Israeli propaganda. They preached peace to all people, and denounced the imperialism, colonialism, dictatorship, and racism of the United States in Nicaragua and of the Israelis against the Palestinian people. After a while I got very bored with the preaching, and turned the radio off.

After breakfast, we went to the fascinating May Day parade, with floats and banners and marching groups of the Komsomol and armed forces. The whole population of the town seemed to be in the streets. Once again, we were separated from Soviet citizens and stood behind our own barrier. No talking with them allowed! We were not to contaminate them with our Western, capitalist ideas, which apparently the Soviet government thought they might find most attractive.

We returned to the hotel for lunch, then had a bus tour of the city, with stops at several churches and a synagogue. The Soviets were eager to convince us of their good attitude to religion, but the whole atmosphere belied the propaganda. I was approached twice by kids begging for chewing gum, which I didn't have. Finally, we went to the hotel for a dinner that was acceptable: a spatchcocked chicken Tabaka, crispy fried chicken cooked in butter under a heavy weight and served with a plum sauce; caviar, and champagne, which was warm, as if there were no ice in Siberia!

In one of the hotel salons, they had dancing with a rock band, as if they were trying to impress the foreigners with how modern they had become. It was fun but odd and altogether a strange experience somehow.

The next morning, before our visit to the art museum, I took a walk by myself down the main street near the hotel. I noticed the there were no elaborate store window displays or signs, just a simple announcement of what the shop was for, so that the street was drab and uninteresting. I went into a bakery, informed by a sign above the door that said *Khlyep* (Bread), and there was almost nothing to be had. I bought a roll, and it tasted as if it had been made with sawdust. I couldn't finish it.

After an unmemorable breakfast, we were taken to the Irkutsk Art Museum, with its amazing collections culled from the mansions of the aforesaid aristocrats and the fur millionaires. Their furniture, a whole room of their antique musical instruments, such as harpsichords and harps, and the extensive art collections they brought with them were all most impressive. There were also more modern displays of African art, and gorgeous seascapes by the Romantic painter Ivan Konstantinovich Aivazovsky, along with paintings by other Russian masters, such as Ilya Yefimovich Repin, both of whom are well represented in the museums of Moscow and Leningrad that we visited later on. There is also an amazing collection of baroque Russian Orthodox icons.

I dislike tours of art museums, preferring to discover everything by myself. So I wandered off, and soon found myself standing next to a young Russian lady. I don't know what possessed me, but I started talking to her, in my limited Russian. She was studying for a diplomatic career at the Diplomatic Academy of Russia, housed in one of those incredibly huge mansions, so she spoke some English, among other foreign languages, and when I told her I was "Amerikanets" she started speaking English to me, and complimented me on my Russian, limited as it is. Like an idiot, I asked her how she liked life under the Communist system, and she replied that she had grown up under it, so it all felt right and natural to her, and she didn't know anything else. "Of course," I said, "silly of me to have asked." I was going to tell her about my left-wing politics, but before I knew it, we were surrounded by three museum guards, and she fled. The guards were all middle-aged ladies in house dresses, no uniforms. One of them pointed at my group, and said, "Vasha gruppa!" (Your group!) "Nu? Shtozhe? Moya gruppa?" (Well? So what? My group?) She asked, "Nye intyeressno nash museum?" (Doesn't our museum interest you?) "Da, da," I replied, "no ya znayu istoria iskustvo, y nye lyublyu tour. Ya znayu shto ya vizhu y khochu vidyet sam." (Yes, yes, but I know art history, and I don't like tours. I know what I'm looking at and I want to see it by myself.) She just looked at me, pointed and said again, "Vasha gruppa!" So I nodded and rejoined the group.

I thought the whole incident very odd. I could not imagine that a Soviet visitor to New York's Metropolitan Museum of Art, for instance, or indeed to any other American art museum, would ever under any circumstances, be warned away by museum guards from talking to an American on any pretext or subject whatsoever.

The next day, we took the five-mile drive in a bus to Lake Baikal, with its scientific expedition ships still frozen in the ice just off the shore. On the way, we stopped so we could see a typical Russian village of small houses at the lake's edge. Parents and their little kids came out, begging for whatever we could give them. We had been supplied with cigarette packets and gum, which we gave them.

We proceeded to a restaurant with a beautiful view of this largest freshwater lake in the world, and had a very good meal of a firm white-fleshed fish called Baikal Omul, a species of whitefish, caught in the lake and only to be found there, and an overbaked raisin cake with seeds in the raisins, plus Russian white wine, not bad but warm. I talked politics with our local guide, who told me they are very scared of Reagan, and she and Vera told me about the news they had heard about underground shelters in the US prepared for the wealthy and for government officials, which made them even more scared.

Afterwards we drove on, and got out of the bus to walk in the "Taiga"—the forest. There was the white Taiga, full of birch trees, some of which had lots of ribbons and strips of cloth tied on them by the local Buddhists. And there was the black Taiga with its coniferous trees, mostly pine and fir. It was quite beautiful, with snow-covered hillsides.

Back in Irkutsk it was a pleasure to see the populace strolling about, kids playing ball in the street, and to see the one-story houses with gardens on the side streets. The evening before our departure, we were taken to a theater to see a Soviet operetta, *Babii Bunt* (Grandma Bunt), beautifully performed. The plot was a sort of combination of *Lysistrata* and Gilbert and Sullivan's *Princess Ida* with folk dances and rousing patriotic music, as well as charming ballads. We were allowed to sit with the Soviet citizens in the audience, for a change, and I talked briefly with a Russian lady sitting next to me. A soldier marched noisily in, and sat in the back of the auditorium, and I had the impression it was to keep an eye on the foreigners.

Back at the hotel, I had a cognac with Kevin, who told me that despite the public stance on equality for all, privately Russian policy was very antisemitic and that Jews were generally regarded with suspicion, with the old canard of dual loyalty, their principal loyalty being really only to Israel. He said plenty of Jewish tourists come to visit the USSR and in his experience just don't really seem to care about the antisemitic and anti-Israel pamphlets they see, like the ones we saw at the Omsk airport. And a French tourist I talked with told me that he had been to a school a few weeks before for a concert, at which one of the songs ended with the line, "How fortunate are we not to live in the United

States!" I said to him, "Et comme je suis heureux de ne pas vivre ici !" (And how happy I am not to live here!) "Bonne soirée tout de même (Good evening all the same)," he said, laughing. I replied, "Merci, bonne soirée ! Et ça ne fait rien, ce n'est pas le peuple, c'est le gouvernement. (Thanks, good evening! And it doesn't matter, it's not the people, it's the government.)" Besides, things are complicated, and the government has its own underground shelters and its inequality of wealth in the "worker's paradise." And how can a country that claims to have justice and equality, which they say does not exist in any capitalist country, be so filled with antisemitic prejudice? No wonder so many Soviet Jews wanted to leave at that point in history. In any case, I was more surrounded by overt political propaganda than I ever felt I was back home.

After breakfast, and before leaving for Central Asia, several of us went privately to the only synagogue in Irkutsk on Karl Liebknecht Street. We met the shammes (sexton), to whom we spoke in Russian and Yiddish, and he told us everything was okay for the Jews in Irkutsk. There are four hundred Jews in Irkutsk and a congregation of two hundred, because young people don't go to synagogue except sometimes on the High Holidays. He had been born in the Oblast (Region), and served four years in the army in World War Two on the Leningrad front. He had a brother who was an engineer and had emigrated with his family to San Francisco, and the shammes was able to visit them three years ago. He implied that in other areas, like Moscow, things were not good for Jews. He was a very sweet, kind old man, and happy to see us. My fellow tourists gave him some money for the shul. Another old man came in, and also said that things were fine, and that there are eight thousand Jews (as opposed to the four hundred the shammes told us lived there) in Irkutsk, many of whom are doctors, lawyers, judges, and professionals of one sort or another. He also told us there is a beautiful Jewish cemetery. There is an itinerant rabbi and a cantor who comes from Odessa occasionally. Before the Revolution, there had been three synagogues.

The next day we flew to Uzbekistan and the city of Tashkent, capital of the Republic, stopping at the Alma Ata airport, now the

Almaty International Airport, in Kazakhstan on the way. We had a superb view of the Altai Mountains in the distance, and I saw more propaganda pamphlets, of which I collected a few.

Our hotel in Tashkent was very nice, surrounded by a lot of modern buildings in a good state of repair, as opposed to what we saw outside Moscow. The food too was okay, for a change.

The day after our arrival we had a guided city tour. There are lots of lush, verdant parks, and it was lovely to hear the melodious Uzbek language spoken. While public transportation is extensive, I also saw a lot of private cars, much more like a western city. There are mosques and churches and two synagogues, because of all the Jews rescued by Stalin and sent to Tashkent to save them from the Germans, and there is a Holocaust memorial that explains what happened. It was fascinating to see all the signs in Uzbek, written in the Cyrillic alphabet. I could read them, but couldn't understand a word.

On a beautiful warm day we took the usual uncomfortable plane ride to the storied city of Samarkand in southeastern Uzbekistan, one of the oldest inhabited cities of Central Asia along with Bukhara. Among the highlights of its amazing history: Samarkand was conquered by Alexander the Great, and in the fourteenth century it was the capital of Timur, known as Tamerlane, whose tomb we visited. A major Islamic center, the city is known for its overwhelmingly beautiful madrassahs (Islamic schools), mosques and minarets intricately and gorgeously decorated in blue, gold, and turquoise, architectural masterpieces on the Registan Square. Samarkand was on the Silk Road from the east, between China, Persia, and Western Europe. During the Medieval and Renaissance centuries, the city was a stopping point with laden caravans that stayed there for the night or for several days in inns called "caravanserai," an Uzbek word.

Partly because it is a major Islamic center, we unbelievers were not supposed to enter the hallowed precincts of the mosques but the Soviets didn't care to observe or respect the religious strictures, so endless hordes of tourists went there all the year round. We saw religious women prostrate in prayer off in the corners, where they would hopefully not be disturbed by the crowds traipsing noisily through.

The city is full of green spaces because of the extensive irrigation system. We visited the subway, beautifully decorated with marble columns and chandeliers, and we went to another *beryozka* (birch tree), a foreign currency shop where you could use dollars and buy souvenirs such as the famous wooden nesting dolls, but they had no film, which was all I wanted. We also visited a medieval observatory in one of the parks, where the local guide explained to us that medieval astronomers knew a great deal that remained unknown in the west for centuries: for instance, they knew the earth was round and could calculate the rate of rotation of the earth.

In the evening, we went to the opera house where we saw *La Traviata* sung in Russian. I was surprised that there was an opera house at all in this heavily Muslim area, where I didn't imagine most people had any interest in opera. The opera house was in fact empty, except for our group and another group of foreign tourists. At one point, an elderly gentleman wandered in and sat down, then got up after a few minutes and left. Judging by his long beard and his dress, he must have been a religious Muslim. He was just allowed by the usher to enter the theater, without paying anything, I'm sure.

The party guests in the first scene were well costumed, and I thought the director was trying to recreate nineteenth-century Paris by even having Oscar Wilde as a character, but he turned out to be the leading tenor! He had quite a nice voice. Most of the performances were pedestrian at best, and the opera, which I dearly loved, dragged on and on in this production. In the last scene, when Violetta sang "Ya stradayu" (I'm suffering), I turned to Vera, whom I was sitting next to, and whispered "Mui tozhe" (we too; so are we), and that was one of the few times I ever saw her crack a smile.

The next day we went on to Bukhara, another one of the most ancient cities, and rather rundown, out in the desert. Once again, we were separated from the local population in the airport. I actually got airsick on the plane for a change. It was the bumpiest, most turbulent ride we had had.

Nevertheless, the breakfast the next day was actually one of the best meals we had had so far, with a copious buffet. I especially enjoyed the *syrniki*, thick puffy Russian pancakes made with cottage cheese and butter and sprinkled with powdered sugar. Later, we had an outdoor lunch, including a glass of champagne.

Bukhara, known for its carpets with their intricate elaborate designs, was fascinating, with possibly the world's oldest shopping center, a bazaar covered with sand domes. There is also a fortress there that we visited, with a view from the ramparts of the oases and small settled areas out in the desert. Rather grisly was the execution tower, a high minaret from which people were thrown to their deaths. They were also executed in the days when Genghis Khan ruled the city on Execution Square, the plaza in front of the mosques and madrassahs.

After the city tour, we returned for a nice nap and dinner. In the evening we went to a concert of lively Uzbek folk dancing and music, quite delightful.

We stayed in a lousy, badly constructed Intourist hotel, the worst I have ever been in. I could hardly believe the conditions. Who in the world could have designed it, and who could have approved the design, and who could have constructed it? The elevator worked one time and not another. In any case, it was better to take the stairs, very carefully because the steps were uneven in height and each step sloped to the left or right. The bed was uncomfortable, and the shower in the dirty bathroom the strangest I have ever experienced. I stepped into the bathtub, took a shower, and expected the water to go down the drain. It did, but when I drew the shower curtain aside, I discovered that the drain gave onto the floor of the bathroom, which had been flooded in no time. The actual drain was at the other end of the room! I waded carefully over to the towel rack and proceeded into the bedroom to dry myself.

The food was the worst yet, and if you asked for milk with your coffee because it was not automatically put on the table, the surly waitress acted as if you were a pain in the neck and gave you dirty looks. Luckily, we weren't there too long. And on the last morning, there was no water, so I couldn't shower or shave, but I had been brushing my teeth with mineral water anyway. And I had been taking aspirin as well, because I got some kind of cold.

As we left, I found it amazing to reflect that these Central Asian cities were two thousand years old. The Kremlin walls were being built a thousand years later.

I felt better even though we got up at 3:15 a.m. to go to the airport for a 4:15 plane to Tbilisi, a beautiful city in Soviet Georgia, which the Russians call Gruzia. The official languages are Abkhaz and Georgian, which has its own beautiful alphabet. The city's architecture reflects the occupying powers over the centuries, especially the majestic Turkish buildings on the main streets. The eclectic styles include gorgeous opulent Art Nouveau mansions and other buildings in many colors with intricately carved balconies.

We went to a beautiful spacious park in the hills above city. It was reached by a funicular railway that took us past the main church of the Georgian Orthodox religion, St. David's, and afforded a spectacular view. I also had a beautiful view of the area of the city where the hotel was located.

In the park, a man approached me. "Hey, mister, you want to change dollars?" I said, "Nyet, nyet" to this strictly illegal transaction, which I wouldn't have done anyway, even if it had been legal.

Afterwards, we had a superb lunch—the best food so far, along with the fish lunch at Lake Baikal—of shashlik, a kind of shish kebab, with skewered grilled lamb and vegetables with tkemali, the Georgian sweet and sour plum sauce we had had with the Chicken Tabaka, served on the side and good Georgian white wine, properly chilled. The Georgian cuisine, with its pilafs, kebabs, and herb salads was particularly delicious, and the cuisine has spread worldwide. In Paris, for instance, there is an excellent Georgian restaurant, La Maison Géorgienne on the rue de Sabot in the sixth arrondissement, not far from the hotel where I have stayed for the last thirty years.

Some of us took the beautiful Tbilisi subway to Lenin Square, and walked to the main synagogue, having gotten directions from a Jewish man in the square who spoke English. He was wearing a yarmulke and was dressed in Orthodox fashion, so we knew he was Jewish. When we left him, he used the only Yiddish he knew, apparently, the common farewell, "Sei gezint!" (Be healthy!)

At the synagogue, we met those elderly Georgian Jews who gathered regularly, we were told, in the courtyard. They were very friendly. The Germans never got there, so they were safe during the war. The stately synagogue was beautifully kept, and they said there was no antisemitism to speak of among the population at large. They were all good neighbors and friends "in my experience," several people said. But they also told us that about half of the thirty-five thousand Jews of Tbilisi have left. They couldn't say why, but I could imagine that the constant anti-Israel propaganda, quickly turning into antisemitic sentiment, was the reason. One of the men said, "Say hi to my cousin Misha! He has an antique shop in New York!"

In the evening, we went to a theater to see a gorgeously costumed and set Georgian folk music and dance concert, quite spectacular. On the street, once again youngsters accosted us and asked for gum and cigarettes, which we didn't have.

And on May 9, after a delicious breakfast of cheese blintzes, we went to the impressive annual VE parade celebrating the end of World War Two, which was actually the day before. At the buffet, I talked with a fellow tourist from East Germany. "Wie ist das Leben in Ostdeutschland? (How is life in East Germany?)," I asked. He shrugged and replied, "Man lebt." (One lives.) Another East German I spoke with was a student doing scientific research in Moscow. He had been to Dallas to do research as well, and loved it. He didn't care for Moscow, which he described as "ein grosser Bahnhof" (a big train station), with two million people coming and going and running around every day.

At the parade, squads of uniformed soldiers, huge old tanks, and floats carrying decorated veterans and bemedalled officers rolled by, cheered on by the huge crowds on either side of the avenue. For a change, we were not separated from the Soviet citizens, many of whom were wearing beautiful native costumes. Many of the young men walked around in pairs holding hands, a Georgian custom, I was informed, and so do women with other women. Men and women do the same, of course. There is a freedom to display affection that is surprising to someone who is not native to the place, and who is from someplace where such free behavior is frowned upon. There were also a lot of youngsters running around happily.

I bought a delicious cup of coffee from a vendor, freshly made on his cart in an ibrik as I watched. An ibrik is a Turkish coffee pot where you let the coffee and sugar, mixed together, rise up and go down again before serving it. This coffee is the preferred one in Gruzia, showing the influence of the historic Turkish occupation.

After the parade we had an excellent lunch of cabbage and potato soup, then took a trip up into the spectacular Caucasus Mountains to view the first capital of Georgia, Mtskheta far below—a superb city architecturally, which we did not descend the mountain to see.

Georgian food is excellent, as I have said, and we had good meals there, and in Central Asia as well. Because the weather was nice in Tbilisi, we ate outdoors a couple of times at long tables. We could eat vegetables there, and there were platters of fresh herbs that are popular as salads, as well as roast chicken and delicious pilaf.

In the evening we went to the gorgeous opera house decorated ornately in Turkish style to hear a performance of Mozart's *Don Giovanni*, sung in Italian. The singers had world-class voices, and were also excellent actors. I thought it a shame that most of those singers would never be heard internationally. The production, strangely staged and with several major arias cut, had an anti-religious aspect. After the Prologue, when Don Giovanni has killed the Commendatore whose stone statue will return at the end of the opera to take his revenge, the first act took place in a church. Don Giovanni has disguised himself as a priest and sits in the confessional to hear Elvira's aria "Mi tradì quell'alma ingrata" (That ungrateful soul betrayed me), delivered as a confession. This production was the least sexy I have ever seen of this opera about a lecherous libertine, and at the end there was no statue to drag Don Giovanni down to hell. In this version, the Commendatore did not return to wreak his vengeance, no doubt because the anti-religious director did not want to acknowledge the existence of Hell. It was all very odd, but beautifully sung and acted, as I said.

Afterwards, we took a trolley back to the hotel through streets thronged with people enjoying the ubiquitous fireworks.

On May 10 we toured the open-air museum of Georgian wooden and stone houses from the early nineteenth to the early twentieth centuries, all quite striking. Our local guide told us a joke, daring for him to tell, I would have thought: A Communist leader says, "Comes the Revolution, everybody will eat strawberries and cream!" A voice in the crowd says, "But I don't like strawberries!" "Comes the Revolution, you'll *eat* strawberries!" This rather reminded me of the apparent Intourist attitude, "We know what you'll be interested in. We will decide what you want to do." That was what happened in the Tbilisi National Art Museum, where we were forbidden to take closer looks at some of the objects in the Treasury room of ancient and more modern artifacts.

At lunch afterwards in the museum restaurant, a man came up to me and asked "Otkuda vui?" (Where are you from?) "Iz Amerika," I replied. "Kharasho tam?" (Are things good there?) "Ochen (Very)," I said, "Ee zdyes?" (And now/here?) "Nyet!" was the surprising answer.

At last, on May 11, we went back up to Moscow. The baggage was picked up in our rooms by a porter who would take it to our bus. He was very pleased that I had only one fairly light valise. "Vot molodyets!" (Atta boy!), he exclaimed. As in Bukhara, when I took a shower, the water drained from the bathtub across the floor to the real drain at the other end of the room! I really wondered who could have thought that was a good idea.

In Moscow we stayed at another gigantic Intourist hotel off the St. Basil end of Red Square. You could see inside the walls of the Kremlin from our upstairs window, which also afforded a view of many of the buildings on Red Square. We had a lunch of shoe leather that was supposed to be steak, and glop that passed for mashed potatoes. At least the mushroom soup that started the meal was good.

In the middle of the night I was awakened when the flimsy plastic green phone on my bedside table rang. When I answered, half asleep, a man started speaking in Russian, then hung up abruptly. I have no idea what he said. I was already up at 7:30 on May 12 when the phone rang again. Apparently it was a wrong number.

I went walking by myself in Red Square on a bright sunny afternoon, with a view to visiting the famous GUM department store, a long sprawling building at one side of it. I noticed immediately that every room was understocked, and I decided to visit the gourmet food department. Not only was there very little food of any kind, not even Russian caviar, but all they had to sell was canned tuna fish. There was no cheese department, nor one for cold fish such as smoked salmon, nor was there a cold cut department. It was very uninteresting, or rather interesting in its lack of anything a New Yorker who goes to Zabar's fabulous food emporium would call a gourmet food store. Similarly, there had been next to nothing even in the open-air markets in Central Asia; only some piles of potatoes and cabbages, and a motto in Russian over the entrance: One must eat to live, not live to eat. That was ironic, to say the least.

We made visits to major art museums, including the Tretyakov Gallery, where there is a major collection of the works of Nicholas Roerich, born Nikolai Konstantinovich Rerikh in St. Petersburg. He was a Russian Symbolist who left during the 1917 Revolution and emigrated to New York. His house on 107th Street near Riverside Drive, not far from where I live, is now the Nicholas Roerich Museum, so I was familiar with his work before I went to the USSR. I was also pleased to see the famous portrait of Anton Chekhov by Osip Braz, with a beautiful landscape by the writer's friend Isaac Levitan on the facing wall.

The Pushkin State Museum of Fine Arts was fabulous, with its notable collection of French Impressionists and Post-Impressionists, including Cézannes and Gauguins as well as its collection of Picassos, and a World War Two poster exhibit.

After a tour of the gorgeous Metro stations, I was allowed to pay a visit on my own to Chekhov's house museum when I didn't want to go to another folk music concert or beryozka. I was given directions on how to get there from the Metro station, and was able to ask the bus driver, "Gde dom Chekhovu, pazhalsta?" and he let me out and pointed out the house across the avenue. It was a very well done, interesting museum. I was given slippers to put on over my shoes. All the signs were in English as well as Russian. The ground floor consisted of rooms furnished as they were when the family lived there. The second floor was full of display cases of programs of original productions lining the walls, with posters and photographs on the walls. The third floor was a miniature theater where productions of the plays were put on. I was delighted to have been able to see the museum.

Of course I retraced my steps to get back to Red Square and out hotel. At dinner, Vera said, "So, you were near the American Embassy?" "Yes," I said, and I could see the American flag and the uniformed guards out front." "Did you go to the embassy?" "Why would I do that? I was going to see Chekhov's house." "I don't know. You tell me," Vera's response, and that was the end of the conversation.

In the evening we went to the Stanislavsky Opera Theater on Pushkin Street to see a museum production, recreating Stanislavsky's staging of *Eugene Onegin* on a postage-stamp stage. The singing was wonderful, and the acting excellent, from everyone. Of course the great dance numbers went for nothing, with a few couples, all there was room for, at the back of the stage while the other characters played out their scenes at the front. In the duel scene, Onegin rushed away and fired from offstage left, running in again as Lensky fell dead. It was actually very effective. The emphasis on acting the roles was exactly what Stanislavsky had insisted upon, as well as the superb singing, and it was the most memorable production of this opera that I have seen.

In the morning, we went to the Soviet Economic Achievement Exhibit, an open-air museum. We saw huge models of factory floors and statues in tribute to the workers. There was also an exhibit about their space achievements, and an impressive display of handicrafts. We then went to another beryozka.

A small group of us went early in the morning of May 14 before our official daily tour started to see the famous Moscow Choral Synagogue on Arkhipova Street, a splendid building housing an Orthodox congregation, a short walk from our hotel. The construction of the building was started several times, but the Russian authorities managed to prevent its being finished completely until 1905, when the ultimately abortive uprising nevertheless forced the authorities to allow construction of various previously forbidden religious institutions. With rare exceptions, until the 1917 Revolution, Jews weren't even allowed to live in Moscow, except by special permission, but had to remain in a limited area called the Pale of Settlement in the west of Russia.

There were a lot of men at their morning prayers, and the shammes was kind enough to show us around. He spoke no English, so I turned out to be the translator. We spoke Yiddish, and his Yiddish was laced with Russian words that I understood. The phenomenon of borrowing words from the majority surrounding language and incorporating them into everyday Yiddish is usual, and in this case, of course, there was vocabulary borrowed from Russian. Pointing to the balcony, the shammes said, "Un dort obn zitsen dee zhenshchinas." No one needed a translation to understand what he meant, but I was interested to hear the Russian word for woman, zhenshchina, with a Yiddishized plural.

We went into the study room near the bima, the platform from which services are conducted, where a number of men dressed in Chassidic fashion and with long beards and side curls were sitting reading at desks. One of them asked where we were from, and I told him that we came from America. He brightened up, and said, "Ikh hob a zun in Chicago! Er schreibt pismos." (I have a son in Chicago! He writes letters!) He stressed the first syllable of *pismos*. Again, there was a Russian word with a Yiddishized plural in his Yiddish. The actual Yiddish word for a letter that one writes to someone is *brievele*, and the Russian word is *pismo*, with the stress on the last syllable.

We did talk about politics and they made it clear that they were happy with their lives, and didn't want to leave the Soviet Union, since they had housing and work and were able to afford various amenities. They expressed their fear of Reagan, and when I told them that "Reagan eto durak" (Reagan is a fool) and "eto bolvan (he's a blockhead)," they laughed. "We all want peace," I said, and they agreed.

Of course, just to even things out after everything I had been learning about the Soviet system, there is a Soviet joke about two state newspapers, *Izvestia* (News; Information) and *Pravda* (Truth): There is no izvestia in pravda and no pravda in izvestia.

We went to see the Novodevichy Cemetery, where Chekhov is buried as are Stanislavsky and actors from the Moscow Art Theater in a special section. For lunch, we went to the great Hotel Baltschug Kempinski, a famous nineteenth-century hotel, its main dining room hung with red velvet curtains and gold braid, very luxurious and much frequented by Soviet officials. Incidentally, Stanislavsky's original family name before he adopted the stage name by which he is known was Alekseyev, and his family was very wealthy, having the monopoly on manufacturing gold braid, used in every czarist uniform and as borders for velvet curtains such as the one in the hotel. I had Chicken Kiev, a chicken roulade coated with egg and breadcrumbs and stuffed with herbed unsalted butter, and crisply sauteed. It's a dish I love, but unfortunately this version was pretty bad, tough, and bland if not tasteless.

We went for a brief picturesque boat ride on the river, with great views of Gorky Park and a bit later on that chilly afternoon, we made a visit to Lenin's Tomb in Red Square. We had to check our cameras at a booth nearby, to be retrieved after the visit, and I buttoned my coat completely. We stood on a very long line, and when I was approaching the actual entrance, a guard held up his hand for me to stop. Pointing with his forefinger up and down, he asked, "Apparat?" (Camera?) "Nyet, u minya nye apparat. (No, to me no camera; I don't have a camera), I replied. With the same forefinger, he waved me on. "Prokhoditye!" (Proceed!) Lenin's body lay in a huge glass case, and was impressively embalmed, perfectly preserved, and rather chilling to see. Afterwards, someone asked me, "What did he look like?" I said, "Dead."

After that, we went back to the hotel for a relaxing evening, and got up on the morning of May 15 very early to take the plane to Leningrad, our last stop before going home, with the usual airport delays.

On the bus touring the city, our local Leningrad guide actually complained about her housing situation, which she said was a very common one. She was in a small ramshackle communal apartment with her daughter, and there were two other small families living there as well. They had put up blankets, roping off the living room into three sections, where they each had their beds and any other furniture, including a sofa and a table and chairs. They shared the kitchen and bathroom. She called her apartment a "barracks." I had heard about this kind of situation and I thought it was American propaganda, but that turns out not to have been the case. You could almost sense that the end of the Soviet Union was drawing near.

Leningrad is so beautiful, and in the age of the czars was a sophisticated cosmopolitan city visited often by wealthy tourists from other European countries. The extraordinary State Hermitage Museum, once the royal palace and a major scene of the 1917 Russian Revolution, and the Neva River waterfront are magnificent, with the splendid St. Isaac's Cathedral particularly striking, its interior lined with green malachite columns, its walls covered with fine mosaics, as I saw when I later visited it. The other rivers, canals, and bridges are so full of affecting memories of scenes in Russian literature that one cannot help but be moved at the remembrance, especially crossing the Neva along the Nevsky Prospekt so often mentioned in Russian novels and stories. Later in the day, I took a walk down that storied street. At one stop during the city tour the guide pointed out the house of Prince Yusupov on one of the canals, where the priest Grigori Rasputin had been brutally assassinated, and told us the chilling tale of the drawn-out murder, ending when he was finally drowned in the icy water. Rasputin had had an incredible influence as a faith healer on Tsarina Alexandra's son Tsarevich Alexei, who had hemophilia, and whom he said he could cure, but of course he was a fake and a con artist.

Also moving is the Tikhvin Cemetery, a kind of Père Lachaise cemetery of Russia, with its composer's corner, where the graves of Tchaikovsky, Borodin, Rimsky-Korsakov, Anton Rubinstein and other great Russian composers are to be found, as well as the grave of Marius Petipa, the original choreographer of Tchaikovsky's ballets *Swan Lake*, *The Nutcracker*, and so forth; and the literary graves, including those of Dostoevsky. It was right across the street from our hotel, and I visited it on my own. I was also deeply moved when we were taken to the Memorial Cemetery, where approximately 470,000 people who died in the siege during World War Two are buried.

On our visit to the Hermitage on May 17 we had a museum guide, who was knowledgeable and unfortunately also dictatorial. At one vast hall we arrived in, with paintings large and small covering the walls all the way to the amazingly high ceiling, I stopped, fascinated. They were all Rembrandts, or at least imitative of Rembrandt. "How interesting! All these Rembrandts!" I exclaimed. "No," she said, "not interesting! Only students of Rembrandt! Come! We go!" And we hurried on out to the superb exhibition of antique porcelain that she loved, and over which we lingered. I love old porcelain too, but I had wanted to see those paintings! I later described our visit as "running through the Rembrandts." I went back on my own the next day, and saw some of their amazing collections of paintings from all periods, including those by the famous students of Rembrandt. On the landing of one of the grand staircases was a statue wearing an original uniform of Peter the Great, who was a very tall and imposing figure.

In the dining room of our hotel, where we were served the usual cold leathery steak and warm salad, we periodically heard the sound of breaking dishes. The waiters, one of the least respected jobs in the Soviet Union, we were told, were inadvertently dropping piles of dishes they had collected. They carelessly tried to put the dishes on side tables without looking, so they missed the tables.

Not wanting to go to another folk music concert, I got a ticket at the hotel desk for the Kirov to see *I Dekabristi* (The Decembrists), a 1953 opera by Soviet composer Yuri Shaporin about the 1825 Decembrist Revolution. I had to reserve a taxi at another desk, and I was given a slip of paper with the license number. I had to confirm my reservation a couple of hours later, which I did. At the appointed time, I went out to look for my taxi, approaching the drivers, who were chatting with each other, and showing them the paper. They all shook their heads. None of them was mine. The same thing was happening to a gentleman who was also looking for his taxi. He turned out to be a British businessman, who was frequently in Leningrad on business, and who said, "It's always like this. I don't know how they get anything done!" His taxi came along finally, but I went back in, and the reservations clerk came out with me, and pointed at a driver, who did all but salute her, and immediately took me to the theater. I talked a bit with the driver, who was interested to learn that I was from America. He liked being a taxi driver, he said in his limited English, because he enjoyed seeing tourists from all over.

The opera was actually exceptionally boring, though the production was gorgeous, with superb sets and costumes, with music in the late Romantic style, very well sung and acted. But I couldn't stand it, and left at the first intermission. I took a long leisurely walk back towards the hotel on the Nevsky Prospekt, then got the Metro for a few stops back to the hotel.

The next morning, once again I had one of the world's worst showers, with the water draining down the tub and flowing across the floor, just as in Bukhara. After breakfast, we went to visit Peter the Great's Peterhof Palace on the shore of the Gulf of Finland just outside the city. On the way we passed more of those dreary, dull, bleak, grim, unimaginably stark housing projects, with cracks in the walls.

Modeled in part on Versailles, the vast palace was gorgeous and very impressive, as were its gardens. Bombed to bits by the vengeful retreating Germans in World War Two, the palace was still being restored when we were there, following the original well preserved plans and drawings. Many of the vast rooms had ropes across the open entrances, so that we could see the expert artists at work on high ladders restoring the floor-to-ceiling wall paintings, ornamental decorations, and ceilings of some of the grand salons that we were not allowed to enter.

As usual, we also went to a beryozka. This one had a wall of books, all very inexpensive. I got several, weighing my baggage down, of course. I got a book about Chekhov that was in both Russian and English and copiously illustrated; a large picture book of all of Stanislavsky's production; a book of Isaac Levitan's paintings, Levitan being a great friend of Chekhov's, as I said, and a marvelous landscape artist; and *Moscou*, a coffee-table book in French about Moscow, with amazing photographs. I also got two small decorative metal tins of Russian tea leaves.

On our last evening, we went for a gala farewell dinner at the Sadko Restaurant. There was a floor show of the type I don't particularly enjoy, but the food was spectacular for a change: caviar, blinis, roast chicken, pork loin stuffed with prunes, and a dessert of vanilla ice cream with chocolate sauce.

As I have indicated, the food on our tour was generally lousy in the Russian cities, with the Sadko being among the exceptions, even in some of the large hotels, such as the Kempinski in Moscow. But in Central Asia and Soviet Georgia, the food was often quite good, as I said above, especially the breakfasts. However, we were warned not to eat any fresh raw fruit or vegetables, or to drink the water because of bacteria and parasites. On the breakfast line in Leningrad, I asked a French tourist what she thought of the food. She grimaced and said, "Trop de fécule !" (Too much starch!)

I rather regretted that we did not visit the Ukrainian Soviet Socialist Republic, so I never saw the glories of Kyiv, Kharkiv, Odessa, or Lviv, nor Ottynia, the small city near Lviv that my grandparents came from when it was part of the Austro-Hungarian Empire before World War One. It would have been quite an exhaustive process to obtain a special visa and permission to leave the group and go with a separate official Intourist guide. Decades later when Ukraine was an independent country after the breakup of the USSR, and long before the present war waged by Russia in Ukraine, my cousin Jonathan Blumenfeld did visit Ottynia, as I related in my book *Memories of a Vanished Time: A Tribute to My Mother and Father.* He telephoned me one day, and said, "Guess where I am!" I could hardly believe it when he said he was in Ottynia. He took some wonderful photographs, of which I have copies.

At the airport on May 19, we had the usual bureaucratic system to deal with, and five lines to stand on: 1) to exchange rubles for dollars; 2) to wait to go through customs; 3) customs inspection; 4) passport inspection; 5) security check. The security officials were pleasant enough, for a change.

Finally, we had to stand in line to get on the Aeroflot plane to the Helsinki Airport, where we transferred to an American plane for the flight to New York, simply reversing the route we had taken to get to the USSR.

I was very glad to be home again, and to experience the kind of individual freedoms we do have in the United States, despite the socioeconomic problems endemic to the American system. The trip had been eye-opening and fascinating, and tiring as well because we were always on the move and as you saw, dear reader, the tour was jam-packed with plane rides, with sight-seeing tours of every place we visited, with evenings at theaters and with visits to art museums and great buildings. My parents were very interested to hear all about what we had seen, and were especially impressed with my observations and impressions of life in the USSR.

CHAPTER TWENTY-ONE

Travels in France and Some Wonderful Friendships

1.

EVENTUALLY I TRAVELED extensively in France. I went to Nice in 1987 on Air France's June 6 inaugural flight, with a ribbon-cutting ceremony at Kennedy Airport. I loved walking along the beachfront, and through the old streets of this picturesque resort. I took the staircase up the eastern cliff for a stunning view of Monte Carlo in the distance. The weather was wonderful, and the food was marvelous, including the authentic bouillabaisse that I ate at an outdoor restaurant in the touristy Cours Saléya.

I took the train to Annecy near the Swiss border a few days later, by a roundabout route passing Antibes, Cannes, and Marseille among other stations, before heading north. After checking in at the hotel, I wandered around Annecy, with its medieval neighborhoods with overhanging balconies and canals. I had the most wonderful dinners at three famous restaurants surrounding the lake in this charming delightful town on the lac d'Annecy, where people who prefer a mountain to a beach vacation go on the long summer break. The most extraordinary was L'Auberge du Père Bise, with a perfect welcoming atmosphere and impeccable service, to which I went on the ferry across the lake to Talloires. It was Winston Churchill's favorite, and a refuge for Papa Doc, the dictator who fled Haiti. Had I known that the owners had sheltered him, I would undoubtedly not have gone there, but I only learned about that later. When I arrived, I was ushered to a seat on the lawn sloping down towards the lake. I had a delicious champagne cocktail with raspberry puree, while gazing at the distant Alps in the sunset. The waiter came to take me into the dining room where I had a truly great meal that included cheese and dessert carts wheeled to the table.

I finished my trip in Paris, seeing the wonderful sights from the train on the way including Arles and Avignon, where you can see the papal palace and medieval city wall in the distance.

In 1991 I went to Toulouse, which I used as a base of operations, taking the train out through the countryside to Carcassonne, the splendid fortified medieval city restored in the mid-nineteenth century by the architect Eugène Viollet-le-Duc, who also restored the crumbling façade of Notre Dame in Paris; and to the small city of Albi, known for its red brick architecture, its gorgeous medieval cathedral, and as the birthplace of Toulouse Lautrec. There is a great museum devoted to his work.

One day I took the train to Boussens, a small country station, where my friend, composer, pianist and professor of music Jean-Philippe Bec, who lives in Paris but grew up in the southwest, picked me up and drove me to the family house in Saleich with its lovely garden, in the department of Haute-Garonne not too far from the Pyrenees. I had the pleasure of meeting his mother, Madame Marcelle Bec, whom some family members call by her sobriquet Marsou. She is a marvelous cook and she made a memorable, delicious lunch. The starter was a salad of lettuce and home-grown tomatoes, topped with delicious *gésiers de canard confit* (duck gizzards, prepared the same way as a confit de canard). The main dish was a mouthwatering stuffed braised rabbit with mustard sauce, followed by *cèpes* (porcini mushrooms) with potatoes, then by cheeses. It was the first time I had had rabbit, and I have never had better. Dessert was an excellent Black Forest cake purchased at the local pâtisserie. It was all wonderful. What a treat! And what a privilege to be invited!

Afterwards Jean-Philippe drove me on tour of the countryside. He showed me the ruins of the donjon and chateau of Saleich, destroyed during the French Revolution. The Count of Saleich, who was lucky to escape with his life, fled with his family through underground passages and made his way to safety. Jean-Philippe also drove me to see St.-Bertrand-de-Comminges, a splendid, impressive Gothic cathedral on top of a hill in the beautiful commune of the same name in Haute Garonne, and other medieval and Renaissance monuments, including the Archbishop's Palace at Comminges.

Jean-Philippe and I have now been close friends for more than thirty years, and I have seen his mother again any number of times when she visits him in Paris. He and I have often had lunch or afternoon coffee on the days when he is not teaching, frequently at one of the places near the Bastille neighborhood where he lives, sometimes at a café near the Michelet Odéon. And I have met his friend, who has also become mine, the brilliant actor Agnès Bove, and her family, and I also met other members of Jean-Philippe's family. I remember when their son Gabriel was born, and I watched him grow up to become one of the soldiers who was given the honor of carrying the torch part of the way for the 2024 Paris Olympic Games.

Agnès Bove, who has a beautiful voice and impeccable diction, studied acting at the Sorbonne and was also trained as an opera singer at the Centre de Formation Lyrique de l'Opéra de la Bastille, and I have seen her in four shows. In October, 1998, she did a superb job of performing Francis Poulenc's forty-minute one-act opera for soprano and orchestra, an adaptation of Jean Cocteau's *La voix humaine* (The Human Voice). She was very moving and sang and acted beautifully. The performance took place in a converted farmhouse made over into a small theater out near Château-Thierry in the province of Champagne, where I went with her aunt and uncle, who drove me, and Jean-Philippe. It was wonderful to see the actual champagne vineyards on the way, and there was a very nice champagne reception afterwards.

I had the pleasure of seeing her in *Et pendant ce temps Simone Veille* (During That Time, Simone Watched). The word *veille* (watch over) rhymes with the name of the famous philosopher and political activist Simone Weil. This fascinating play is about the conditions of women's lives in France and how they changed in the direction of greater equality over the years. The four-woman show was first performed in 2015, and has often been on tour in the years since.

She was astonishing, just superb in *Colorature* is a two-person American play translated from *Glorious!*, an American comedy by Stephen Temperley about Florence Foster Jenkins, which Agnès Bove took on tour. Grégori Baquet, the actor playing her pianist was also excellent, and accompanied her very well. She told me that the hardest thing was to learn to sing off pitch, and at the end of the show, she tells the audience that she now knows what people heard when she sang, but what she heard inside her head was this: and she sings Franz Schubert's *Ave Maria* so beautifully that it brings tears to your eyes. I saw that show twice, once at an invited reading in September 2010 at a tiny theater at the unlikely address 0 rue Darwin, and then much later on at a theater in the picturesque town of Herblay, close to Paris, when it was fully produced.

I was fortunate too to see her in Nantes, not far from Paris, in a touring production of Offenbach's Opéra Bouffe Féerie *Le roi Carotte* (King Carrot), considerably cut but very well done, and she was wonderful as the student Robin-Luron. Her superb diction made the marvelous lyrics by Victorien Sardou eminently clear. It's one of my favorite works by Jacques Offenbach, a great political satire with a spectacular score, about a sorceress angry with the authoritarian reigning King Fridolin. She brings the vegetables in the garden to life, mounts a revolution, deposes him, and makes the carrot king. Eventually there is a counter-revolution, since the kingdom is tired of being ruled by vegetables, and Fridolin, having learned his lesson, resumes the throne. Victorien Sardou's libretto is based on a tale by Hoffmann. Sardou is known for his melodramas such as *La Tosca*, in which Sarah Bernhardt was the triumphant star, and which was adapted by Puccini for his famous opera.

After the excursion to Toulouse and its environs, I continued on to Paris for the rest of my vacation. I also went on September 12, 1990, a splendid sunny day, to Dijon and toured Beaune, with its fascinating medieval architecture, and the Burgundy wine country. Everywhere you walk in Beaune are small shops owned by a particular winemaker and you can taste each of the wines as you make your way through the winding streets. I sampled a lot of them, and was a bit tipsy by the time I got on the train back to Paris.

And eventually I went out to Normandy and Brittany, and took a day trip through the verdant countryside on June 10, 1989 to Mont St. Michel. The abbey on top of the mountain was built in the eleventh century, then restored and rebuilt in the twelfth century. We had two very informative guides on the bus tour I took because it was the easiest way for me to get there. There is a famous Michelin-starred restaurant, La Mère Poulard, near the crowded parking lot at the foot of the mountain. Lunch had been included in the tour in a restaurant about halfway up it on the main tourist street, with its plethora of souvenir shops, but I decided to have lunch at the celebrated restaurant. One of the guides objected indignantly that I had already paid for lunch, but I insisted, and said I would join them later. "I may never be here again for the rest of my life," I said, "and I don't want to miss this opportunity." The other guide agreed with me.

Lunch was great, with a starter of their famous puffy, light, and frothy omelet cooked on a wood fire. Just inside the entrance I saw girls making them in huge kettles, beating the eggs by hand, near a giant hearth where omelets were cooking. My main dish was a succulent, tender lamb roast *en croûte* (in a pastry crust), with an excellent apple tart for dessert; the latter two dishes, typical of Normandy, known for its sheep farms and apple orchards. I then went on up the hill and rejoined the group in time for another piece of apple tart. The view of the surrounding countryside from the top of the Mont was truly spectacular. After a short history lecture, we were allowed to wander about at will. On the way back to Paris, we stopped in a country restaurant, very touristy, and not very good, I am sorry to say.

I also went to Cabourg to see the hotel where Proust had stayed, and to Deauville and Trouville. To get to Cabourg, where I went on September 13, 2002, I took the train from the Gare St.-Lazare to Trouville-Deauville, a splendid ride through the gorgeous countryside of Normandy, then had a beautiful bus ride down the coast past Houlgate, and walked along the beach. I had a delicious lunch at the Grand Hôtel, where Proust describes the dining room as being like a fishbowl with passers-by continually looking in through the floor to ceiling glass windows. The lunch was delicious, with a grilled red snapper with an orange butter sauce as the main dish, and a chocolate tartlet with cacao ice cream for dessert. I took the bus back to Deauville, and walked out to the water before returning to take the train back to Paris.

On September 18, I took the train from the Gare du Nord to Pontoise, where the French Impressionist Camille Pissarro lived, and which many artists painted, to change trains for Auvers-sur-Oise, where Van Gogh spent his last days in a tiny bedroom at the Auberge Ravoux, which is still open as a restaurant. They have an upstairs room where they show a short documentary about Van Gogh's stay, and then you can go and see his actual depressing bedroom. Walking around town, you see the buildings he painted, with display cases on the street near them showing reproductions of his paintings of them. Leaving town for the long walk up the hill to the cemetery, and looking back, you see the gorgeous fields that look just like his paintings. The sky was a pure bright blue when I was there. He and his brother Theo are buried sided by side. Later that afternoon I went to Château d'Auvers to see an exhibit about life there in the Victorian era before taking the train back to Paris, and waiting once again in Pontoise, for about an hour.

I also traveled through northern France, passing through Lille and Arras on my way to Belgium, where I went on the TGV to Brussels, with its magnificent restaurants, and at other times to the seaside resort of Koksijde in Flemish, Coxyde in French, to visit my friends Joanna and Paul, who have a house there. To go to Coxyde, I took a TGV to Dunkerque (Dunkirk), where you can see three-masted sailing ships in the harbor and monuments to the evacuation of the British troops in World War Two, and they picked me up at the train station to drive across the border. We went to Anvers and Ostend as well. I saw Ghent from the train, and spent a marvelous few days in the capital of the province of West Flanders, Bruges, a beautifully preserved medieval city of canals, the Venice of the north, with amazing architecture and art, and excellent food.

One of the occasional problems with traveling in France and sometimes Belgium is the frequency of transport striked, which can be announced in advance, or can be wildcat. I once had to deal with it when I arrived in France, and I had to take a taxi to my hotel. Not only was it expensive, but since it was rush hour, the ride seemed to take forever.

On Friday, September 14, 1990 I was supposed to go to Brussels to have lunch at the superb three-star Michelin restaurant Comme Chez Soi (As In Your Own Home), where the cooking is anything but like what you make at home. The brilliant chef Pierre Wynants published a wonderful cookbook, *Comme Chez Soi: Les Recettes Originales de Pierre Wynants* (As In Your Own Home: The Original Recipes of Pierre Wynants; 1985), and I have made a number of the recipes that I first enjoyed in the restaurant, where I went several times. I arrived at the Gare du Nord at 7:45 a.m. only to be informed that there was a National Railway strike in Belgium, and I could only get to the border on French trains. "Rien ne circule sur le réseau belge. Ça dure 24 heures de 22h00 hier à 22h00 aujourd'hui. (Nothing is circulating on the Belgian network. It lasts for twenty-four hours, from 10 p.m. yesterday until 10 p.m. today)," said the railway official who informed me about the strike. I asked him if I could get to Brussels. "Oui, à pied à la frontière, où vous prenez un taxi. Ça vous coûtera des milliers de francs, si ça vous intéresse (Yes, on foot to the border, where you take a taxi. That will cost you thousands of francs, if that interests you)," he said. "Mais non, ça ne m'intéresse pas du tout (But no, that doesn't interest me at all)," I replied, and we laughed. I was easily able to change the reservation to Tuesday, September 18, when I took a nice walk from the train station to the restaurant and had a superb meal, but on the 14th I had no choice but to return to the Odéon whence I had come.

CHAPTER TWENTY-TWO

Travels in Other European Countries

I HAVE BEEN TO Germany, first of all to Munich in 1984 to see my friends David, an American whom I had known as an actor in New York before he quit the business, and his German partner. They had a car, and we drove out to visit the three famous and magnificent Bavarian castles built by the eccentric but highly creative King Ludwig II of Bavaria. Linderhof, with its Venus Grotto inspired by Wagner's *Tannhäuser*, some of which was performed for his royal patron, King Ludwig. The grotto is provided with a golden boat sailing on the tiny interior lake. King Ludwig did not share Wagner's horrible prejudices, but loved his music. He also built Neuschwannstein and Herrenchiemsee, modeled on Versailles. We had a magnificent lunch at Bavarian inn, sitting outdoors in the balmy sunny weather.

On other trips, I went to see different friends in the charming German university town of Tübingen, a charming university town, once home to eighteenth- and nineteenth-century great writes, such as Schiller and Goethe.

In Austria I went to Salzburg, very busy and very touristy, where I saw Mozart's birthplace; and to Vienna, that gorgeous imperial capital city with its many stately and impressive buildings from the old days of the Austro-Hungarian Empire, where I visited the great art museums and also the house of Mozart, with its bare utilitarian kitchen and small rooms, near St. Stephen's Cathedral where you can see flags high up on the walls surrounding the nave representing all the old Austro-Hungarian provinces, including Galicia. It was a great pleasure to wander the nearby streets.

I also went to the house of Sigmund Freud at Berggasse 19. There were display cases, some furniture, and pictures, but very little of his famous collection of antique miniature statues. And the famous consulting couch covered with a Persian rug was not there either. I asked the guard, "Bitte sehr, mein Herr, wo ist der berühmte Divan?" (Please, sir, where is the famous couch?) He replied curtly and almost as if I had offended him, "In London."

Having purchased a copy in the gift shop of Freud's *Drei Abhandlungen zur Sexualtheorie* (Three Essays on Sexual Theory), I went back to the city center and sat reading it over a cup of coffee and a slice of delicious chocolate Sachertorte. The hotel is right behind the newly opened, sumptuously renovated Staatsoper, the Vienna Opera, where I had the great pleasure that evening of seeing a magnificent production of Verdi's *Simon Boccanegra*.

A couple of times, I had the great pleasure of lunching at Demel, a superb emporium in the city center near the Hofburg, the principal winter palace of the Habsburg dynasty, to whom Demel was an official purveyor of pastries and chocolate since its founding in 1768. The salads and desserts, including the various tortes, are first rate. The Hotel Sacher sued them for serving Sachertorte, because the hotel owners said only they had the right to use the name, since that torte had been invented at the hotel. They won the case, and Demel simply changed the name to Schokoladentorte. The other Viennese restaurants I dined in were also excellent.

I saw two great shows in splendid productions at the Wiener Volksoper, the operetta theater: Friedrich von Flotow's *Martha*, and *Im weissen Rössl am Wolfgangsee* (The White Horse Inn on the Wolfgangsee) by Ralph Benatzky and Robert Stolz. Emperor Franz Josef is a character in the operetta, a speaking role, and when he disembarked at the dock near the inn, not only did the on-stage crowd go wild, but so did the audience, out of a sense of nostalgia for the days before World War One, I presume, and with regret for what came after. The actor spoke with a heavy Viennese accent, which I doubt would have been the way the emperor actually spoke, but which gave great joy to the audience.

As I was walking past the Hofburg, the principal winter palace of the Habsburg dynasty, and around the stately, impressive Opernring, the grand circular boulevard that rings the historic city center, and stopping to admire the buildings, a man stopped and looked at me, then asked me in his Viennese accent if I thought the buildings impressive. I said yes, and he shook his head, and said, "Wien ist eine ausgestorbene Stadt." (Vienna is an extinct/deserted city.) He nodded and moved on. Of course, I didn't see it that way, what with the lively shopping streets, such as the Mariahilfersstrasse, the great restaurants, and the beautiful architecture. But I knew what he meant: Here on the Opernring were the visible vestiges of the power of the Austro-Hungarian Empire. Another vestige was the summer palace of the Habsburgs, Schönbrunn, now a wonderful museum with its extensive park and gorgeous vistas.

One evening I went to a Heurige, a new wine festival with lively Schrammelmusik. When I purchased my ticket at a train station, the box office attendant said in her broad Viennese accent, "Und Sie bekommen ein Schnitzel damit." (Und you get a breaded veal cutlet with it.) "Ah," I replied in the same accent, "wenn Ich ein Schnitzel bekomme, dann muss Ich da gehen!" (Oh, if I get a Schnitzel with it, then I have to go there!) And we laughed. It was a delightful event with delicious white wine, and the Schnitzel was indeed delicious. In the background traditional Schrammelmusik, a style of nineteenth-century folk music composed by the Schrammel brothers Johann and Josef, and played by a live band added to the festivity.

I loved Vienna, and if it weren't for the present state of Austrian politics, with the far right taking power once again, I would be tempted to go for another visit, just as I would love to go to those other major cities of the former empire, Budapest and Prague.

I loved Switzerland, too, where I was in Geneva, Lausanne, Lucerne, Zurich and Winterthur, where I went to see the extraordinary collection of paintings by Manet, Van Gogh, Courbet, Daumier, and many others at the Oskar Reinhardt Foundation in the gorgeous mansion that had belonged to him.

In Zurich I had dinner at the well reputed Grill Room in the prestigious Baur au Lac, a luxury hotel. It was delightful, and the when the waiter approached my table, I said, "Guten Abend, mein Herr. Wie geht es Ihnen? (Good evening, sir. How are you?) He looked at me blankly, clearly not understanding a word. "Ah," I thought, "wrong language. Bonsoir, monsieur. Comment ça va?" Again, I got a blank look. "What language would you like to speak?" I asked. "English," he said, I'm from near London." The way he pronounced "near London," it sounded like Nederlanden, slurring the d and almost skipping the last syllable, Nederland being the Dutch name for the Netherlands. "Oh! You're Dutch?" I asked in astonishment. "No! I'm from near London!" he said. Then, of course, I understood. He was training for the hotel and restaurant business, taking his courses at the school run by the Baur au Lac. I don't know how he got by, because I am pretty sure the classes could not have been taught in English. The restaurant was empty by the time I had finished my first course, and the waiter was very attentive and actually quite charming in his service, putting the dishes on the table and removing them with an elegant but unobtrusive flourish. Later in the meal, I said, "Thank you! Your service is excellent!" He replied in his heavy Thames Estuary, near-Cockney accent, "Well, sir, it's a pleasure to be able to serve this way. When the restaurant is full, we don't generally have the chance."

In 1973, I also went to Scandinavia. I was the one speaking actor with the Little Theater of the Deaf, the children's division of the National Theater of the Deaf, on our tour of Bergen, Oslo, Stockholm and Copenhagen, accompanied by our artistic director, David Hays. When we arrived in Bergen, where we would be performing in the Bergen International Festival, jet-lagged as we were, David Hays greeted us, and said he would take anyone who wanted to go on a boat trip up the nearby fjord. It would be our only chance to do that. We immediately accepted. It was truly amazing and gorgeous, and I slept nearly all the way back to the town.

On our one day off, I took a short bus trip up the coast past farm country by myself to see the composer Edvard Grieg's house and museum, with a spectacular view of the countryside. Unfortunately, the museum was closed to visitors that day, because there was a piano concert being performed inside. The concert, which consisted of excerpts from Grieg's score to Henrik Ibsen's *Peer Gynt*, was broadcast through loudspeakers, so I sat and listened to it before going back to Bergen.

On that second trip of mine to Copenhagen, we went up the coast a short way to Helsingør (Elsinore), to see Hamlet's castle, where summer performances of Shakespeare's play have often taken place. By special permission of the museum guard, whom David Hays persuaded by telling him we were actors eager to see the view, we were able to go up on the roof for a splendid sight of the surrounding countryside.

2.

In Italy, I went to Rome, Florence, Milan, and four times to Venice, which I adored.

On my first trip to Italy, in 1983, I arrived st the airport in Rome on Alitalia, and took a train into the city, where I stayed at a pensione near the central railway station, Roma Termini. The clerk at the reception desk felt compelled for some reason to tell me, after looking at my American passport, that he was sorry the fascists had lost power and that Italy was better off under Mussolini. I didn't bother arguing with him although I am sure I looked at him with great surprise, quickly suppressed. There would have been no point in saying anything. But I was astonished that anyone had that point of view, although I needn't have been, in light of everything that has gone on since.

I took busses from the train station everywhere. I went first to the Coliseum and walked around inside it, thrilled to be there. The next day I went to see Mussolini's sports stadium the Foro Italico, originally called the Foro Mussolini. This complex is one of the last remaining monuments to fascism. It is built like an ancient Roman amphitheater, with huge statures of naked athletes surrounding it at the top representing the different provinces and bearing fascist mottos on their bases. Some jokers had stuck Coca Cola cans on some of the athletes' penises, and I did laugh.

Near the entrance is a huge obelisk with the name Mussolini Dux (Latin for leader, or Duce in Italian) in huge letters. Some boys were having fun playing soccer and kicking the ball against it. A man approached and chased them away as they shouted obscenities back at him and laughed. He said hello, and told me he thought the stadium was most impressive. I agreed. And then he said it was a shame that respect was not paid to one of the great eras of Italian history. So I knew I was talking with another fascist. He pointed out the house in the distance of Clara Petacci, Mussolini's mistress, who was executed in 1945 by partisans at the same time as the dictator. Again, he said how great Mussolini was. And again I didn't see any point in arguing, so I simply said, "Buona giornata (Have a good day)!" and left to go back to the pensione.

As an opera lover, I wanted to see the three settings for Giacomo Puccini's *Tosca*, so guidebook in hand, I set out to find the baroque Church of Sant-Andrea della Valle, where the first act takes place. It is gorgeously decorated with its ornate painted ceilings depicting various biblical scenes surrounded in gold, and its amazing side chapels, and it was beautifully reproduced on stage in Franco Zefirelli's 1985 production at the Metropolitan Opera in New York.

Then I went over to the setting for the second act, the Palazzo Farnese, a Renaissance palace, which turned out to be the French Embassy, and of course there was no admittance except with authorization, so I couldn't go inside. There was a huge Communist demonstration outside the embassy, with posters informing the world of who they were, and of course I wondered what was going on. Were they opposing the French for some reason? So I asked one of the demonstrators, and he explained that it had nothing to do with the French, but that it was one of the largest open spaces in the neighborhood surrounding the embassy and that in this area and in certain other poor quarters of Rome, there was still no electricity and they were demonstrating against the city government in an effort to get them to complete the city's necessary services so that all Rome would have what it needed. The embassy itself had all it needed in the way of municipal services. I was amazed at what he told me. No electricity in that day and age!

Lastly, I made my way to the Castel Sant-Angelo, Hadrian's Mausoleum, a huge towering rotunda on the Tiber, and climbed all the way to the top, for the superb view of the city and surrounding countryside. It is from the parapets of this imposing monument that Floria Tosca leaps to her death.

On one of my last days in Rome, I took a train out to Ostia Antica (Ancient Ostia), the seaport of ancient Rome at the mouth of the Tiber. The sand had covered the ancient city when the Roman Empire fell, and the harbor was virtually abandoned. Starting in 1939 under Mussolini, the city was excavated like Pompeii, which I never did go south to see. I wandered Ostia Antica's streets with a guidebook, and saw the gorgeous baths with their black and white mosaics, and the colorful mosaics on the floor of the house of Cupid and Psyche, the impressive frescoes on the inside walls of some of the buildings, and the grand Temple area, with temples to Jupiter, Juno, and Minerva. A way out on the edge of the town I found the ancient synagogue, the oldest one on the European continent, decorated with such Jewish symbols as the Star of David and the Menorah. Its main monumental gate faces southeast towards Jerusalem. The Jews, whose Sabbath duty was to walk to synagogue, lived near it in their own separate area. The authorities had decreed that the synagogue could not be in the Temple area, because the Jews refused to accept or worship the Roman gods.

I also had a great time in the splendid Piazza Navona, with its fountains and statues. And at my Uncle Sy and Aunt Shirley's urging I went to Tre Scalini, an excellent caffè, and sat outdoors and had a *tartuffo*, a delicious preparation of vanilla ice cream surrounded with a hard chocolate icing, and with a secret inside, which Sy and Shirley said would be a nice surprise for me. It was indeed: a brandied cherry, quite wonderful.

I walked from the incredibly impressive Spanish Steps to the splendid sculpted Trevi Fountain, the one that is featured in the movie *Three Coins in the Fountain*. And I marveled as I passed by in a bus at the incredibly ornate huge sculpted Monumento Nazionale a Vittorio Emmanuele II, which many called the Wedding Cake.

I went to the excavated ancient Roman Forum, with the Senate House where Julius Caesar was assassinated, and I was surprised to see that it was a low-lying building without columns and a huge flight of steps leading up to the entrance, as one sees it depicted in various film and stage productions of Shakespeare's play. Nearby is the Arch of Titus depicting the sacking of the Second Temple during the Roman conquest of Jerusalem. The entrance to the forum is right near the old Roman ghetto and the Great Synagogue of Rome, an Orthodox congregation on the Tiber. As a police officer informed me, the synagogue was guarded by police for fear of terror attacks, so I couldn't go inside. I had an excellent lunch at a kosher meat restaurant in the old ghetto, lasagna with no cheeses, of course, but fine nonetheless. And for the first time I had the delectable *Carciofi alla giudia* (deep-fried artichoke hearts, Roman-Jewish style), among the best known dishes of the Jewish Roman cuisine. My waiter was an older man, who wore an obvious toupee, and spoke with a heavy Roman accent, diphthongizing the "o" sounds, for instance in the name of the city Roma, instead of pronouncing them as the pure vowels of standard Italian. He was a survivor of the Holocaust and had been in a concentration camp, and he told me a little about what had happened to the Jews of Rome, and to him, but he found it too upsetting to talk much about it. He also told me that Jews were not to walk under the Arch of Titus, because of what it depicted. Many people walk under and around it, but I refrained from doing so, out of respect for what the waiter had told me, and for the ancient suffering of those who had been conquered.

Having loved my time in Rome, I took the train to Florence through the beautiful countryside of Tuscany, and spent a few delightful days touring the Uffizi and other art galleries, and glorying in the Duomo and the great central plaza, and the crossing the Arno on the Ponte Vecchio to wander around the city.

I took the train from Florence to Venice, and when I arrived, I found a hotel right near the train station, and after my stay of several days, during which I fell in love with the city, I took the night train up to Paris, a fantastic ride past Bologna, until it got dark. I didn't have a sleeping berth, but I dozed off in my seat, arriving tired but happy in Paris. Again, I didn't have a hotel reservation, but I went over to the Odéon area and found a room at the Hôtel du Pas de Calais on the rue des Saints-Pères for a week before I got the Alitalia plane from Charles de Gaulle airport back to New York.

Another time, in May 1984, I took the train to Milan over the Alps from Munich with my American friend David who had lived there for several years before going to Germany. The central section of Milan is a magnificent impressive delight, including the opera museum in the famous La Scala opera house. We were on the Metropolitana di Milano public transport on our way to see Leonardo da Vinci's *Last Supper*, when my pocket was picked. We were just getting out of the train, and he asked me if my passport were in a safe pocket, because there were notorious pickpockets around. I tapped the left-hand lower pocket of my jacket and said it was fine, and then I felt a hand in that pocket just as the train doors closed and I had gotten out. I yelled out in Italian, "Aiuto! Aiuto! Fu rubato!" (Help! Help! I've been robbed), and the police came running over. I explained what had happened, but there was nothing they could do except to commiserate with me. Fortunately, my friend knew where the American consulate was located, only a couple of blocks away. Happily for me, the thieves didn't get any money, because I kept my money and traveler's checks in another pocket.

The clerk at the consulate was very sympathetic. He had a pile of empty United States passport booklets next to the typewriter, because this happened all the time. There were a couple of gangs working the subway, an Italian and a Turkish gang, who would sell the passports to forgers, apparently a lucrative and thriving market. I filled out a form and paid the required fee, then went to a photographer the clerk directed me to, just around the corner. After giving the clerk the photo, I had to wait a couple of hours, until I finally had my new passport. My friend David asked me if I wanted to go see the famous fresco, but I said I was no longer in the mood, and went straight on to Venice for my second of four trips, while he waited for the train to Munich. I never did see Leonardo da Vinci's *Last Supper*.

Incidentally, when I was already back home, I got a letter from the consulate telling me that the Italian police had found my passport and leather folder in a garbage bin near the train station. I haven't the slightest idea why they didn't think them worth keeping. The consulate sent them back to me for a small fee.

I had no hotel reservation in Venice, and the hotel I had stayed in near the railway station was full up, but I got a room at the deluxe hotel Monaco e Canal Grande right near the justly famous Harry's Bar, with its excellent upstairs restaurant. The Monaco e Canal Grande's restaurant faces the canal, and I had dinner there. At one point a gondolier rose up right at the wall of the outside dining area so that I thought he might actually come over the wall. We were all very startled, but of course we laughed afterwards.

In 2004, having flown to Venice from Orly Airport in Paris, and taken the spectacular boat ride from the Venice airport into the city, past the Lido and other islands, I stayed at the very expensive Hotel Danieli, which had been built as the Palazzo Dandolo by the wealthy Dandolo family in the fourteenth century, and went through various structural changes during the heyday of Venetian power. The hotel, with its gold balustraded staircases in the lobby, was gorgeously decorated with antique furniture and Old Master paintings on every floor like a museum, eminently worth the stay, and a short walk along the waterfront to the Piazza San Marco, with its splendid Basilica di San Marco and grand Campanile, and the Doge's Palace, where I had a marvelous, informative guided tour through its spacious ornate halls and to the immense Grand Council Chamber, as splendid as that for any monarchy. It was in this chamber that the Council elected the Doge of the Venetian Republic. The word *Doge* is Venetian for the standard Italian word *Duce* (Duke; Leader).

The Danieli is not far from the beautiful enclosed Ponte dei Sospiri (Bridge of Sighs), so named because prisoners were conducted across it from the Doge's Palace to their cells on the other side of the small canal next to the palace, and the hapless souls supposedly sighed at their last view of Venice through the bridge's windows, before being led down into their oubliettes, from the French word *oublier* (to forget), cells where they could and often did die, starving and forgotten. Among other places I went to the Caffè Florian, opened in 1720 and still decorated as it had been when Lord Byron went there.

The reason I chose to stay at the Danieli, with its gorgeous view of the Grand Canal from the breakfast toom at the top, was that Marcel

Proust had stayed there, as well as many others of the French literary establishment, wealthy classes, and the French artistic establishment, including Claude Monet and his wife, in the late nineteenth and early twentieth centuries. So of course I had to splurge and stay there at least once.

On one of my long walks, I went to the sixteenth-century Chiesa di San Sebastiano, where the artist Paolo Veronese is buried. He decorated the church and some of his paintings are displayed there as well. I had a guided tour in Italian, and translated for two French high school boys who were also there. Afterwards, I went round the corner to the excellent Trattoria Anzolo Raffaele, *anzolo* being Venetian dialect for Italian *angiolo* (angel). They have no menu, but serve whatever they have found in the market that morning. That day's feast was spaghetti with squid ink sauce, followed by a grilled fish, *orata* (bream) and a small salad. The waiter asked if I would like dessert, and when I said yes, he told me there was no dessert, but that I could go around the corner to an excellent gelateria with some of the best ice cream in Venice, so I did, and he was right: it was superb. I think Italian gelati and sorbetti are the best I ever have. After dessert, I took the long walk back to the hotel, and had a good nap.

I took a boat trip on the Grand Canal on one of the city busses, a great way to see the Venetian palazzi, and on every trip I walked all over, losing myself in the almost deserted back streets and squares, and carrying a small map of the city, although it would be extremely difficult to get lost because there are signs everywhere pointing the way back to the Piazza San Marco. Walking along the canal and going to the Rialto is one of the great pleasures of a visit to Venice. I was also fascinated to hear the Venetian dialect of Italian spoken in the streets. It had rather a French sound to it. For instance, the word for open-air market where linens were sold, among other goods, is *merceria*, pronounced "mehr tcheh REE ah," but the Venetians called it the "mahr zhahr EE."

I visited the medieval ghetto with its German Ashkenazic and Spanish Sephardic synagogues, and sat on a bench just outside the Ghetto to contemplate the Holocaust memorial on one of its walls, with bas-reliefs depicting what had happened. This ghetto is where Shylock would have lived in Shakespeare's *The Merchant of Venice*. The gates, long gone, were closed and barred every evening, and opened during the day so people could go back and forth.

The etymology of the word "ghetto," while not certain, may actually be from the Venetian for foundry, as the ghetto was set up in the unsavory, odiferous area of the foundry where tar was melted for the ships, and where there was noise day and night. The *campo*, which is what the open squares and plazas are called in Venice, still retains its Jewish character, with its synagogues and kosher food stores.

I took a trip to the colorful island of Burano to its famous glass and glass-making establishments. And of course I went to the major art museums, including the Peggy Guggenheim collection of modern art. On one of my trips, I stayed in a pensione right near the museum, and wandered around the streets in that much less frequented neighborhood.

When I left for Paris, I again took that breathtaking boat ride to the airport. We took off, only to have to put back almost immediately, because a bird had flown into one of the engines. We were in the airport for a couple of hours, but eventually got back to Paris.

I never got to Spain, because I refused to go while Franco was still in power. When I went to the Canary Islands in February, 1986 for a couple of weeks to visit that same American friend David and his German apartment mate, who were renting a house there on the small island of La Palma, very popular with German tourists, the fascist dictator was long gone, but the street named for him in the main town had not had its name changed.

La Palma was very interesting, with its volcanic caldera at the center, its mountain observatory, its banana plantations and black sand lava beaches in the south, and fertile farmland with groves of almond trees in the north. Their house was in the south, and we drove north through the mountains to the farm country, and ate in a small restaurant near the orchards. It was fun to see that our waitress in the walled garden next to our table, picking the vegetables for the mixed salad we had ordered. We also had goat stew, the first and only time I have ever eaten that dish, which slightly resembled lamb, but which I can't say I liked very much. And I was happily there in time to enjoy the old custom of Carnival back down south. It was self-indulgent, hedonistic and celebrated with colorful costumes, loud music, fireworks, parades, and dancing in the streets, just prior to Ash Wednesday and Lent with its austerity and deprivations.

CHAPTER TWENTY-THREE

Friends in the Worlds of Books and Restaurants

I WAS ECSTATIC TO be able to return annually to Paris, sometimes twice a year, and sorry to have to skip my trips there during the Covid pandemic, when thanks to modern technology I was at least able to keep in touch regularly with my friends through email, FaceTime, WhatsApp, and Zoom, which I do all year in any case. In the course of my visits in 1983 and beyond, I had made many friends: rare book dealers, people in the restaurant business, and other people in show business. It was easy to befriend the book dealers, since we had many interests in common from literature and music to gastronomy. I would enter the store, browse, have a conversation, perhaps make a purchase, and return again and again for conversations, and eventually we would go for a meal or coffee.

One of my very greatest friends is François Roulmann, the most noted expert on rare music in France today, and also one of the experts on the polymath, popular novelist, and musician Boris Vian (1920-1959). François has received the well-deserved honor of being made a Chevalier des Arts et des Lettres in the French government's cultural organization, the Ordre des Arts et des Lettres. He is one of the editors of the authoritative 2013 Pléiade edition of Boris Vian's works, and has written books about Vian in collaboration with Christelle Gonzalo, another one of the editors. She is also a great friend of mine, whose marvelous rare *librairie* (bookshop) Sur le fil de Paris, is in the Marais close to the Seine is devoted to the history of Paris.

I was talking with Jean-Philippe about my interest in Offenbach and in finding out-of-print Offenbach vocal scores, and he told me to go see François in his bookstore on the rue de la Grande Chaumière off the boulevard du Montparnasse. When I did, we had a wonderful conversation about Offenbach, and he showed me some of the rare vocal scores he had. I went to see him there innumerable times on subsequent trips to Paris.

He moved his shop eventually to the rue Beautreillis across the rue St.-Antoine just south of the place des Vosges. Long after we had already become friends and I had made an appointment to visit him in his bookstore, which I had to do in advance because he is always so busy, often evaluating lots of rare books and music for the great auction house Drouot, or lots he had purchased from private collectors, I would arrive early in the neighborhood so I could sit for a brief time in the place des Vosges. In later years after that first meeting, I purchased a first edition of *Du côté de chez Swann* (1913) when he was still on the rue de la Grande Chaumière; and after he had moved, a first edition of Proust's first book *Les plaisirs et les jours* (Pleasures and Days;1896), a collection of short stories and prose poems, both volumes beautifully bound and at very reasonable prices. He also gives me presents frequently of books and catalogs of rare books that I love to look through.

Sotheby's, whose auction house is right near the Palais de l'Élysée, the official residence of the French president, had an auction of Proustian materials at the end of May, 2016, and a public showing of everything on offer for two days several weeks before the auction. I unfortunately missed the public showing. François was well acquainted with the expert who was handling the auction, and very kindly put me in touch with him. So I went to Sotheby's a couple of days after the public showing, told the receptionist why I was there, and their expert came out to the lobby to meet me. After some amicable discussion, he took me back to the storage area, leaving me alone for a half hour or so to look through everything, which had already been put back there after the showing. I very carefully held some of Proust's letters in my hand and read them, and looked through the photographs and autographed copies of first editions of his books, and other documents. I was thrilled and so grateful to François and to his expert acquaintance for this unique experience.

Among the many marvelous rare scores François showed me over the years were first editions of Schubert's *Die Winterreise* (The Winter Journey), published in two parts, the first one autographed, the second published just after his death; and a 1725 edition of Vivaldi's *The Four Seasons*, with four poems meant to be read aloud as the concertos were played. He also showed me a magnificent 1887 album of photos of a production of Offenbach's *Orphée aux enfers*; a hand-written note with a bar of music by Offenbach; and a poster from the original production of *The Tales of Hoffmann*. We had the most interesting, conversations about everything from art to politics, and we have so much in common with regard to both. Among other people I was fascinated to meet in the bookstore was Laurent Fraison, who owns the greatest collection of Offenbachiana in the world. He has every vocal score, original production set models, costume designs, countless photographs, manuscripts, and other documents. François and I had wonderful lunches more times than I can say. And I always had a great time browsing while he dealt with customers who came in.

On September 15, 2015, when I was seventy-two, he and Jean-Philippe Bec, who lives not far away from the bookstore in the Marais, gave me a marvelous surprise birthday celebration in his shop after Jean-Philippe and I had had lunch at the Grand Véfour, the gorgeous eighteenth-century restaurant with its authentic Rococo décor at the northwest end of the Jardin du Palais Royal. We were stuffed, but we managed to walk slowly over to the bookstore, and they gave me a concert. Jean-Philippe played a wonderful recital of Beethoven's *Moonlight Sonata*, pieces by Scriabin, and others on the grand piano, and François played the violin, which he does very well, even sometimes participating in concerts. I was so delighted, and truly surprised.

Madame Blanche Buffet, niece of the famous modern artist Bernard Buffet, is another wonderful very dear friend, and we occasionally correspond during the year when I am in New York. She always sends me Thanksgiving and New Year's greetings. Her rare bookshop, very near the Michelet-Odéon, is on the rue St.-Sulpice, heading towards the magnificent Cathedral of Saint-Sulpice with its splendid, ornate baroque interior, and with a place and a magnificent fountain in front of it. You can sit there and relax and gaze at the church. The two towers have little holes near their tops, from bullets fired when shots were exchanged during the Revolution of 1830.

Madame Buffet inherited the Libraire Claude Buffet from her father and she is an expert in late-nineteenth and early twentieth-century French literature. I went in one day by chance to see what she had on Proust, and found immediately that she was a great, amazing expert not only on Proust, but also on Balzac, and nineteenth- and twentieth-century French literature in general. I bought a great many books from her that added immensely to my Proust collection, including one by Dr. Adrien Proust and his colleague Albert Mathieu, *L'Hygiène de l'Obèse* (The Hygiene of the Obese; 1897), who wrote some thirty books on medicine, some in collaboration. They are so rare that even a bookstore devoted to rare medical books on the rue Jacob didn't have any. She also very kindly gives me presents of books and catalogs that are treasures I love to browse in.

I kept stopping by to say hello and talk with Madame Buffet and her late mother, when she was still working there, and we had the most wonderful conversations about literature and many other subjects. Blanche and I got to know each other's personal life stories, and talked about food and cooking and the dishes we make, and then we started having lunch and occasionally early morning coffee at the Danton at 9:30 or 10, just before she opened the bookstore. We have had countless lunches and dinners together over the many years of our wonderful friendship. She is a great cook from everything she has told me about what she makes, and the photos she has shown me, and a great gourmet, and has a place in the country right near Paris, with a garden. She speaks excellent English, and we had a dinner with my Uncle Sy at the Brasserie Bofinger *sous la coupole* (under the cupola), a gorgeous stained glass dome ceiling in the large dining room. If you make a reservation, you ask to be seated there, but even without a reservation there is usually no problem. In any case, the other downstairs dining room and the upstairs are also beautiful.

And I also had a lot in common with the people I befriended in the restaurant and hotel business, from waiters to managers, experts in gastronomy and oenology who were happy to tell me what they knew, and who appreciated my interest. From common interests to an interest in our personal lives was an easy jump after a time. I have now been friends for more than thirty or thirty-five years with a number of them.

In fact, the reason I return every year for a month or so is to visit with those old friends. People drift in and out of my life, sometimes never to return, even if I had been friends with them for a long time, and even if sometimes I want them to come back into my life, and that is true in Paris as well as in the United States. Then there are those who remain lifelong friends, and I am very lucky to have them. I am sure everyone goes through the same kind of thing, with friends who prove true and are loyal, and others who simply disappear and whom you don't hear from again. There are also those people whom I have been happy to have out of my life, who proved their incompatibility. But enough philosophizing, to paraphrase Chekhov in *Uncle Vanya*! Let us return to the story of my travels.

As the well known line from *Casablanca*, one of my very favorite films, has it, "We'll always have Paris." I always will. I spend a month at a time in Paris, usually in May. One year, I couldn't afford to go in May, but I earned enough money doing television commercials to go in September, and that became my usual month to visit what I considered my second home, partly because of those lifelong friends I just mentioned, and partly because I have stayed in the same place for some thirty or more years now, since 1992, the Hôtel Michelet Odéon in the place de l'Odéon, except for when I was doing Moisés Kaufman's *Gross Indecency: The Three Trials of Oscar Wilde* for a two-year Off-Broadway run. I had a week's Equity vacation each year, in October, 1997 and April, 1998, and I went to Paris both times and stayed with friends, returning in the autumn of 1998 after the show had closed. The hotel is right near the Luxembourg Gardens and Palace, so the St.-Germain *quartier* (neighborhood) has become my quartier. Part of what made the hotel such an agreeable place to stay, aside from its wonderful location, is that I have mostly had the same room, so that is it as if I am returning to a Paris apartment, and also, most importantly, I got to know all the personnel over the years, and we are always very friendly.

One of my very greatest friends ever, Dimitri Devenne, became the manager of the Hôtel Michelet Odéon in 1996, after having worked as head of reception, and on my return to the hotel after lunch or a visit to a museum, I would sit for a while in the lobby and we would talk as he did his work at the reception desk. He enjoyed his job as hotel manager a lot, until the Covid pandemic closed the hotel, since sold, renovated, and reopened, and still where I stay on every Paris trip. So of course I saw him nearly every weekday at the hotel, and we talked a great deal. We often had coffee in the mornings when he arrived for work. I would be in the breakfast area near the reception desk in the lobby, having my petit déjeuner and he would join me for a coffee before starting his workday in the manager's office, and before I started the rest of my own day. We also had excellent restaurant lunches occasionally And we used to go often for walks in the Luxembourg when he took his afternoon break, so we really got to know each other, we have shared views on many subjects.

In 2000 he married the charming, beautiful Nathalie, and when he returned from his honeymoon, we went to the Café de Flore one afternoon, and he showed me the album of his wonderful wedding pictures. I remember when his two daughters, Clara and Aurore, were born. When they were little girls, I had the pleasure of meeting them one weekend. Dimitri brought them to the hotel and we went to the Luxembourg, then I bought them ice cream. It was a charming visit, and I heard all about them and their activities as they grew up.

He invited me once for a superb Sunday family lunch at his house in the suburbs from which he commuted every weekday on the D line of the RER. I traveled out there with two friends of his family who were also staying at the hotel. I was very happy to meet other members of his extended family there, and by that time I was fully established as a family friend.

Dimitri oversaw the closing of the hotel during the pandemic, and we used to FaceTime when he was there winding things up. He would show me on his iPhone what was happening in the place de l'Odéon. Eventually, when their daughters were old enough the be on their own, he and Nathalie moved out to Charente-Maritime, and acquired a restaurant, L'Eau à la Bouche, in the town of Châtellaillon-Plage, a delightful and very popular beach resort on the Île de Ré near La Rochelle, to which I took the TGV from Paris. The joke is that Paris has twenty arrondissements, and this is the twenty-first.

The restaurant ambience is charming, warm, and welcoming, the food is superb, and I ate there for most of my meals. I went out to Châtellaillon-Plage twice once the pandemic had ended and I could travel to France again. I stayed the first time at a really nice hotel on the main street, because their new house was not ready, and the second time at their charming house with its upstairs guest bedroom. On the restaurant's weekly closing day, Monday, we drove around the gorgeous countryside and they showed me the sights at La Rochelle and Rochefort. I also got to know his delightful warm and friendly aunt and uncle, Michele and Bruno, who live in a small town nearby, and who invited us for a magnificent lunch on my first visit, with oysters on the half shell to start and roast duck for a main course; and for a light supper on my second visit, after Dimitri, Nathalie, and I had been traveling around all day. In short, I had perfectly marvelous visits. When I am not in France, and even when I am in Paris, we keep in touch regularly on WhatsApp.

CHAPTER TWENTY-FOUR

Some Marvelous Paris Museums

L IKE EVERYONE, I love the museums in Paris. Aside from the Louvre, the Marmottan, and the Musée d'Orsay, each of which I have visited several times, making an effort to visit the latter on every trip, I have very much enjoyed the special exhibits at the gorgeous Petit Palais, the Museum of Fine Arts of the City of Paris, which also has a wonderful permanent collection; and those special exhibits at the Grand Palais, also home every year to a rare book fair, for which I always get a free ticket from my bookseller friends who have stands there. Both splendid ornate buildings were constructed for the Exposition Universelle (Universal Exhibition) of 1900. I usually take a bus from near the Michelet Odéon to the ornate pont Alexandre III with its gold ornamentation, and cross it to go to one or other of those buildings.

At the Musée d'Orsay I always went slowly through the galleries with the beautiful landscapes by Corot, Millet, and others, and then all the way upstairs to see the Impressionists. I then descended to see all the other collections. I always make my way through the rooms with Art Nouveau furniture to see the portrait of Marcel Proust as a young man painted in 1892 by his friend Jacques-Émile Blanche on one of the walls near a window with a view of the Seine. One September day in 2015, I went as usual, only to find that the portrait was not there. So I approached a guard a few rooms away and asked about it. She told me where it was, and I explained that I had just been there and the painting was gone. "It can't be," sh said. She got up and peremptorily told me to follow her. When we got there, she was astonished to see that I was right, and told me she had not been informed. Motioning me to follow her, she went out onto the central museum balcony and phoned her boss. "Monsieur Proust est parti. Où est-il ? (Monsieur Proust has left.

Where is he)," she said. And I had all I could do not to laugh. It turned out that the portrait was on loan for a special exhibit at the Musée des Arts Décoratifs in the Louvre's northwest wing, to which I made my way, but I was too late, because it was just before closing time.

Also fascinating is the Musée des Arts et Métiers, where among many intriguing and informative exhibits is a reproduction of the laboratory, with all the original equipment, of the celebrated eighteenth-century polymath and father of modern chemistry, the nobleman Antoine-Laurent de Lavoisier, known for his recognition of oxygen and hydrogen as elements. He famously said, "Rien ne se perd, rien ne se crée, tout se transforme." (Nothing is lost, nothing is created, everything is transformed.) My father loved what I told him of the exhibit, and the photographs I took of the laboratory.

I also love the museums devoted to individual artists, among them the Musée Zadkine, the house and studio where the Russian-born sculptor Ossip Zadkine lived and worked. And I went to the magnificent Rodin Museum in the gorgeous eighteenth-century town house, the Hôtel Biron with its lovely gardens where you can see Auguste Rodin's amazing, sometimes turbulent, deeply impressive, and innovative, and occasionally massive sculptures, with smaller works inside the house. Wandering in the garden, I was overawed by *La Porte de l'Enfer* (The Gate of Hell), a complicated bronze group sculpture illustrating the scene from Dante's *Inferno*, Canto 3, verses 1-9 that ends with the famous sentence, "Lasciate ogni speranza, voi ch'entrate" (Abandon all hope, ye who enter) over the gate to Hell.

The charming house and studio of Eugène Delacroix, with a peaceful garden where you can sit and contemplate life, just off the place de Furstenberg, is easily visited in an hour. There is also a superb museum devoted to Gustave Moreau, in the town house where he lived and worked on the rue de la Rochefoucauld in the ninth arrondissement.

The literary museums include the Victor Hugo Museum, his house in the place des Vosges, furnished as it was when the family lived there, and with a splendid view of that corner of the park from the upstairs windows. He didn't feel he could write there, however, so he used to go to write upstairs at the wonderful restaurant Lapérouse on the Quai des Grands-Augustins, the view from the upstairs window being very different from what it is today, although of course he could see the Louvre. He observed the passers-by and the traffic on the river, and all of that gave him some ideas. He also had lunch there every Sunday with his family in one of the private upstairs dining rooms, now named for him.

At the present day, the head waiter at the restaurant is happy to give people a guided tour of the upstairs of this historic establishment, there since 1766, which I have done a couple of times with friends. Aside from Victor Hugo, famous authors frequented the beautiful restaurant, including Mark Twain, Robert Louis Stevenson, and Sholem Aleichem, aside from the French literary luminaries, and other celebrities such as Jacques Offenbach. Their portraits line the walls outside the salons.

Politicians also dined there, sometimes with courtesans in the private dining rooms, called "salons privés." The scratches the women made on the mirrors to test whether the diamonds their mentors, Senators among them, had given them were real are still there, as is the entrance to the underground tunnel that led all the way to the Senate at the Palais du Luxembourg. You can rent one of the private upstairs salons, which were formerly free in the days when smoking was permitted in the main dining room and diners wanted a smoke-free environment, or eat in that elegant dining room, with views of the Seine, or have a drink in the plush bar on the street level, with its dark wood and red velvet seats.

I gave myself literary walking tours of Paris, having made lists of the addresses in the novels of Honoré de Balzac and those of Marcel Proust, and the places he visited, including the Parc Monceau and the Musée Nissim de Camondo, a historic mansion built starting in 1911 and now a decorative arts museum where Proust was sometimes invited to parties when the family lived there. There is a framed letter from him on one of the tables amidst various objets d'art; and there is a magnificent collection of eighteenth-century furniture amassed by the Count Moïse de Camondo, whose son Nissim was killed as a pilot in action in World War One. He gave the mansion and its collection to the private non-profit organization that manages museums of decorative arts in Paris as a memorial tribute to his son. The Camondo family were called the Rothschilds of the East. They were Sephardic Jews originally from Turkey, and very wealthy bankers. During World War Two, most of the surviving members of the family were sent to Auschwitz, where they were murdered. I had never heard of them before I went to the museum, and was very saddened when I learned their fate, even more so when I read a biography of the family that I had purchased in the gift shop. The museum is a memorial not just to Nissim de Camondo but to the whole family. I also saw the houses where the other aristocrats whose salons Proust frequented lived, and the places where he himself lived. There are so many places mentioned in Balzac's and Proust's novels that I found myself happily walking all over Paris.

In the case of Charles Baudelaire, who was born in Paris, I saw the plaque marking where his birthplace at 17 rue Hautefeuille near the rue Monsieur-le-Prince had been until it was torn down during Baron Haussmann's rebuilding of Paris in the 1850s; the rue de Buci, where he manned the barricades during the Revolution of 1848; the Île Saint-Louis and the place Vendôme, where he lived at various times.

I went to the Alexandre Dumas Museum in Villers-Cotterêts, a short way outside Paris, and a long walk up the slopes of Port-Marly not too far from the local train station. It is a magnificent estate, and he called the main house the Château de Monte-Cristo. A short way from the chateau, there is a small house on the grounds in Gothic style reached by crossing a bridge over a moat. Dumas called it the Château d'If after the prison on the island in the Marseille harbor where Edmond Dantès is imprisoned, and from which he will escape to become the Count of Monte-Cristo. Dumas spent his days there, reading, researching, and writing. The main house is full of exhibits of original editions, advertisements, newspapers, and drawings and paintings, all concerning his amazing career, but very little is furnished the way it was when he lived there, although each room is decorated in a different period style.

Also worth visiting is the Balzac Museum, his house from 1840 to 1847, which is now in the sixteenth arrondissement, and was in the village of Passy before it was annexed to Paris. You can sit in the garden and enjoy a splendid view of Paris. The house is on top of a steep hill, and there was a door from the house to the street below, with a carriage and horses kept waiting, so that Balzac could flee his creditors. When you enter, you see display cases with original manuscripts, editions, paintings and drawings, and other mementoes of his career, as well as personal belongings. Farther on in the house, you come to the darkened room where he used to spend his nights writing and drinking endless cups of strong coffee that he made right at the side of his desk, where you can see his coffee bean grinder and pot.

Incidentally, three of the greatest writers I know spent their nights writing: Balzac, Proust, and Louis de Rouvroy, duc de Saint-Simon, whose extraordinary detailed memoirs of life at the court of Louis XIV and the beginning of the reign of Louis XV fill eight volumes in the fully annotated authoritative Pléiade edition, covering the years 1691-1723. He wrote during the night because he had to attend court for part of the day, and his memoirs are lots of fun to read, full of scurrilous, scandalous anecdotes and an exposé of the political shenanigans and intrigues of the era. I don't imagine he ever got much sleep.

George Sand's house, the Musée de la Vie Romantique in the ninth arrondissement, also has a charming garden where you can sit and have tea or coffee under the trees after visiting the beautifully furnished, spacious house, with its splendid paintings and mementoes of her life. That part of the ninth was once all country estates, until the city expanded outwards and they were replaced by the present-day streets and smaller houses.

Among the chateaux that I visited near Paris is the very popular Chantilly, where I went twice, the first time on my own, and the second with my friend Jean-Philippe Bec and his cousins. It is a charming picturesque moated chateau, with an unpicturesque parking lot nearby that was filled with cars. But when you turn your back on the parking lot and walk a few feet, you have a great view of the chateau. The notable library is extraordinary, and so are the gorgeously furnished stately rooms. The chateau houses one of France's greatest art galleries, the Musée Condé. It was built in the 1550s and 1560s for Anne de Montmorency, duc de Montmorency, who served under five French kings and was known for his service in the wars of religion. There are actually two houses that are part of Chantilly, the Petit Château and the Grand Château. The latter was destroyed during the French Revolution and rebuilt in the 1870s. It is now owned and run by the Institut de France, an organization that includes the Académie Française, which oversees the purity of the language and honors literary figures. The town of Chantilly is also known for its stables and for the prestigious Chantilly Racecourse, where noted races are run each year. Crème Chantilly, the famous sweetened whipped cream, which can be flavored with vanilla, kirsch liqueur, or anything one wishes, owes its name to the village, where it was created in the seventeenth century for a banquet at the chateau for King Louis XIV.

Another great museum is Malmaison, the Empress Josephine's house right near Paris at Rueil-Malmaison, accessible by RER (regional transport) train, line A. The park and house are a short walk from the station. Among its memorable displays is Napoleon's uniform as Consul, and he really was as small as his reputation would have it, when he was given the nickname the *Petit Caporal*, the Little Corporal. The obligatory guided tour was excellent, and I learned many details of aristocratic daily life. People ate so much at the banquets that they had to sleep sitting up in bed. They cleaned their teeth with ashes from the fireplace. Napoleon stayed there very often with Josephine at this stately, beautifully furnished, elegant home with its lovely gardens and grounds.

On September 18, 1991, I also took the train to Reims, where I wandered around for almost two hours and visited the famous Gothic cathedral, twice destroyed by cannon fire in the two world wars of the twentieth century, and twice rebuilt. The cathedral museum also holds some fascinating artifacts, including the brown coronation robe of Louis XVI's youngest brother Charles X, the reactionary monarch overthrown in the Revolution of 1830. I actually went there to have a memorable, superb lunch prepared by Gérard Boyer in the Michelin three-starred restaurant Les Crayères, which is in a small chateau on an estate that used to belong to the Polignac family, who were friends of Marcel Proust. He spent time there visiting the Princesse de Polignac, and there are some wonderful photographs of those days. The restaurant has its own kitchen garden and fruit trees in the grounds, so all the herbs, vegetables, and fruits are the freshest possible. Since I arrived early, before the time of my reservation, I was able to wander around the gardens.

I also visited Chartres, another easy train ride from Paris. I climbed one of the towers of the splendid, gorgeous cathedral. Ahead of me on the stairs were a French couple and their English friends with their little girl, who complained about having to climb all those steep stairs. The Frenchman asked, "Mais qu'est-ce qu'elle a, cette petite?" (But what's the matter with the little girl?) "Oh," replied the Englishman in a perfect Oxford accent in French, "elle rêve peut-être." (She's probably dreaming.)

After my visit to the cathedral, I went on to visit Illiers-Combray, formerly Illiers, a village renamed in honor of Marcel Proust, who fictionalized it under the name Combray. A stop or so on the local train line past Chartres, it is the setting for the first part of *In Search of Lost Time*, where the Narrator spends his childhood summer vacations. There is a museum very much worth visiting, the Maison de Tante Léonie, so named in the novel. The person on whom Tante Léonie is based was Proust's paternal aunt Elizabeth (née Proust) Amiot. There is a great photo gallery just inside the entrance gate. The gallery visit is free, and, continuing on along, you get to the house where you have to pay for admission.

Nobody except me was interested in seeing the house, so I was alone with the guide, a guided tour being obligatory. Nobody is supposed to be left alone in any of the rooms, but the guide, realizing my interest in Proust, trusted me and did agree to leave me alone in the downstairs room where the magic lantern that is featured in the book, as well as other artifacts were on display. She had things to take care of, and came back a short while later to continue the tour, and I really enjoyed talking with here, and I think she enjoyed talking with me too. Among other things, she told me that the family name was pronounced "prou" (prooh) by the locals, and the "st" was silent.

After the museum tour, I walked around the municipal park, and saw the *aubépine* (hawthorn) bushes that Proust describes so beautifully. I then strolled around the town, lingering in the town square where

I saw the Church of Saint-Jacques, which Proust describes under the name the Church of Saint-Hilaire. The church interior is beautiful and somewhat austere in its medieval décor. Afterwards I crossed the square to buy madeleines in a bakery that advertised that it sold the authentic madeleines of Proust—how could I resist? They were very good, too! The entire world of the novel arises when the Narrator tastes a morsel of madeleine, a small sponge cake in the shape of a scallop shell, dunked in a spoonful of tea, that arouses his memories of lost time. I walked back to the train station, munching a madeleine on the way, and returned to Paris changing trains again at Chartres.

For several years, the apartment at 102, boulevard Haussmann where Proust wrote most of his book could be seen on certain days of the week. The bank that had purchased the building from Proust's aunt, thus obliging him to move to what turned out to be his last apartment at 44 rue Hamelin, decided to let people visit the rooms with a guide who explained everything. For some reason, the bank eventually discontinued the visits, but I was happy to go twice to see all the rooms, refurnished similarly to the way they were when he lived there, including the cork-lined walls in his bedroom. However, Proust's bedroom, with all the original furniture, is recreated at the Musée Carnavalet, in a section called the Chambres Littéraires (Literary Bedrooms). The fur coat he always wore is on display in a cabinet, and portraits of his parents are on the wall. The second time I went to the apartment at the bank was in 2000 with my Uncle Sy. Since he didn't speak French, I translated for him as we went from room to room. He was also in Paris when I was there in 2005, and we spent a lot of time together.

I also went to see where Proust was born in 1871 in what is now the sixteenth arrondissement, but was then the rural borough of Auteuil, to which his mother fled from Paris during the violence that filled the city during the suppression of the Commune following the Franco-Prussian war, to the safety of her uncle's farm. The area is now completely built up, and there is a commemorative plaque on the building at 96 rue Jean-de-la-Fontaine near his birthplace that I was very moved to see.

My brother Donald Blumenfeld-Jones and my sister-in-law Kathryn were also there one year, as were she and my niece Rebecca another time, and it was a pleasure to show them around as much as I could, their time being limited. American friends of mine have also visited Paris at the same time as myself, and I have enjoyed giving them my historical walking tours of a couple of neighborhoods I know particularly well: St.-Germain and the Marais.

On Tuesday, June 13, 1989 I got a ticket at the box office of the Théâtre Français to the evening performance of Molière's *L'Avare* (The Miser) by the Comédie Française, then proceeded the short distance to the rue de Rivoli to meet the bus at the Paris-Vision tourist office for a round trip to Giverny. I made the afternoon trip to Giverny to visit Claude Monet's splendid house and superb idyllic gardens, where among the other splendors you see the pond with the water lilies and the Japanese bridge that he painted. "En dehors de la peinture et du jardinage, je ne suis bon à rien. Mon plus beau chef-d'oeuvre, c'est mon jardin," he said. (Aside from painting and gardening, I am good for nothing. My most beautiful masterpiece is my garden.)

I took the guided bus tour because it was the easiest way to get there and back, rather than taking a train to Vernon and a taxi to Giverny. Of course, there was a lecture on Impressionism that I could have done without, because I was already very knowledgeable on the subject, but it was well done. There were mostly Americans on the bus, and the lecture was in English. When we got off the bus, we were all free to wander in the gardens on our own, and told to be back at a certain time.

I sat next to a young lady on the bus, and then walked with her around the gardens, all beautifully in bloom, and we sat on a bench surrounded by flowering bushes. She told me her story at some length. She had recovered a couple of years ago from a nervous breakdown and now worked for Ethiopian Airlines in Rome, where she had been adopted by an Italian family when she was around four. Her mother was a maid in the family, and she was born out of wedlock, then abandoned when her mother simply left. Her adoptive parents knew who her father was, but refused to tell her. Then one day, her adoptive parents handed her a letter her mother had left for her. It was written in Amharic, her first language, her second being Italian, and her third French, which is what we spoke. The letter led her to believe that her father was a member of the Ethiopian royal family so that she was actually a relative of Haile Selassie, and therefore an Ethiopian princess, and she was thinking of having the letter translated into Italian and trying to regain her inheritance by legal means. She didn't know what she should do, and I didn't know what to say or what to tell her to do, or even whether to believe her or not. We parted ways in a friendly fashion, so I could go and visit the house and gardens.

In the gardens you have a simultaneous sense of vitality, surrounded by everything in flower, and of great peace and tranquility. The house is charming and spacious and the kitchen at Giverny is beautifully equipped and magnificent, as is the yellow, white, and blue-rimmed dinnerware Monet designed. *Monet's Table: The Cooking Journals of Claude Monet* by Claire Joyes (Simon & Schuster, 1990), translated from the French, is a superb cookbook. He loved good food and enjoyed having his fellow artists to dinner. I've tried several of the recipes with great success.

Decades later, in 2023, there was an exhibit about his brother Léon Monet at the Luxembourg Museum. He was a color chemist, and went into business as a manufacturer of dyes for cloth, widely used by the great fashion houses of his day. He became rich and was a great supporter of his brother and other Impressionists, and he collected their works, so the wonderful exhibit featured paintings, drawings, and sketches by Claude Monet and other Impressionists that are rarely seen in public, as well as family photographs and documents, and a brief silent film of Claude Monet painting in his garden.

The performance of *L'Avare* that evening was excellent, superb, dark, realistic, very funny, and very tragic. Michel Aumont was wonderful, head bowed, always deep within himself, laughing ironically, a miser with his feelings as well as with his money, and treating people as if they were his possessions.

CHAPTER TWENTY-FIVE

The Ancient Sites of Greece

I N 1994, I took a guided tour of the ancient sites in Greece. I flew from John F Kennedy International Airport to Athens on Olympic a couple of days ahead of our tour group. I don't need tours of cities, generally speaking, and I prefer to explore them on my own, as I did Athens. I had a room where we all stayed at Novotel, and I was very pleased to see myself on an AT&T commercial on CNN on the television in my room.

We were near the fascinating National Archaeological Museum, which I visited the day after my arrival, and which was not on our itinerary, so I would never have seen it otherwise. I was fascinated by the collection of pre-historic artifacts, the incredible collection of statues, vases and other relics of antiquity; the Mycenean art collection including gold funerary masks, and the treasure trove of other ancient artifacts discovered by the German amateur archaeologist Heinrich Schliemann during his excavations of Mycenae. Schliemann was well known for his work on excavating ancient Troy in the 1870s near the Sea of Marmara and the straits that lead from the Aegean to the Black Sea in what is now Turkey.

There was a rooftop restaurant at our hotel with a splendid view of the Parthenon in the distance and of Athens lit up at night. I had dinner there, and the food was quite good: Greek hors d'oeuvres, tender grilled, marinated lamb souvlaki, and ice cream. There was a live band playing banal American music that rather ruined the moonlit atmosphere, at least for me.

I got up early and took a taxi to the Plaka, the old historical district built over the ancient neighborhood surrounding the Acropolis on its northern and eastern slopes, where I had excellent Greek coffee. Then

I walked up to the superbly impressive Acropolis to see the Parthenon and the Acropolis Museum, and afterwards explored the neighborhood of narrow winding streets with its whitewashed houses. I also had a wonderful meal at a restaurant near the Plaka.

I discovered almost immediately on my taxi ride, as I passed a number of huge barricaded holes in the ground, that the government was building an underground transport system, which was taking forever to complete, because the crews would come across some ancient artifacts and by law would have to stop digging while teams of government archeologists were called in to inspect the site. Everything halted as they continued their explorations, only giving their no doubt reluctant go-ahead when they were pretty sure there was nothing more to be found.

Our tour group had arrived by the time I got back to the hotel late that afternoon and we had a relaxed, friendly meeting to introduce ourselves and to explain what we would be doing, then dinner at the rooftop restaurant again.

On the first day of our tour, after a spectacularly good breakfast buffet, we boarded the bus and proceeded out of the city, arriving eventually at the great modern Corinth canal between its two hugely high rocky walls, and continuing on through the plains of Arcadia to the spectacular ruins of the palace and tomb of Agamemnon and the Lion's Gate at Mycenae.

On the winding mountain roads all over the areas we visited, the views were breathtaking, the valleys so green and full of olive groves, even if the ride on the exceptionally narrow roads was a bit unnerving at times. I thought that even if I drove, it would be a better idea to take a bus tour and leave the driving to someone who was experienced. When the guide pointed it out, I was thrilled to see Mt. Olympus, home of the gods, cloud-capped, its summit lost in the mists even on that sunny day. Our driver, Yannis, was friendly, bluff, and hearty, and a very good driver, but struck me as occasionally foolhardy, taking turns around the bends a bit too quickly for my taste. I sat on the side looking straight down the mountains and cliffs.

Our brilliant guide, Elena, was excellent. She had been a French major and then switched to archeology, which she left to become a tour guide because she wanted to "transmit the culture," as she said. We spoke French quite a lot. She lived in Athens, but was from Olympia.

Our next stop, ancient Corinth, was very impressive with its well-preserved extensive agora or marketplace. Above the ancient site on the hills is the modern town of Corinth, and it was interesting to see how totally different the modern houses were. They almost looked out of place.

Just inside the main entrance are rows of public toilets, not closed off in any way like modern toilets, but simply open. People on the way into the market would stop there before continuing into the main area. They used pieces of cloth to clean themselves, and would then throw them into the toilet wells.

Farther on, in the open area of the marketplace are the ruins of columns. Most prominent is the rostrum from which St. Paul is said to have addressed the crowds.

Our next stop was another particularly impressive site, the perfectly preserved amphitheater of the Theater at Epidaurus, where we sat in the tiered stadium while our guide whispered below on the flat plain of the theater, and we could hear perfectly. She also described the theatrical technology of the time, the masks all actors wore, and the fact that only men were allowed on stage.

Then we went on to the seaport of Nauplia, which we reached by evening on September 4, and we had an excellent seaside dinner looking out over the harbor with the many boats and yachts moored there, beautiful in the moonlight.

We continued on the next day to the ancient stadium and Zeus's Temple at Olympia where our guide told the group all about the ancient games, and about her role in carrying the torch. She had been a torchbearer for the Olympic Games one year when she was a high school star athlete, carrying it from the ancient stadium, where the torch was lit, to its next stage on the way to the site of the games.

We had another delicious fresh seafood dinner at a seaside taverna with a wonderful view on the way to what turned out to be my favorite of all the antique sites we visited, Apollo's Oracle at Delphi, just outside the modern town of Delphi where we stayed in a very nice hotel.

The Oracle is splendidly situated on the slopes of Mt. Parnassus, home of the Muses, and with a view straight down the mountain to the Gulf of Corinth, an inlet of the Ionian Sea that separates the Peloponnese from western mainland Greece. The extensive Temple of Apollo included the actual place where the oracle's priest relayed its pronouncements, sitting in a cave on a stool just above a gaseous steam spring. The priest would go into a trance and then make pronouncements to those who had come to consult the oracle.

I had plenty of time to wander through the place by myself, after listening to the wonderfully informative lecture given by our guide, as she pointed out the different places at the site, including the treasury where all the taxes and donations were stored.

The next day, we had the pleasure of seeing the awe-inspiring, amazing Greek Orthodox monasteries placed on the incredibly high pinnacles of Meteora, a geological phenomenon. The bus parked down below, and we climbed the narrow staircase up to see one of them, with its exhibit of ancient icons in one of the monastery halls. I had some difficulty when we were leaving because we were so high up and the stairs were so narrow that I had a touch of acrophobia, and Elena told me to go straight ahead all the way without looking down, which was a huge help.

I was amazed that some of the people in our group were there at all. The only thing they seemed to want to do was to go back to our hotels, and sit around the swimming pool sipping martinis. A few of us were there to see the antique sights, but when our guide would start one of her excellent lectures, I could hear one of these uninterested vacationers whispering, "There she goes again!"

That was nearly the end of our tour, and we went back to the Novotel in Athens. I left the group early, but I was with them for part of my last day for a fascinating bus ride, which included a view of the ancient hillside amphitheater and another climb to the Acropolis. I went to the airport later in the afternoon and took a plane to Paris, finishing my vacation at the Michelet Odéon hotel.

CHAPTER TWENTY-SIX

More about the Pleasures of Paris and My Wonderful Friendships

I HAD A MARVELOUS rest of my trip. Upon arriving at the hotel, I phoned my parents, and talked with my father, who was doing well and was looking forward to my return home. He had suffered from a stroke a number of years before and was mostly confined to a wheelchair, although he could use a walker when he had to get up. He had told us to send him to a nursing home, but none of us wanted that. My brother Richard moved back in to help take care of him, and I myself went out there to Princeton from New York on most weekends.

I took a nap, then got up and walked over to the Ritz to have a superb dinner with Joanna and Paul at L'Espadon, returning to the hotel happy and very tired, and I had good night's sleep, as you can imagine.

On Saturday, September 24 I arranged to have a drink with Jean-Frédéric when his service at Taillevent was concluded, and he met me at the Michelet Odéon, with his fiancée Delphine. I was meeting her for the first time. We went over to the Café de Flore. I immediately thought her very nice and very beautiful. She was M. Vrinat's secretary and was always in the office, so I had never seen her before. The weather was very pleasant and we sat outside. We all had refreshing citrus fruit juice cocktails of orange, lemon, and grapefruit, and scrambled eggs with smoked salmon. We had a delightful time talking of politics and restaurants, and he insisted on paying, even though I had invited them. By next September, when I returned to Paris, they were already married.

This meeting was most auspicious, we really hit it off, and they became among my dearest friends in all the world. I have met other members of their families, and I remember when they were married, and when each of their three sons was born. Victor, the oldest, is now a doctor; Alexandre, the middle son is a very talented baker; and Paul, the youngest is currently studying automotive engineering. I held them in my arms when they were babies, and watched them grow up, at first in their apartment in Levallois-Perret near the banks of the Seine, where they invited me frequently for lunch, then in a chateau in Normandy they purchased.

With a pond in front of it and what had been stables off to one side, the main building was on the site of a thirteenth-century chateau that had belonged to Joan of Arc's brother. Foundations of the chateau dated from the sixteenth century, and everything built above them was from the seventeenth, with some possible eighteenth-century renovations. There was a medieval dovecote on the grounds, and an old long stone shed, which had been the laundry. Outlines of the estate walls are also there in the fields. The inside was completely renovated with all modern conveniences and appliances.

It was my pleasure to be invited for many wonderful joyous weekends, when, among other pleasures such as walks in the countryside and visits to their neighbors, Delphine served superb meals. Jean-Frédéric would drive me out from Paris and back, or I would take the train out with Delphine and one of their sons, stopping at Vire where he would pick us up and continue on to the chateau in the car.

When they were still moving in, I went out one weekend to help, and sat in the back of the car, with a number of cartons, while more were on the front seat. When Jean-Frédéric and I drove all the way, I was amazed to see so many ruined, bombed out sections of villages in the Normandy countryside that had never been completely repaired since the end of World War Two, even all those decades afterwards. There were quite a few new housing blocks also, sometimes near the old villages. In one town, the only old building was a ruined church, its tower more or less intact. Unfortunately, it was the Americans who had done a lot of the bombing, and not the Germans. The Americans dropped leaflets to warn the population to evacuate, but the leaflets were often not picked up and read.

We went once to see the Omaha landing beach on the Normandy coast and the American Cemetery. The boys had been there on a school trip, but Jean-Frédéric and Delphine had never seen the beach. The experience was very moving, and it was fascinating to see the sculpted Monument to the Fallen on the beach, a landmarked site, where almost nobody was swimming or lounging, and to climb up to see the ruined German bunkers on the hill overlooking the beach. I had tears in my eyes as I gazed at the clear blue, almost cloudless sky and the calm water, and visualized the newsreels I had seen of the invasion, and of course I thought of my Uncle Sy who had been there on D-Day, June 6, 1944.

Jean-Frédéric and Delphine have sold the chateau and their restaurant a long time ago, and now live in an apartment that has a beautiful view overlooking the Canal St.-Martin in the tenth arrondissement.

Starting on September 27, I enrolled with Joanna in a series of cooking lessons at the École Ritz Escoffier at the Ritz Hotel, the series paid for in advance. The lessons were in the form of lecture demonstrations, not hands on at a cooking station, so we sat in comfortable seats watching the chef.

The entrance to the school is on the rue Cambon, on the west side of the place Vendôme, at the back of the Ritz Hotel. They offer professional training as well as lessons for tourists. There was a group of Japanese tourists in the class, many of whom apparently spoke English, but no French. A translator gave a simultaneous translation of what the chef said into English. The chef was quite funny and cracked jokes, at which Joanna and I were the only ones to laugh. The other attendees didn't get the jokes even in translation. After a while, the chef addressed everything directly to us, since he realized we understood French. We were given sheets of paper with basic recipes and tips, one side in English, the other in French, and I took notes. The chef demonstrated the recipes, and at the end of each class, we tasted the results. I still occasionally make the quiche lorraine and other recipes we learned how to prepare. All the food was just delicious, and the tasting was a good reason all by itself for taking the classes.

I still use cooking techniques that I learned there: for instance, to cook green vegetables such as asparagus, green beans, spinach, and other leafy greens, bring a pot of water to a boil, plunge the vegetables into the boiling water and cook for the required number of minutes, then drain well before continuing the preparation. To cook root vegetables such as potatoes and carrots, peel them or not, cut them up or not, clean them well, and put them into a pot of cold water, which you bring to a boil. Leaving the pot on the boil, allow the water to evaporate almost entirely, and the vegetables will be done. Make sure to keep an eye on the pot so the root vegetables don't burn and test them with a knife from time to time to see if they are cooked.

We also had a guided visit to the Ritz kitchens that served both the main Michelin-starred restaurant, L'Espadon, and the two bars, the Vendôme and the Hemingway. We got to taste some of the food, too, and to watch the chefs preparing it. They keep huge stockpots on some of the burners, with stock for soups and sauces perpetually simmering and constantly replenished.

On Sunday, Sept. 25 I went with Paul and Joanna to visit the Chateau of Vaux-le-Vicomte and then the town of Barbizon, to the southeast of Paris. On the way to the chateau, we stopped at Sèvres to browse in the *brocante* (flea market), lots of fun. The elegant chateau is one of the few privately owned and maintained, and it is very well kept up. It was built between 1658 and 1661 by Nicolas Fouquet, and he opened it with a banquet for King Louis XIV. When the king arrived, Fouquet knelt in front of him and presented him with the chateau as a gift. The king replied that the chateau already belonged to him, because everything did. The banquet was prepared by the greatest chef of the era, François Vatel, who ran himself on his sword when the freshly caught seafood he had ordered failed to arrive from the Normandy coast. The fish eventually did arrive, too late to save Vatel, and the banquet proceeded. Fouquet was accused of financial malfeasance by his rival Jean-Baptiste Colbert, and sentenced to prison for life. The king allowed him to live, and he spent the rest of his life as a prisoner in a downstairs dungeon of his own chateau. The rooms are furnished in a stately manner, very elegant, and superbly decorated, and even the dungeon is comfortably outfitted.

We drove from there to Barbizon, on the edge of the Fontainebleau Forest. On another occasion, I went by myself to visit the famous chateau of Fontainebleau, a splendid Renaissance building, with a double staircase in the courtyard, from which Napoleon departed into what turned out to be a temporary exile on the isle of Elba.

The picturesque village is known for the Barbizon school of artists, including Jean-François Millet and Théodore Rousseau. Since it was Sunday, the museums and galleries were unfortunately closed, but we got a good glimpse of the famous artists' studios behind closed gates.

Before heading back to Paris, we had an excellent dinner in town at the reputable restaurant Les Pléiades, with a memorable grilled *magret de canard aux jus de truffes* (duck breast with truffle juice) as my main dish and a chestnut soufflé for dessert.

The drive was horrendous going out of Paris, the roads jam-packed and the traffic hardly moving. The *bouchons* (traffic jams) on the Périphérique, the boulevard surrounding Paris, were especially onerous, but going back was not nearly so bad, perhaps because it was so late. They dropped me off at the hotel before proceeding to park and go upstairs to their apartment on the top floor above the Méditerranée restaurant.

In 1995 on my return to Paris, I found that they had moved to an apartment in the ninth arrondissement on the rue de la Rochefoucauld. Their flat, which they have since given up, was a short way south of the place Pigalle, where the famous Moulin Rouge nightclub is still open. It was in a co-op that had been a *maison de passe* (a house you just pass through), a euphemism for brothel, in the nineteenth century. The apartments, each occupying one floor, used to be *chambres séparées* (separate rooms), each occupied by one of the prostitutes under the supervision of a madam. Their apartment, a seven-flight walkup, was once the first studio of the impressionist painter Pierre-Auguste Renoir, advertised as such when it was on the market, and he used to invite the girls upstairs and pay them to pose for him.

September 29 was my last day in Paris for 1994. I had lunch at the rooftop restaurant at La Samaritaine on the Right Bank just across the Pont Neuf with my friend Jean-Philippe Bec and cousins of his. It was balmy and sunny, and we sat outside. The view to the south over the Left Bank is spectacular, with the Eiffel Tower off to the west and Notre Dame to the east. Lunch was excellent: shrimp and cucumber salad; chicken fricassee à l'orange with polenta; and a scoop each of orange, lemon, and passionfruit sorbets.

I had my last cooking lesson at the Ritz afterwards, and bade a fond farewell to Joanna and Paul. The excellent, very useful lesson was on salads of different kinds, from vegetables such as cabbage and carrots to chicken, to a delicious lentil salad, and a nice technique for making vinaigrette: Take one part vinegar and put it in a small bowl with salt and a small amount of Dijon mustard, to taste. Whisk together. In another small bowl, put olive oil and freshly ground pepper, and whisk together. Pour vinegar mixture into the olive oil mixture just before serving, whisk, pour over the salad, and toss well.

When I returned home to New York the next day, I immediately phoned my parents to let them know I was back and to see how everything was going. "Are you sitting down?" my mother asked. "Yes," I said, "why?" She told me that my beloved father had collapsed the night before from congestive heart failure and fallen into a coma, from which he never emerged. He been taken to a nursing home uptown because he required intravenous feeding and round the clock care, impossible to manage at home. She hadn't phoned me, because I was returning the next day anyway. I went to Princeton right away, and we all went to see my father in the nursing home, lying there quietly, his eyes occasionally blinking, but seeing nothing. As it turned out, that conversation with my father when I phoned from Paris was the last one I would ever have with him. He died peacefully in his sleep on December 26, 1994.

My mother survived him by twenty-one years and died on August 18, 2015, at more than one hundred years old. It is still hard to fathom that I, who was once one of the youngest generation of my family, am now a member of the oldest.

As Prospero says in Shakespeare's *The Tempest*,
"The cloud-capp'd towers, the gorgeous palaces,
The solemn temples, the great globe itself,
Ye all which it inherit, shall dissolve,
And, like this insubstantial pageant faded,
Leave not a wrack behind. We are such stuff
As dreams are made on, and our little life
Is rounded with a sleep…"

EPILOGUE

GRIEF, WHICH EVER dwells within, recedes into the background after a time as the necessities of life take over, only to reassert itself at any moment. Along with the sadness and losses that life inevitably entails, I have also had the great good fortune to be able to fulfill my dreams, and to live as I have wanted to do, and to have had many happy and wonderful times. The fantastic trips to Paris and elsewhere and spending time with my friends there as well as with my friends here in the United States have given me immense joy. As Alfred, Lord Tennyson says in his poem *Ulysses*, "Though much is taken, much abides…"

It has been my custom for many years now to spend time in the Jardin du Luxembourg on my last afternoon in Paris, rain or shine. Leaving the Michelet Odéon, I turn right and take the rue Rotrou to the rue de Vaugirard, cross the street and enter the park. Sometimes there is an organ grinder at the entrance playing delightful light music. And there are always joggers emerging from the path behind the Fontaine Médicis just inside the gates. I have had the great pleasure on Sunday afternoons of attending free open-air concerts performed by different bands and orchestras playing everything from jazz to short classical pieces.

Walking past the side of the palais du Luxembourg, I sit at my favorite places in my favorite park, as I do almost every morning before starting my program for the day, at either the great bassin where children play with their toy sailboats, or next to the Fontaine Médicis; or most often, I climb the stairs, enjoying the view past the statue of the ancient Greek actor Thespis of the place Edmond-Rostand and the Panthéon in the distance, looking closer than it is up the rue Soufflot, and sit on the terrace above the fontaine, looking out over the park in the direction of the Tour Montparnasse in the distance. I inevitably think of my parents. I look up, and can imagine their faces in the sky above.

I love being in the Luxembourg so much, watching all the people enjoying themselves, from the children with their parents, to the joggers, and the groups of tourists with their guides, and the individuals walking around. And I especially love contemplating the beauty and serenity of the park. I spend a nostalgic few hours there before returning to the hotel, finishing my packing, and perhaps having dinner with friends. I get up at 5:30 the next morning, and get a taxi reserved for me by the receptionists of the Michelet Odéon from the hotel to Charles de Gaulle for an early flight home, enjoying the view of the early morning streets and buildings on the way. The flights have usually been restful, with only occasional turbulence. I sit in the last row of the coach section most of the time, so there is nobody sitting behind me. And after taking the AirTrain train on the monorail at Newark Liberty International Airport to the NJ Transit train station, and then the subway from Penn Station, I arrive at my apartment in New York at around lunchtime. Every trip for many years has ended in this happy manner. I hope there will be many more trips to Paris in my future.

THE END

ABOUT THE AUTHOR

ROBERT BLUMENFELD IS the author of the historical novels *The Count of Saint-Hélène, or The Lure of Infamy* (CreateSpace Publishing Platform, 2014) and *The Vampires of Morève: A Family Chronicle* (Xlibris, 2019); as well as of *Accents: A Manual for Actors* (1998; Revised and Expanded Edition, 2002); *Acting with the Voice: The Art of Recording Books* (2004); *Tools and Techniques for Character Interpretation: A Handbook of Psychology for Actors, Writers, and Directors* (2006); *Using the Stanislavsky System: A Practical Guide to Character Creation and Period Styles* (2008); *Blumenfeld's Dictionary of Acting and Show Business* (2009); *Blumenfeld's Dictionary of Musical Theater: Opera, Operetta, Musical Comedy* (2010); *Stagecraft: Stanislavsky and External Acting Technique---A Companion to Using the Stanislavsky System* (2011); *Teach Yourself Accents: The British Isles* (2013); *Teach Yourself Accents: North America* (2013); *Teach Yourself Accents: Europe* (2014); and the collaborator with noted teacher, acting coach and actress Alice Spivak on the writing of her book *How to Rehearse When There Is No Rehearsal: Acting and the Media* (2007)---all published by Limelight. He lives and works as an actor, dialect coach and writer in New York City, and is a longtime member of Equity, AFTRA, and SAG. He has worked in numerous regional and New York theaters, as well as in television and independent films, and performed in many comedies and farces. For ACT Seattle he played the title role in Ronald Harwood's *The Dresser*, and he has performed many roles in plays by Shakespeare and Chekhov, as well as doing an Off-Broadway season of six Gilbert and Sullivan comic operas for Dorothy Raedler's American Savoyards (under the name Robert Fields), for which he played the Lord Chancellor in *Iolanthe*, Sir Joseph Porter in *H.M.S. Pinafore*, and other leading comedian patter-song roles. In 1994, he performed in Michael John LaChiusa's musical *The Petrified Prince*, directed by Harold Prince at the New York Shakespeare Festival's Public Theater. He created the roles of the Marquis of Queensberry and two prosecuting attorneys in Moisés Kaufman's Off-Broadway hit play *Gross Indecency: The Three Trials of Oscar Wilde*, and was also the production's dialect coach, a job which he did as well for the Broadway musicals, *Saturday Night Fever* and *The Scarlet Pimpernel* (third version and national tour), and for the New York workshop of David Henry Hwang's rewritten version of Rodgers and Hammerstein's *Flower Drum Song*. At the Manhattan School of Music, he was dialect coach for Dona D. Vaughn's production of Strauss's *Die Fledermaus* (2009); and for Jay Lesenger's production of Weill's *Street Scene* (2008), which he also coached for Mr. Lesenger at the Chautauqua Opera. Mr. Blumenfeld has recorded many books for Audible, among them *Pale Fire* and *Invitation to a Beheading* by Vladimir Nabokov and *A Modest Proposal* by Jonathan Swift. He has recorded more than 320 Talking Books for the American Foundation for the Blind, including the complete Sherlock Holmes canon (four novels and fifty-six short stories), Victor Hugo's *The Hunchback of Notre-Dame*, Alexandre Dumas' *The Count of Monte Cristo*, a bilingual edition of Rainer Maria Rilke's previously unpublished poetry, and a bilingual edition of Samuel Beckett's *Waiting for Godot*, which he recorded in Beckett's original French and the playwright's own English translation. He received the 1997 Canadian National Institute for the Blind's Torgi Award for the Talking Book of the Year in the Fiction category, for his recording of Pat Conroy's *Beach Music*; and the 1999 Alexander Scourby Talking Book Narrator of the Year Award in the Fiction category. He holds a B.A. in French from Rutgers University and an M.A. from Columbia University in French Language and Literature. Mr. Blumenfeld speaks French, German, and Italian fluently, and has smatterings of Russian, Spanish, and Yiddish.